Living a Radical Life

Astonishing Ideas
Hidden in Plain Sight in
A Course in Miracles

James K Anderson

Oceanic Surrealism Press

Copyright © 2021 James K Anderson All rights reserved

ISBN: 979-8-7865-9364-9

The characters and events portrayed in this book are fictitious. Any similarity to real persons, living or dead, is coincidental and not intended by the author.

No part of this book may be reproduced, or stored in a retrieval system, or transmitted in any form or by any means, electronic, mechanical, photocopying, recording, or otherwise, without express written permission of the publisher.

Cover photo and design by: James K Anderson
Printed in the United States of America
www.jameskanderson.com

Table of Contents

Preface 1
Chapter 1 – A Disturbing Idea 9
   Get Ready 9
   Tiny and Mad 12
   Forget it! 18
   All I Have to Do is Dream 21
   Difference #2 23
   Creation 25
   Insanity Plea #1 27
   Give it up 28
   How about Global Thermonuclear War? 29
   Vigilance 33
Chapter 2 – A Little Bit More on the Dream 35
   Elephant 35
   Insanity Plea #2 35
   Let's Split 38
   Inception? 40
   Specialness 41
   The Purpose 44
   Magic 48
   Death, by the way 50
   This is a Holdup! 50
   Goal 52
   Important? 54
Chapter 3 – My Journey 57
   Atheists 57
   My Journey 60
   Loathing in Las Vegas 63
   Reality 65
   The Path 71
Chapter 4 – The Solution 75
   Your Role 75
   The Answers 76
   The Atonement—The Master Plan 77

Communication Breakdown	80
Eliminating Conflict	82
Forgiveness	82
Attack!	84
Is It Real?	85
Forgiveness to Destroy	89
Real Forgiveness	91
Guilt	93
Subtlety	97
Looking Within	98
Miracles	99
Eliminate the Past	100
The Real Purpose of Forgiveness	103
Judgment	105
Timing	108
Your Brother	109
Chapter 5 – Your Mind, Your Life	**111**
The Mind	111
Tiny and Mad	114
Send in the Clowns	115
The Source	117
Projection	118
The Old Ideas	119
My life	120
The Law of Creation	122
Hold Onto Your Horses	127
Chapter 6 – Problem Solving	**135**
Quiet, We're Taping	135
Solutions	137
Give It Away	140
Time and Space	141
Your Brother	142
Bigger Still	143
Ego	145
Choice	147
So Easy	149

Chapter 7 – Symbols and a Bigger Picture 155
More on Symbols 155
Emotional Response 159
Creating Lack 161
The Big Start 167
Opposites 169

Chapter 8 – Relationships and Chaos 173
Special Function 173
Relationships 175
The Holy Relationship 179
Laws of Chaos 180
Your Power 183
More Magic 186
Two Ways 187
See it Differently 188
The Guy 189

Chapter 9 – Letting Go of Control 193
The Universal Curriculum 193
We Like It 194
No, Not Frozen 199
Defense 206
Holy Spirit 210
Lucid Dream 212
Acceptance 215

Chapter 10 – Guidance 217
God's Mind 217
Guidance 220
No Decisions 225
Dropping Away 226
What do you want? 228
The Path 230
Hear This! 235
Dying 236

Chapter 11 – The Two Worlds 239
My Fake World 243
Three Levels 248

Vigilance	255
Truth	258
Love	263
Change	266
The Context	267
About the Author…	**273**
Bibliography	**275**

Preface

I apologize for starting a book this way, knowing that you're probably standing in a bookstore somewhere, or looking through it on Amazon deciding whether or not to buy it, flipping through it in the hopes of finding that enticing hook, that savory morsel that will compel you to reach into your virtual wallet—but alas, then, you take the unfortunate step of reading the next paragraph. . .

You, my friend, are insane. I am not calling you a name or invoking some humorous bon mot; I am merely describing you accurately. You are absolutely loony, daft, deranged, out of your mind, non compos mentis! That's the bad news. The good news is that it's not just you: we're all nuts. Well, maybe that's worse news. Even if you're the smartest person on the planet, you're crazy. We are all out of our minds because we have collectively created a bizarrely cruel and unjust world, and we have decided that this life is really great, with just a few minor bumps and unpleasantries (like ubiquitous sickness and suffering, not to mention certain death), so we're all going to accept it and shut up about it, cramming our true feelings way down into our unconscious minds while putting on a perfect smile as we rearrange our Titanic deck chairs.

This book is the reflection of the path I have been on since 1974—the year I graduated from college—when I finally had time to read something other than a textbook and start the search for God that I had decided to make after a number of interesting events that occurred during college. Like so many of us, that search has led me to some strange and amazing places. I have gone through many phases and stages, stumbling over my ego and stubbornness, latching onto some wonderful ideas that turned out to be not so good after all, reevaluating what I believed until I reached a point in the late 1980s, after I had read book after incredible book, when I realized without doubt, that I knew absolutely everything I could possibly know, or could possibly be known, about God. I'm not sure if I can express how hilarious that is to me now.

Besides the obvious hubris behind that thought was my unrelenting disappointment with the surface life I was living. I wasn't happy on any level, and yet I was doing everything I thought I should be doing, and believing everything I thought I should be believing, according to everything I thought God expected of me. I wasn't happy with any aspect of my life. There was a serious disconnect happening, and I needed to know why.

That led me to the first major positive change in my life since my search began; I began meditating in 1990. It was a remarkable change and as important a decision as I have ever made. This was also around the time Marianne Williamson's book *A Return to Love* came out. After I read her book, I immediately went out and bought a copy of *A Course in Miracles* to add to my ever-expanding library of spiritual books.

Meditation satisfied my yearning for self-discovery for many years, even as I kept reading more and more interesting and obscure books on every aspect of God I could get my hands on. Unfortunately, every time I picked up the Course over the next 20 years, I couldn't get very far into it before I gave up in frustration. It seemed it was just not for me. I eventually read it, as I explain in Chapter 3.

This book is about what I discovered as I grew in spiritual knowledge and eventually came to embrace what the Course had been trying to tell me all along. Because of my habit of trying to understand each book I read in the context of every previous book I had read, I discovered ideas in *A Course in Miracles* that I have not heard any other Course teachers talk about at all. The Course is rich in its depth and profound in ways that most Course teachers have yet to uncover.

If you are a student of *A Course in Miracles* or not, you will find information in this book that you have never seen before. There is an amazing amount of information hidden in plain sight within the writings of the Course, and the only way to uncover it is to read it over and over again, while listening to your inner guidance. You can read the words of the Course casually on the surface, or you can delve deep within it to uncover a treasure trove of information that reveals itself as you are ready for it.

I have always thought this world was insane, and most likely, so do you. You know this world is nuts! I believe the time has come to dredge up that suppressed belief, and we must all say it out loud together, and take responsibility for our part in it, and stop blaming someone else, like hate groups or terrorists, or political parties, or your parents or spouse or boss, not to mention the devil or just plain old bad luck. You are not a victim. We have to accept that we each have created this, and then do what we each can to change what we have made.

You are not *certifiably* insane by any measure on this planet simply because insanity has been defined by the insane. Oh, and by the way, it also means that we would have to admit the Truth of what's going on here and understand why this world even exists and who we are and what our role in it is. You know, just the purpose and context of life. That's easy enough for us all to agree to, don't you think?

There is no absolute metric here that can determine that you are nuts. That would have to be an admission that we all are, and we certainly can't have that. Everything we believe is automatically determined from the point of view of a bonkers world. Like children who grow up in abusive families never knowing that it's not right, because it's all they know. We don't know anything else besides living in insanity because we don't know what sanity looks like. We don't understand why it is this way, but it *is* this way and the only reasonable thing to do is to salute it and carry on with life as usual.

We may not understand why things are the way they are, but we

Preface – *Living a Radical Life*

do our best, and because we don't understand life on earth, that means life must not be possible to understand any more than we do now. When we do acknowledge how screwed up things are here, we make token attempts to fix the small pieces that are screwed up. But those attempts haven't worked out very well, have they? It seems that the next guy just comes along and screws it all up again. And after all, if it were possible to understand this life, someone would have figured it out and told us for God's sake!

Our general course of action is to temporarily fix the stuff we can, one item at a time, by taking action; by manipulating our external lives and inventing or buying better stuff to help us cope and make our lives easier, hoping for a better result. We then suppress any inconsistencies or problems that are beyond us, and continue to live our ignorant lives going from one personal crisis and shopping mall to the next, hoping for the small respites that come on occasion. The entire time most of us are here on earth, we never come to the realization that the whole purpose of life is to *figure it out*!

But it's even worse than that. We have taken our ignorance to the next level by justifying this mess. We don't understand life, and so we not only accept it the way it is, we defend it! We live lives that are chaotic, perplexing and unjust. We observe all of the ridiculous things that we do collectively and, out of frustration, assign meaning to the meaningless, importance to the unimportant, and do our best not to take responsibility for any of it. *They*'re the ones doing it, for God's sake! It's the Democrats! No, it's the Republicans! It's the Jews! No, it's the Palestinians! It's the women! It's aliens! It's the devil! It's my next-door neighbor! It's AT&T!

We dislike life immensely if things aren't going well for us, but we go along with it easily if things are going our way, no matter how poorly it may be going for everyone else. We regularly ignore all of the things we see and do that are contrary to sanity, whatever that is. We focus very little on understanding who or what God really might be (which might explain a whole lot). Because of that, we pray for things to be better without a clue as to why or how prayer works. We worship a god who has come more and more to resemble us at our psychological worst.

Yet we pretend to believe that God is wonderful, even with His strict rules and vengeance and smiting, even though we refuse to try to reconcile why a wonderful God would create such a painful and unjust world as this. We accept that we are condemned to hell or rewarded with heaven if we play or don't play the game that God wants us to play. Many of us ignore a god altogether because the god game just wears us out.

What we don't understand, we redefine. We don't care what Jesus actually said because long ago, we discarded the message and focused on the messenger. Be perfect? Gimme a break! Forgive seven times seventy? Ha! The message did not fit our explanation of life—it is *way* too difficult to live, so the message was lost and replaced with a focus on accepting the messenger into our hearts—something much safer, less radical, totally meaningless, and requiring much less work. This readjustment is true for all major religions. We change the fundamental ideas behind each religion because we don't know *why* we're supposed to do the things we were originally taught, because we don't know who we are, and we don't know who or what God really is! We are complacent because of our ignorance, and this book is asking you to stop reading books like this and go out into your world and remake it. Of course, read this book *first*, so you know what to do and why to do it. But *then*, stop reading books and start taking action. The time for life as usual is over.

So, if not life as usual, then what? What is the alternative? Before you can answer that question, your life has to fit into a context that makes sense. What you now believe about everything, from God to ghosts to fate and luck, is the context of your life. That context determines how you live in every detail, even if you aren't aware of it. The best place to start changing your life is to think seriously about the odd context you are holding onto. Before we understand how we can live a life that actually makes sense, we first need to understand why we're here. We need to understand God and we need to start taking an honest look at what we're doing to each other on this tiny, floating dirtball.

Before we start, you need to know what you're up against. As I hinted, this book is based on the ideas in *A Course in Miracles*. The Course is not your normal spiritual book. It is a self-study course and a complete philosophy that describes, in detail, the context of the lives we live. Up until I was truly able to read the Course for the first time, I had never before read anything that gave a description of life that made any sense to me, including the refreshing idea that there could indeed be a God of unconditional love along with an explanation of why (as I mentioned above) there is so much suffering here on earth that ends in our certain death. Those two conflicting ideas never sat well with me and caused me to reject a lot of spiritual teachings and teachers.

The Course states that it has been written clearly with "words that are almost impossible to distort," but many teachers and students of whom I am aware have little more than a basic understanding of the meaning of the Course at all. My experience with the Course has been breathtaking. Therefore, with this writing, I intend to share what it is really telling us and take Course students (and everyone else) to a place they have never been before by putting it into a larger context based on all of the other very important spiritual teachings that are out there. I want to do this because there is so much information in the Course that is glossed over. So much wonderful material is ignored by so many because it seems to be mentioned only in passing, or is bewildering in its message.

The Course presents all the whys and wherefores of life in a straightforward manner and, even from a cursory overview, it all makes incredible sense to me. Of course, I could be nuts. Whether it makes sense to you is up to you. The Course is not fooling around. It's not just different; it's world-shattering, literally. It goes far beyond vague, religious dogma, rituals, healing techniques, special diets, pendulums and crystals. It combines profound insights into psychology and the human condition, coupled with a beautifully logical description of the construct of this universe and that unconditionally loving God I mentioned. It is unique in that it describes, in exquisite detail, the one, very odd little problem we face here on earth, as well as the elegant solution to that problem. It is not required that you accept the quite strange context it describes right away.

But, after all of those other spiritual practices you have been studying, if you want to move forward in your life in a meaningful way and experience something real—something that actually works if you can get it into your head—then you will understand the Course's descriptions as inevitable truth. In any event, we will *all* learn to move to this amazing worldview through our natural evolutionary progression, as all other explanations fade away. I am certain that there are many people who absolutely do not want to hear any of this—yet. The Course takes everything I have ever understood about "spirituality" and takes it to the next level and beyond. These are not your standard ideas of God and life. It answers the most fundamental questions of life clearly and directly, and some indirectly, and does it in a way that makes more sense than any other belief system I have encountered—and I have encountered a lot. Who exactly are we and why are we here? Who and where and what is God and why does He seem so absent from this place? And the deal breakers; why would God create a world with so much suffering and pain? Why does it end in death? How can any honest thinker possibly believe in a God of unconditional love and still justify this world in any way? I have not found any other belief system that could adequately answer these questions without jumping through some large and rather specious hoops, or simply ignoring any idea of a god. I have come to see the Course, not as another competing philosophy or another spiritual book, but simply as the first true description of whatever "this" is.

And along the way, a lot of other questions also get answered, including behavior and psychology questions. What about all of the extreme anger we seem to have? Doesn't it seem that we spend an awful lot of time being angry at people for things they do to us? Our relationships are so dysfunctional. Our lives didn't go in the direction we hoped. Things go terribly wrong so often for most of us. And there are so many of us who want everyone else to stop being who they are and start being who we want them to be. And in the meantime, we are so, so angry about it. They are so wrong and we are so right! What the hell is wrong with them? Don't they see what

Preface – *Living a Radical Life*

idiots they are? It's so obvious they are! How can we ever come together in even the smallest way to reconcile our differences? It certainly does not seem to be happening now.

I wrote this book because, as I said, I have been a spiritual seeker for my entire adult life, and even a bit before that. After over 50 years of reading and teachers and practicing and hoping and praying and visualizing and meditating, and many years of exhilaration and disappointment and failure and hope, I finally came to the end of my seeking. I found *A Course in Miracles*. There is no way to describe the significance of this book unless you have read all of the others. I have read most of them. With my spiritual background, I quickly noticed that my grasp of the Course seemed significantly deeper than other students and teachers I encountered. Most had limited knowledge outside of the Course, so the context I brought to it made it very rich to me. I could see the huge connections to other spiritual ideas, but I could also see where it took off in entirely different directions than any other book I had ever read.

One important thing about the Course is that it is very repetitive in an unusual way. This repetition is a vital part of its structure. If you are able to read the Course more than once, you will notice that each time you read it, it is an entirely new book. The old and obvious revelations from your last reading will fall away and new, wonderful insights will be revealed. It keeps taking you deeper as your understanding deepens. The confusing ideas that you had to skip over before are now obvious and breathtaking. This doesn't happen just once; it happens every time through it.

I am writing this not only for Course people who could use a deeper understanding; I am writing this for everyone who wants to know about life and their place in it. It's for everyone who wants to know more, whatever level you find yourself at right now. I hope to open up the Course for those who keep reading it but still may feel stuck. It's another way to read a book that is, in my opinion, the most profound book ever written. If you're not interested in looking at the deepest questions about life and God, then put down this book now pick up another one. And I'm sorry I called you crazy. Not really.

Chapter 1 – A Disturbing Idea

Get Ready

What if you woke up one morning and suddenly realized that you have been absolutely, totally incorrect about the world we are living in? What if you discovered that every person, event and object has a meaning that is different from the one you thought it had? And since you didn't know what life was about before, you now realize that every choice you previously made was inadvertently creating conflicts that you could have easily corrected if you only knew what was really going on here. Those conflicts were causing you immeasurable suffering, pain and anxiety. What if you realized upon waking that everything you have accomplished has been mostly a waste of time, because now, you suddenly understand that the true purpose of life is something you never even thought of before, and everything you have been striving for has been based on an entirely pointless purpose?

On the other hand, in spite of yourself, all of your earlier striving has led you to this new realization, and now that you have had this shift in your understanding, you can actually start to live a life that matters. Unless you are already a student of *A Course in Miracles*, then know that what I just wrote about this world is true: you have been wrong about it. Very wrong.

If you can slow yourself down for just a few moments and take some deep breaths and allow yourself to sink into a totally honest moment, and dwell on the essence of this world, you have to admit that this life on earth is a phenomenal mess. If you are reading this, you are most likely a believer in God, whatever form that belief may take. Have you thought about how tolerant you are of this world, and how conflicting your beliefs about God's role in it may be? There is certainly plenty of good here, but where does all the rest of that bad stuff fit in with a god who cares about anything? So many people aren't honest, or polite, or in the least bit concerned with anyone except themselves. Natural disasters are occurring at an unprecedented level. And, as usual, there is poverty, unrest, fear, war, torture, starvation and every negative idea you can imagine taking place all over the planet on a regular basis. Mankind's best efforts have never made a lasting or significant change in our condition.

But then, after the introspection is over, isn't it easier to forget and move on, allowing the truth, once again, to be replaced by the crazy? After all, it's so impossible for us as individuals to know how to change something so vast. And we all have our own piece of the pie to strive for, and when we aren't striving for that, all we can hope for is a few moments of peace, away from the insanity.

In the current state of the world, no matter when and where you are reading this, most of us believe that God created us along with this world, and that inevitably leaves us with one huge, unanswered question: what the heck was He thinking? Does he even deserve that capital "H"? Today, many of us have rejected the idea of a god, because we are very angry that he could cause, or even allow, the incredible amount of suffering that must eventually come to each of us. A God of love is inconceivable, and incongruous with a world such as this. If you do believe in God, he's ultimately in charge of everything, right? He must not be such a great guy if he has let it come to this. Where the hell is he while all this crap is happening? Sipping a bottomless cappuccino?

And so, as more and more people actually try to think about life in a real way, the trend has been to slowly but surely simply let go of the possibility of a god, any god. Of course, we also blame other humans for this suffering because most of the pain is caused by seeming injustice and outright cruelty that we mete out to each other. We feel incredibly angry, and we're not sure how or why it has come to this. We feel guilty, yet very justified for being so angry. Many wallow in their sadness, and many others ignore what's outside their own perimeter, with a tunnel vision that just allows them to see the next item on their personal agenda.

We live in crippling anger and blame and regret and confusion and guilt. A lot of our anger is passionate and very intense. There is so much repressed anger that when people could finally begin expressing that anger openly and anonymously on the internet, the scope of it has revealed itself, and it is overwhelming. The anger and the pain we are all expressing is clearly accelerating.

So, what if you were to face this insanity head on instead of accepting it as the way things are supposed to be? What if you decided to really look at it, why it exists, and who you are in the grand scheme of things? Our collective world mind is out of control and there seems to be no way back to sanity. We have avoided thinking too seriously about God, because He seems to be so hard to find, and it seems to be way beyond our feeble human ability to make any sense of the world. In any event, God certainly doesn't seem to want, or be able, to do anything about it. Our anger demonstrates that we are in an almost constant state of feeling victimized by everything and everyone around us. What kind of a world is this? Why would a so-called loving god do this to us?

Are you spending any time asking yourself meaningful questions about life and God and who you are? Do you believe that the answers to all of your questions are available, or do you feel they are beyond your pay grade?

What if those answers are not only available, but they are *necessary* for you to understand before you can make any meaningful changes in your life? The answers to this bunch of insoluble problems are offered by, and many are unique to, *A Course in Miracles*. It gives us the big picture in a way that feels very logical, detailed and, in my mind, correct. Although the Course puts our lives into a perspective and a context that is unbelievably beautiful and satisfying at the deepest level of the soul, the Course is also based on one very disturbing and difficult idea. Before you can accept the teachings of the Course, you must be open to this rather apple-cart-upsetting concept and to seeing this life very differently than you ever have before.

Warning! For most of you, this idea will cause an immediate and strong negative reaction because it goes against everything you have believed in for your entire life. It goes against what every major religion teaches—at least on the surface. Your ego will have a powerful inclination to reject it firmly and without consideration. And yet I ask you to consider it. I don't ask that you *believe* it—at least not right away. I only ask that you keep an open mind to this idea, because it is a very difficult idea to process, and also, because if you do, if and when it finally starts to sink in, it will change your world forever, literally.

Tiny and Mad

That idea is this: this world is an illusion. This world does not exist. Quite literally, it is simply the collective dream of the Son of God, who is all of us together. You and I are asleep, and this world is as unreal as the dreams we now have at night. It is powerful and real to us because we have dreamed it up using the immense power of the mind of God, which we share. It is an illusion born of a very understandable, but strange and insane idea.

According to *A Course in Miracles*, this is how it all happened. God created his only Son in perfect love as an extension of Himself, yet still one with Him, part of God forever, endowed with every quality and ounce of power and creativity of God. God creates through extension; in other words, whatever God creates always remains a permanent part of Him, and what God extends is love. This Son of God (us) has absolutely all of the attributes of God because when God creates something, He can put no less than all of Himself into it. That means that the Son of God is exactly like God in every way except one; God is the Father. The Son did not create himself. God did. The Son of God lives within the body of God, one with God forever, having everything, lacking nothing.

> *T-28.V.7. You who believe there is a little gap between you and your brother, do not see that it is here you are as prisoners in a world perceived to be existing here.* ²***The world you see does not exist, because the place where you perceive it is not real.***

This is what the Course teaches. The idea that life is an illusion also exists in many other writings, like the ancient Vedas, but what they say can be confusing because of the many conflicting and puzzling ways life is explained. *A Course in Miracles* puts forth a very beautiful context for this life, and it fits together in an amazing way. There are no gaps or missteps in the entire work. There is nothing senseless. It doesn't demand or coerce you to believe anything. It merely offers you something to help you lessen your suffering. Yet it is all based on this one, incredible, unbelievable, incomprehensible bombshell of an idea; this universe doesn't exist. The Truth of this idea has always existed and, therefore, it has always been available to those who are able to access it. You must decide for yourself if you can take this teaching into your heart or not. If you do, your life will change dramatically and for the better.

The Course is clear, and repeats the idea many times and in many consistent ways, constantly cajoling us to consider it as inevitable truth. The Course simply describes what happened within the body of God and the troubling idea that arose from His Son. It tells us the *why* of everything.

At the very moment of creation of the Son of God, what the Course calls a tiny, mad idea occurred. That tiny, mad idea, thought by the Son of God, was actually a fairly deep thought with layers of meaning and is the basis for everything we now believe about ourselves, as well as this crazy dream world. The Son of God was curious about the only things he did not know and could not experience. The main idea behind this universe, and what the Son did not know, came with the desire to understand the concept of uniqueness, or specialness. This is anathema to God. In the real world of God and oneness, there can be no specialness. God and love can only be absolutely equal and fair in all things, so the idea that some aspect of God could be different, or special, from another aspect of God, and deserving different treatment, immediately creates the necessity of judgment, because judgment is automatic when different things need to be compared. God knew that specialness was an idea that undermined everything that love was. So when the Son of God asked for uniqueness, God said, "Like, no way," or cosmic words to that effect. That idea of specialness is outside of what can be true, for oneness means that there are no parts, no separation, no comparisons.

If the Son of God could not experience uniqueness within himself as part of God, then the only way to experience it was to add another mind-blowing concept to the original tiny, mad idea. The Son of God wanted to know something else he did not know; "OK if I can't be special within God, then what would it be like *not* to be God?" That's a pretty significant idea for someone who knows everything; a part of God wants to know what it would be like to be something other than himself, so he could experience the opposite of God. And if he could experience what it felt like *not* to be God, then what would that possibly look like? What would be the ramifications of the goofy idea of specialness that God was so against? Who or what would someone living according to a different framework be like? What would life be like without the perfection of God, or the perfection of oneness? How could there be something else? And if there was life without God, where would or could that life come from? How could any life arise without a creator, from nothing?

All of these thoughts are very related. In this theoretical daydream, the Son of God simply began to question his origin and his nature. If he were not God, he would certainly not be part of God, so who would he be, and where could he have come from? If he wanted to experience specialness, then there would have to be things that were different from each other, so comparisons could be made. Also, in this theoretical scenario, the Son wouldn't be the "son" of anyone anymore; he would somehow be responsible for his own creation and his own life, or he would have to spring forth from some spontaneous cosmic randomness.

Now, why would the Son of God be so interested in being different from God, or experiencing specialness? This entire scenario of specialness seems to have come about because the Son of God recognized immediately that He was an offspring, and because of that, He was a tiny bit different from God, because He didn't create Himself, so he was a Son to His Father, His Creator. The Course mentions that the one problem we have here is caused by what it calls Authorship. This just means that God is the father and the Son is the son, and God created the Son, and that small difference determines the cosmic pecking order of existence, as the Son must now also create His own children. If that slight difference existed, it also meant that difference was built into creation somehow, and it seemed natural for the Son to explore differences. So, this world was a natural outgrowth of the Son taking the idea of differences to their most insane level. This universe seems to be a part of the Son's birth process that He is experiencing as He settles into the truth of His reality. He must let go of this vestigial baggage of ideas of differences before He can become the pure Son of God as He travels through the birth canal to His true identity. Our entire universe may just be this process of the Son of God finally coming to the realization of Who He really is and shaking off the chaff of random ideas and reckless thinking of His natal disorientation, as He settles into the majesty of perfection.

As I said, this is the basis of everything we believe about *this* world. Many of us believe in God, but this is a world where belief in God is a choice, not a fact. We just don't *know*, unless we strongly pretend we know, just like we pretend everything else. Knowing God will never be a provable concept, shared by one human with another. God can only be known or experienced individually. Many of us really *hope* there is a God. But here, we have imagined a world where God has been eliminated, and we have separated ourselves from our source and from each other. But because we really *were* created by God, there is something way down inside each one of us that still knows Who we are. So, God seeps through into our beliefs. The more we let go of this world that is based on no God, the more we can feel our connection to God.

In the meantime, we imagined a world where we arose from something other than God. We have, in essence, become our own creators, and in so doing, we have symbolically overthrown God. If there is no God, we had to come from somewhere! So, we created a universe that arose spontaneously from nothing in a big bang, that is also self-sustaining and self-contained; a universe that we believe, in turn, created us. Now we can put our finger on the starting point of life, and also experience what it is like not to be God. We can each be special.

I don't know about you but this is unbelievably clever to me. This isn't really that radical, but just a simple matter of curiosity. We just want to know what we don't know. We want to experience something outside the box. We are just the rebellious, petulant child, acting out against our parent. We weren't being mean with this tiny idea. That's against our true nature. We were being curious and we wanted to experience something outside of the boundaries of perfect love. We needed to experience smart phones and croissants and falling leaves and kangaroos—badly. Simple as it is, this will take a while to process for most of us.

Here is something even more amazing. As I said, the tiny, mad idea was a complex thought with many layers, so add this to the first part of that idea; the source of the tiny, mad idea isn't just that the Son of God wanted to know what it would be like to be unique or not to be God: its true origin is that the Son of God felt there was something else he wanted that he did not have or know. He felt the idea of *lack*. The tiny, mad idea was remarkable in that it comes from the mind of the Son of God, that complete, unbelievably perfect mind imagining for the tiniest moment, just after He was born, that there was something lacking. There was something out there that God could not provide. The Son had a question that lacked an answer.

Based on the original tiny, mad idea, this entire universe is built on the foundation of lack, and the corollary to that idea, which is desire. Desire is the idea that you need something because there is something missing. This is an amazingly rich idea. The tiny, mad idea is not merely the thought that created the universe billions of years ago, it is also the idea that sustains it to this day. We live our lives in a world that expresses lack and therefore, desire, in every form. The Son of God wanted to experience concepts and ideas that were outside of the boundaries of truth.

> T-1.VI.2. ²*This sense of separation would never have arisen if you had not distorted your perception of truth, and had thus perceived yourself as lacking.*

The three-dimensional world of form is a place of separation and lack, of specialness and the absence of God, and it is the entire theme of this life we are living. We do not ever believe ourselves to be complete or whole, or "finished." We can only *have* what we take from someone else, making them less complete. Every single moment of the day, we are absorbed in the struggle of give and take, of what we lack and in the striving for it, whether it's food, love, money, health or respect, or any of a billion variations on those themes. We are in the constant search for more; some sort of completion. No matter what we have, there is always something missing. There will be no feeling of completion until we realize that we have, at this moment, absolutely everything we could ever want or need. This doesn't translate well into the world of solid matter, because this world is incomplete by its very nature, so it stands to reason that your completeness lies beyond this world.

Another way to understand the tiny, mad idea is that, with the request for specialness, the Son of God wanted God to change the Truth. But what could be changed in perfection? Any change to perfection must result in something that isn't true; something that falls outside of perfection. The Son began to recognize and give importance to what wasn't true: lack, specialness, separation. We began to believe that our insane desires *were* true. This still holds true today in our lives, and the result is the world you see around you. This world isn't true and therefore, it isn't real, but in our collective insanity, we have utterly convinced ourselves that it is, and most of us are still really attached to it—for the most part.

This is an amazing thing to wrap your head around. The goal of this life is to return to God, and that means to accept, without any doubt, there is nothing lacking in your life, because the *real* you is already with God, safe and perfect and lacking nothing.

Forget it!

OK, so with that tiny, mad idea came a host of implications. When the Son of God thought the tiny, mad idea, there had to be a way to really grasp it and follow through with it. Not to be God means to be apart from God, and the only way to really *know* that, for the Son of God to really experience the mad idea fully, was to *forget* the truth about himself and lose all memory of who he really is. Of course, being separate from God is impossible on the face of it because there is nothing that is not God. God is everything. The only way for the idea of separation from God—and the so-called reality of this dream universe—to occur would be for it to occur, not in reality, but only as a thought or an imagining of separation; a *dream* of separation. When this idea came to the Son of God, the vast power of the Son of God's intention and focus immediately gave birth to an immense dream world where separation could exist; separate consciousnesses, separate objects, and above all, the single most powerful and frightening thought ever considered—loss of all memory that he is really God.

Because the Son of God is still God, separation from God also meant the Son of God had to "separate" from himself to undermine the idea of perfect oneness, and to provide a venue for the specialness he craved. As I said, for this to be truly experienced, the Son of God had to imagine the existence of a *place of separation* where this idea could thrive. It had to be a "place" (since there was no precedent for the idea of a "place") and it had to contain, and have built within it, a structure of rules that didn't need God for it to function, which would also fulfill the idea of separation from God—a self-sustaining place that appeared without explanation and needed no God. We call these rules the laws of physics or the laws of nature, and they must never stop working, because that would break our firm belief in the reality of this place. So, the Son of God imagined a neutral, three-dimensional "place," a world of form, where objects could exist separate from each other; where one object could not be in two places. In order for one object to occupy more than one space, another fascinating concept was imagined—time. For an object to be in two places, it had to move from one place to the other—over time.

Without time, a three-dimensional place of separation falls apart. Time is needed in order to facilitate the movement of solid objects, and also to allow for interaction between the multiple things that occupy space. And further, two separate objects could not be in the same place at the same time. The idea was that, since we are now imagining separateness, each separate piece had to be somewhere where there was nothing else. The body you now occupy completed that desire. The Son of God split into billions, or even trillions, of pieces of individual consciousnesses and they are now all separate from each other, occupying their own meaty, leafy or rocky containers. Time also means that this universe is in constant motion and change, and can never be completed. This dream was unfathomably all-encompassing and detailed, with every subatomic particle playing its part in the play. It is as real as it can be, within itself, because the power of the mind of the Son of God is unlimited, just as God's mind is. In other words, it's real because we want it to be real, so we can experience a different "truth" apart from God. The only reality this dream has is the one we give it, through the immense power of our mind. But to God, it's only our temporary, unreal and tiny, meaningless experiment in self-discovery.

This place that the Son of God imagines is absolutely neutral and harbors no need of God. It only contains whatever the separate consciousnesses decide it contains, fulfilling their own individual versions of desire, for the separate consciousnesses are merely tiny fragments of the mind of the Son of God. The only way for the idea of separation to work is if those separate consciousnesses do not remember who they are, for if a tiny part of their minds remembered they were God, they couldn't really immerse themselves into the world of the original, tiny, mad idea; they would not experience what it was like not to be God. So, we fell asleep to our true Self, and pretended to wake up inside a strangely upside-down dream.

Since we don't remember we are God, that means we also don't have any memories of God that in any way come close to the truth. Since we don't remember our creator, our vast, natural curiosity had to come up with a scenario to explain where we humans and this universe came from. So, we had to create a creation story. We created an idea of God, or rather, we created hundreds of ideas about different types of gods and/or no gods at all, including the god of scientific research. We created as many scenarios about our origin as we liked, because we are free to do that in this dream. Some of those scenarios speak of gods, some do not. We believe in a tremendous variety of gods, all with widely different attributes. Collectively speaking, together we have usurped the throne of God, and way deep down inside all of us, we are feeling extremely guilty about it, because we know how far away from the truth this whole world is. We have created a dream in which we are responsible for ourselves individually, and therefore, we can believe in a god or no god, but what we really believe without question, is that we are small, separate beings, living alone in a scary world.

The Course states that we are thoughts of God, and that God Himself is a thought. When the Son of God fell asleep, what really happened is that He merely thought a countless number of thoughts in His desire to experience separation, and layered them over Himself. They are thoughts of separation, untrue and temporary. They are thoughts that brought to life individuals that are separate from each other, also known as "egos." We believe these ego thoughts to be true. We believe these thoughts are "us," and that we exist as humans. It is up to us to see these thoughts of individuality and humanity and let them go into the nothingness that they are.

The Son of God made these ego thoughts so he could become the creator. The Son of God created these unreal children, living in an unreal world, disconnected from their source, in charge of their own existence. It is the manifestation of our "specialness." The ego's entire purpose is to support the tiny, mad idea, to convince us that we are in this alone, that we are special, and "I" am responsible only for "me." Oh sure, there may be a god, but the Christian god many of us are most familiar with and all the other versions of God that are thriving today on the planet are reflections of our ego. We haven't created a God of oneness who is unconditionally loving, as much as a god who, at the least, is very intimidating, demanding, contradictory and mysterious—and scary. More like the Wizard of Oz, or a flawed, angry human.

We wiped our memory of our reality by falling asleep to it. We shifted our focus so totally into this tiny, mad idea that it became our only reality. This is our *dream*! But it's almost impossible for us to know this because it was made using the incredible mind of the Son of God, who made it out of a desire *not* to remember that it *is* a dream.

All I Have to Do is Dream

I understand that the idea about this being a dream or illusion is very daunting. So let me ask you this; What makes you think that this *isn't* a dream? This is a good way to begin to undo the idea that this world is real. There are only two main differences between our nighttime dreams and this waking dream, as far as I can discern. These two things firmly keep us from realizing this is a dream. The first one is *consistency*. For this dream to serve its original purpose, it has to be consistent so we can have faith in its stability and not question its reality. Clever Son of God! If things started getting weird and inconsistent, like an episode of the Twilight Zone, we would start to question it, and our doubts would begin to crumble its foundation, and that would undermine its purpose. There is nothing more earth shattering than understanding that this is a universe that has been designed very specifically for a particular purpose. We have to believe in it. The consistency is the linchpin of its hold on us.

Every day, when you wake up, it has followed the flow of time, and everything that happened overnight made consistent sense. Everything is the same; the world is still spinning, the people on the other side of the world woke up and lived their lives. The only differences from yesterday are the easily understandable things that have happened during your sleep; other people moved things around, it snowed, the world stock markets went up and down according to their natures, the news events from all across the world, etc. All the people you know seem to have the same personalities as yesterday, and they remember and share what you remember about this world. Some people die and some new ones are born. Everything that happens, no matter how large or small, is easily understood, because it always flows from the previous day and the weeks and months before. It appears that the dream doesn't stop when you are asleep, for the world seems to continue seamlessly around the clock. You left it for a few moments of sleep, and re-entered it like jumping off and back on a carousel. The laws of the universe have held everything in place. The rules always function, and the rules account for everything. The powerful grip of these rules means that patents can be filed, businesses can make and sell things, physicists can keep looking at the rules more intensely, and trains can run on time.

The consistency is the *only* reason we have to go to school—to learn how it works day in and day out, and to learn what other people discovered about this world in the past that still works today. It is empirically provable. Whatever you do stays done. Knowing that everything continues is what keeps us believing in it. Whatever you remember life to be like the previous day, remains. Your car keys are always right where you left them the night before—OK, so maybe that's a bad example.

The consistency of this dream is the only thing that gives it credibility. If it were not consistent, there would be nothing to learn, because nothing would be predictable. There would be no schools because it would be pointless teaching something that was constantly changing. There could be no lawyers, or scientists, or any other vocation, because what consistency *really* means is that this dream is based on the *past*. Every day, another solid and real 24 hours is added to the history of the world. As long as we believe in the existence of the past, this dream will reflect it. All of our ideas about this world (scientific, psychological, etc.) are only valid because we know that what we discovered last year is still valid today. We may modify our ideas, but that's because we are really understanding them better; and therefore, understanding ideas from the past better.

Without consistency, this world would instantly fall apart. We could never draw any conclusions—about anything. This life would have absolutely no point and no substance. This life would be like your nighttime dreams, and you would wander aimlessly inside of it. And we, powerful pieces of the Son of God, are using our incredibly powerful minds to give this consistent dream reality. Our focus on it, our belief in it, and our steadfast buy-in to it, are making it real—but only making it real within itself, to us humans. We created this powerful dream to convince ourselves that it is real and we are separate from God, so we can really live that tiny, mad desire of knowing what it is like *not* to be God, what it's like to be incomplete and unique. We had to make this world believable! It *has* to be consistent! This is the single most powerful aspect of the dream. The consistency of the dream has the power to convince us that it is real. The Son of God constructed this dream world so well, that ironically, this unrelenting consistency and logic is the source of all the arguments for science *against* God, as well as all of the arguments *for* an amazing god who created such a complex universe. The remarkable complexity of this universe will support anything you can think up. You are free to choose. Pretty clever stuff.

Difference #2

The other difference between this waking dream and our nighttime dreams is that we *know* our nighttime dreams are dreams, because every morning *we wake up* from them! But when you are dreaming them at night, you firmly believe you are living within that dream. It is as real to you as this waking life. It is all you've got at the moment you're in it. But we have not awakened from this daytime dream; at least not yet, so we've got nothing to compare this dream to. **There is no way to know you're in a dream until you're out of it!** That is the incredible power of our minds. After the Buddha became enlightened, he came to a place where they didn't know him, and a group of men asked him if he was a god? He said, "No." They asked him if he was a reincarnation of a god, and he said, "No." He also said, "No" when they asked him if he was a wizard, or a man. Finally, they asked, "Then, what are you?" and the Buddha said, "I am awake!"

So, you've probably heard that story before, but have you really understood the implication of it? He woke up! The very name "Buddha" means "awakened one." Yet, the impact of the idea that this world is a dream has not gotten any real traction throughout history, no matter how often we hear it, because it's so radical, and so threatening to the ego, so impossible to believe. We continue to go through our lives being Buddhists or Christians or Jews but never understand the idea that we are literally here to wake up from a dream, because that idea gets buried and twisted within all of the other many ideas of every belief system. **It is the single most important concept to understand**. On its face, it is a completely ridiculous idea! The grip this dream has on us is powerful and unquestionable. But then again, no matter what you believe, you still have to pay the rent and eat something once in a while. Not to mention all of the other things that revolve around your imaginary body's needs. We are very easily distracted by our clever and conniving egos, but the goal is to wake up!

Now, think about this in a thoughtful way; do these two differences between your nighttime and daytime dreams really convince you that one is a dream and one isn't? Is there anything of any real substance to convince you that this waking life you are living is more real than your nighttime dreams? Do you think that if you are really the Son of God, that any suffering at all could possibly be the result of God, or the wish of God? Do you think there is anything *real* outside of God? Do you really think this is real? Really? Do you really think that an unconditionally loving God would create a world that contained any anguish for His Son?

If you are a part of God, and share the mind of God, then you must admit to yourself that anything you can conjure up with your infinitely powerful mind can appear to be real. This is just a dream. It's a dream that is constructed just a little bit better than your nighttime dreams, because it was created for a specific purpose by an immensely powerful, collective mind, so it has us all sucked into it in a persuasive way.

Chapter 1 – *A Disturbing Idea*

Creation

So, that brings us to God. This world, this universe, was *not* created by God. **God did not create this!** Try telling that to anyone on the planet with religious beliefs without being chased down the block. This is the most important concept to take away from the idea that this is a dream. The reason God appears to be so absent from this world is because, as I said, we have chosen to exclude Him from it. God also does not acknowledge this world because of the error built into it. That's a big concept to wrap your head around. God cannot see this universe (this world of form) because God only acknowledges what is Real, what is True and what is Love. If God were to acknowledge this world, that would give it reality, because the power of God's mind is what creates. God can only experience and acknowledge and create perfection, which is love.

Those of us who do believe in God, and that God created us, have quite naturally and automatically tied that belief to the idea that God *must* also have created this world and universe. After all, we're part of it and it seems like a package deal. And where the heck else could it have come from? Nothing is powerful enough to create something this big and complicated except God. If you can suspend that thought for a moment, consider allowing yourself to now believe that God could have created you without also creating this world. The fact that God seems not to be in attendance here should make it a distinct possibility.

We can still find God here, and indeed, that's exactly what we are here to do. But in order to do that, we have to let go of this world and believe in another world of God that we aren't even aware of; a world of oneness and unconditional love. Our egos want to keep God away from this world in every practical sense because that's the whole idea. But because we know on a very deep level that we *are* God, it is impossible for many of us who feel that presence to keep that knowledge hidden. When the ego realizes that we are getting close to the truth of something, it panics, and does whatever it can to undermine that truth. The ego's reaction to the truth is always the same; twist it into a perverted version of the truth as a disruption to stop the searching. Swift and clever distraction. The ego takes our potential for remembering a perfect God and twists it into a perverted idea of God; one who punishes and loves conditionally, a god who hates certain things about us, and is capable of punishing us in hell for all eternity for stealing a few office supplies. The ego has created a god that is as silly and confusing as the world we are now in. This is a very effective way to keep us from wanting to really find Him. It creates a strange god and then says, "Here you go! Here's God" but the god it has created is not really worth the trouble for most of us to find.

The ego resorts to absolutely every trick it can come up with to make us believe that we are on the path to finding God or the truth, while behind our conscious backs, it is doing everything it possibly can to make sure that discovery never happens. There is no adversary you will ever come across that is as formidable, devious or confusing as your own ego. The ego's goal is to keep you totally convinced that all of your decisions are the right ones and all of your seeking is leading you to the truth, while its true agenda is to deceive you into believing without question that the wrong direction you are heading in is the right one. The ego's god is the tiny, mad idea.

Another thing that immediately happened when we decided to pretend that we were separate from God is that we lost our belief in our unlimited nature. We suddenly became very, very small and separate individuals, fending for ourselves against a hoard of other individuals, scary external events and unknown forces, conspiring to use our smallness to conquer us in every possible way. We immediately became subject to attack. The idea of attack is built into the idea of separation, because each individual is expressing its own desires, and when those desires conflict, they must compete, and then there can only be fear and suffering, and winners and losers. In this dream, we feel we are being attacked by everything we can imagine, quite literally: disease, aging, decay, poverty, physical attack, mental attack, verbal attack, lack of anything. We became immersed in our fear of attack. We didn't make this silly world to feel the support and power of God, but to eliminate it. Because the belief that the world is a dream is a difficult one to grasp, here are some more thoughts to wrap your powerful mind around to see if they help you open up a little more to these ideas:

Insanity Plea #1

A Course in Miracles is vastly different from all major religions or belief systems, because it teaches that God is one. Other religions hint at the idea of oneness, but the simplicity of it gets lost in all of the obfuscating baggage they bring along for the ride. There is only God and nothing is separate from God. Whatever God creates remains forever part of God. The mind of God is a shared mind, where everything is known to all of God. "We" humans are not separate beings; we are the collective Son of God, part of God, merely demonstrating separateness in a dream.

So, what about this idea of oneness? Do you truly believe in the idea? You've heard about oneness a lot but have you ever asked yourself what that really *means*? Do you believe (correctly) that you and I are part of and one with God, and that the reason we don't know it is because we share a misperception of who we are? If you believe in oneness, can you then believe in the duality of this world as well? Can you believe yourself (incorrectly) to be an individual with a separate identity? Duality is this universe we live in, where things have opposites and degrees, and where everything is separate from everything else. Duality is the idea of perception, where what you believe is true for you but not necessarily for someone else. Do you believe in oneness or duality? **You can't believe in both!** There is no "unified theory" that could possibly account for both. You are either one with God, or you aren't. God would never create duality because it is against His nature, and God cannot create against his nature. And if duality actually existed, that would mean oneness couldn't exist, because that would mean there would be something else besides "oneness," which takes us right back to duality.

So, that's the insanity. If you believe in duality, then you believe in this 3-D universe, and have somehow justified in your mind the insane idea that duality can exist within oneness. Seriously? So the question then becomes, if you believe in oneness, how can you possibly explain this world we live in? And if you believe in duality, then you can't believe in oneness. Or, you could believe in the ego's version of oneness, which is a watered down, new age catch phrase that means absolutely nothing. Oneness is easy to say, but it is a hard thing to consider in reality, since this universe of twoness and threeness is the only thing we know. Of course, this is another way of seeing this world as a dream, so I'm asking you, do you believe that this life you are living and the planet you are living on right now, is real!? Especially because if this dualistic world isn't real, how can something that *seems* so real not be real? What else is there? What *is* real?

Also, if you truly understand oneness, then you can't exist as a separate being. This is *the* fundamental fear of discovering who we really are, because we would have to acknowledge that this thing, this person we are now, cannot possibly be explained, and cannot possibly exist. We fear total annihilation, but that's exactly what's going to happen to all of us—but in a good way, he said cheerfully.

Give it up

Here's the really scary part (it just keeps getting better, doesn't it?): this is another, very difficult concept to accept that is based on this world being a dream. If this world is a dream, and you're not really a human, and you're not really here, then that means that *everything* you have worked so hard for, and spent so much time validating, confirming, dramatizing, defending and working for, is not real. I'm asking you to consider that everything in this world of form means absolutely nothing. I am telling you that all of the stuff that you have given so much importance to, means nothing! Nothing you believe in means anything; your job, your body, your name, your social standing, your possessions, *nothing*! Well, there is one thing: the only thing that is real is your mind, and the only real thoughts you have are thoughts of love. All thoughts that conflict with love are just part of the dream, and have no substance or importance. This is attacking the very foundation of your life! Is it even possible for you to consider giving up everything you've ever believed in for a vague idea that has almost no real support from anyone else? Can you believe in something the entire world rejects? Can you break away from all of your societal, religious and personal beliefs?

If this world doesn't exist, then there must be a way to get out of it. Indeed, the *purpose* of life must be somehow to get out of this dualistic world, and see and join what must be another, or Real, world of Oneness, if you can get over your fear of not existing as you anymore. Because you can't see that real world now, or even conceive of it, you may not be inclined to give up the only thing you know for what seems like a pipedream. Ironic, eh? But if I'm asking you to consider giving up everything that you are now, then I'm asking you to consider that a life containing the dualities of health and sickness, happiness and sorrow, joy and suffering, birth and certain death, is just a construct of your ego and, in fact, is not even here in front of your eyes at all. There is something about this life that we cling to because we fashioned it to experience something very specific, and so it will not go away easily, as long as we still want these experiences. If you can believe in the power of the mind to create anything, then try to understand that the power of the mind is responsible for you and me believing this dream is actually real, and it is also our ticket out of here.

How about Global Thermonuclear War?

The collective mind of the Son of God is many orders of magnitude smarter than any of us individually. This collective mind of ours has created an amazingly complex scenario designed to keep us here to experience a life of specialness and lack, without God. By keeping us separate from each other, it limits our ability to come together to figure this out, and it uses our separateness to convince us that this is what we are—humans; tiny, dumb, helpless, victims of a ruthless world, disempowered and alone, powerless to go beyond this. No matter how you look at it, it's up to *you* to see something beyond your humanity. It's up to you to figure it out and relentlessly search for yourself.

Imagine this:

This universe we have created is an incredibly complex, three-dimensional, multi-sensory, full immersion video game. And just like any video game, we made it so we could experience something other than our usual life. Winning this game is a complicated process because it is a very clever game. The first step is to figure out that you're even playing a game! This game is not real, but accepting that is a very difficult hurdle, because all of the players have had their memories erased as to who they really are; that they're really living in an entirely different and perfect world while just imagining they're in a game. When we play a video game, we can immerse ourselves into it to the point where we will give up all food and drink and just about everything else. But we are always aware that it's a game and that's because we remember another life beyond it that we can come back to. Not in *this* game. We don't even know we're playing. We have put the controller inside of the game and severed our contact with everything outside of the game.

After taking the first incredible step of realizing that this is a game, the second step is the conscious understanding that winning this game means ending it, unlike a normal game, where the goal is to win something *within* the game. We don't even know why we're playing, so discovering the "why" seems to be a reasonable goal. This game is designed to keep going as long as you keep playing. Our focus on and belief in the game is what creates it and perpetuates it. In order to create something with your mind, you have to concentrate on it. This game will go on as long as you believe it has credibility, reality and purpose: keep playing and it keeps going.

The third step is to take action; we have to take the necessary steps to end the game. The only way to do that is to stop playing. You learn when you meditate, that in order to hold a constant image in your mind, you have to constantly re-create the image. The present moment is all there is, so in order for the image to always remain in your mind's eye, you have to re-think it, re-think it, re-think it over and over again to keep the image, because that image only exists right now, in your mind. The second you let your mind wander into memories or future worries, your mental image goes away and is replaced by whatever has grabbed your attention.

What we are doing as the Son of God to create this world is to focus on it so completely in every moment that it has become real to our subconscious minds, and so we project it constantly. It is what we have decided to believe is real. In order to end the game, we have to focus completely and intensely outside of the game, knowing there is something else beyond the game. We must focus so intently that we can break the spell of the collective mind until our proper vision begins to return.

Like the movie *War Games*, every move is a losing move and the only way to win is not to play. We need to learn the futility of this life. But unfortunately, to learn that, we first have to play every move we can, until we realize that none of the moves really work. Nothing in this world is ultimately satisfying. Eventually, everything gets old and tired and frustrating here, but the only way to know that is to find out for yourself. We will not stop playing until we lose interest, because this world is initially so compelling.

If you believe we are here to figure out life on earth, and you are having difficulty accepting this world as a dream, then consider this: for centuries, our current way of thinking hasn't been able to figure anything out. We are all still pretty much guessing about life. A huge percentage of the world population is religious. We have widely different practices and views about life and God, most of which amount to superficial rituals, judgment, anger, violence and groveling. The same as it's been for centuries with minor adjustments. A spiritual, non-religious approach may seem more natural but in general, spiritual people have just as much trouble with this world as everyone else. Most people are trying to win something inside the game. Have our countless clever gizmos and gadgets done anything to really make us happier as a human race? Doesn't that tell you right away that in order to figure it out, we have to approach this world in a different way?

How long will we continue in the same direction before we realize we're no further along with real answers? We are doing everything we can to fix ourselves by manipulating the things in this world. We continue to try to make the world better with gadgets and inventions and think tanks, but unfathomable poverty, cruelty and suffering go on unabated. We think very hard about the right way to proceed, and we create more and more clever drugs, but we always come up against more and more clever diseases. We go to workshops and seminars and learn what we need to know. We diet and exercise. We believe in spiritual "places" and a million other things within this world that have some special power. We never stop looking for our completion within this world.

So, how do we stop playing the game? We have created this game in a way that allows us to reincarnate over and over again, to be rich and poor, healthy and sick, gay and straight, white and black, living as many different scenarios as it takes for our individual souls to suddenly get it and say, "Hey, none of this works!" Other advanced players may tell you that, but you won't believe it until you experience it for yourself. We have to withdraw from it, one step at a time. We have to give up the imaginary bodies, the drama, the money, our careers, personalities, all of the things our imaginary five senses tell us we desperately need and seem inextricably attached to. But most of all, we have to give up the fear and guilt. If we really tried, we could hear our Mother gently calling us to give up the game and come and have some dinner. We have to give up the guilt of playing the game so long and letting go of our real life, and ignoring our Mother. We have to give up the fear of what She will do to us for playing the game, even though She is unbelievably nice and would never think to punish us in any way or even make us feel bad about our little indulgence.

That last step is the most difficult, because this game seems to be the only thing that exists, so giving it up seems to mean giving up *everything* with nothing to replace it when we stop, because we have had our memory erased, and we fear that annihilation thing. Also, how does one stop playing when the game keeps going? The game won't stop until we stop it, but we won't stop playing until it's over but it's not over until we stop... Whew! The ego has designed this world with all of the exits seemingly closed. But God has given us a way out, and until we recognize that, we will not understand how to stop the game.

Chapter 1 – *A Disturbing Idea*

Vigilance

Because we have made it so clever and all-consuming, and because we have forgotten everything about ourselves, we have convinced ourselves that this game is extremely important somehow. As a matter of fact, it is *everything* to us. It is the only thing. The only way for us to see the alternative, that is, the real world of God, is to withdraw our attention from this illusory world. But how do we do that?

It takes as much vigilance to turn off the world as we currently expend energy in creating it. To break its hold on us, we have to keep our minds focused on God more than we focus on this world. We create this world by living in it, participating in it, believing in it, focusing on it. We *want* to be in this world. To turn it off, we must put as much energy into letting this world go, while striving for another one.

You have to stop wanting it.

You have to drop out of this life more than 50% of the time, and give yourself over to God's world. And that's only to get started! Are you discouraged yet? These ideas are not for people who still love this life because giving up this life means trying to grasp another, more real world that currently exists beyond our comprehension. We have very little understanding of a world without form, without specialness or judgment, where perfection is as normal as it is impossible here on earth. We have no idea what it means to be a non-self. It is also why many people have trouble with the Course. They simply cannot see giving up this life, and they make many different excuses for not only modifying what the Course says but modifying the words of all the great teachers who have come here before with the same message. **This is not who you are!**

We are here to wake up. Nothing more. You must realize that your ego is enticing you to believe something that isn't true. All of the resistance you feel right now to these words is your ego trying to stay alive. The ego's self-imposed, and only job, is to keep this world going, and to maintain the tiny, mad idea. We must be vigilant for God and His kingdom, just as we are vigilant now for the ego and its illusory kingdom. Our egos trick us into looking for stability in this chaotic world, and into thinking stability can be found in consistency, or lots of money—which we equate with security—or a good job, or raising a family, or whatever else we put importance in. But those things only work for a while—until they inevitably stop working altogether. Just because the ego wants and justifies everything here doesn't mean those things are true or worthwhile or valuable.

Think of all the things you used to want. Think of all the crazy things you hear people say about what they want and believe. Every wacky idea ever accomplished or attempted by every single human who has ever lived, has been justified by them, and eventually, those desires all fade into nothingness by their very nature. The Course says that we, as humans, believe we have to give up everything to gain nothing, but in truth, we are giving up nothing to gain Everything.

Chapter 2 – A Little Bit More on the Dream

Elephant

The idea that we are living within a dream is the elephant in the room of *A Course in Miracles*. This is the single most difficult concept to understand, accept and believe about life on earth. It is not an intellectual idea. It is literal. We are not here. There is no Jim or Betty or Sally. There are no such things as human beings or separate identities. Yet, how can something so ridiculous be true? This world is, and has been, obviously very, very real to us for as long as we've been humans, even over many lifetimes. How much mental work do you have to do before you can even begin to believe that it might be a dream? I have known many Course students and I feel that many ardent followers are still having tremendous difficulty understanding this idea in a meaningful way. The shift in consciousness that is required to believe it is impossible to describe. This idea is not taught in any religion or alternative belief system, except for the ancient texts of Hinduism. If this is a dream, what does that mean to you? It means quite a bit.

Insanity Plea #2

Here's a little bit more to help you think about this world as a dream. If you believe in God, do you believe that there could be anything except God? In other words, do you believe that something could exist outside of God? Like hell, for instance? Or purgatory? Or the devil? And where exactly would these things be? God would have to exist within some larger "thing" that contains other things as well. Wouldn't that mean that God is limited because He's next to something else, and that means He must have a border of some kind to keep Himself separate from those other things? If hell is within the body of God, then can God still be unconditional love, with an eternity of torture enclosed within Him?

So, here's the insanity; if this world exists and was created by God and is truly part of a God of unconditional love, could it contain suffering of any kind? Does your definition of God allow you to believe that He's limited, or *not* unconditional love? What allows you to believe in a god who would accept suffering in any form? Examine that thought in yourself to see how you may have adjusted your definition of God based merely on the cruelty of this world. If you believe that God is love, then either your idea of love has gotten very tenuous (probably because our love relationships seem to be so strange), or the God you believe in must be far from perfect. Is it OK for you to accept a flawed, cruel, humanlike god, or do you just not think about it?

Just to make it easy for you, there is nothing that exists that is not God, particularly if you accept a God of oneness. Therefore, there is no hell, and everything that *does* exist is one with God and made of unconditional love. That's the definition of the only kind of God I want to believe in, but I have no way to make you believe what I believe. But, if I'm right, then where does that leave you and me? If you believe in the idea of oneness, if only intellectually, there is only one solution to the problem of Oneness vs. Duality from that first Insanity Plea in the previous chapter: the solution is that duality can't possibly exist, so this duality we are experiencing doesn't fit into a rational definition of a loving God. This world can't exist! Once again, what do you think God is? How much are you willing to alter or compromise your definition of "Oneness" or "Unconditional Love" to explain and justify this toxic world that ends in death? I know how

Chapter 2 – A Little Bit More on the Dream

difficult these concepts are, and that these ideas go against that big basket you and I have put all of our religious and philosophical eggs into up until now, but this is why it matters to engage in some healthy thinking about what's really going on here. No matter what anyone says, this world just seems like it must be real! That idea has never been seriously challenged and it seems almost ridiculous to consider that it isn't real.

The experience of specialness that the Son of God wants has taken over everything in our thinking, because the world we live in is nothing *but* specialness. It's all special and separate and there is nothing we can imagine that counters that idea. Can you even imagine what Oneness is, where everyone is the same, totally equal? Or where there aren't even separate consciousnesses, where we all share one mind? Does that sound possible or even appealing in any way? Even if it sounds remotely desirable, how can one even start to think like that or imagine getting there from here? This can seem like quite a mountain to climb, and it is also why there are so many watered-down versions of the idea of God and non-duality. We have to change our thinking in easy-to-take, non-threatening doses because the goal is so far from where we now are. We may want God, but we also want our house, our car and our Chardonnay, not to mention our bank account, just in case.

Can you accept a definition of God that is based on the best possible idea of God you can possibly imagine, such as a God who is unconditionally loving, in the true sense of that word? Can you believe in a God who doesn't want or need anything from you, except to reconnect with you? Can you believe in the joy and unbelievable bliss that you will feel when you return to God that will be so overwhelmingly good, that you will never want this world again? If you can even fathom something as wonderful as that, maybe you can let go of this world just a little bit more, and know that there really is something better than this, even if you can't grasp the idea yet. Maybe you need to immerse yourself in this world for a little longer before you can be sure that you want to let it go. Or maybe this world of suffering is just an odd choice we have all made, and you have now decided that it has overstayed its welcome.

Let's Split

At the moment the tiny, mad idea occurred to the Son of God, there was an explosion of imagined separation—of millions, billions, trillions of "things"—causing everything to exist on its own—an instantaneous Big Bang. When our imagined consciousnesses began to look out from within our separate places, called "bodies," we needed to be in charge of our own lives, because we were no longer part of God, no longer part of each other or something bigger—or part of anything else at all—and there *was* no longer a God or anyone or anything else taking care of us. We were just our dreaming selves, alone and separate, responsible for ourselves. This is the moment when the mind of the Son of God imagined a split; one part of his (our) mind remained with the Truth, forever one with God, in perfect happiness, while another very small part fell asleep into an imagined world of separation.

This world of separation caused two very important ideas to originate; fear—because we were now alone in a strange, new world where we had to survive and fend for ourselves against all the other separated beings and objects, and depended only on ourselves for our own survival—and guilt, because we had done the unthinkable; we had abandoned our perfect home and loving Father to explore something else, as if there was something better, as if there could even be something *else* out there that was better than having everything and being totally loved and part of everything.

We also feel guilty because we are acting out our desire to be special, and we have discovered in a very real way why God wasn't so crazy about the idea. Maybe God is showing specialness to us, so we can understand that, why it may seem to work in the short-term, it certainly doesn't in the long run. Specialness can only exist when things are separate, but when things are separate from each other with unique characteristics, it gets very scary very quickly. We are afraid because our uniqueness has given us each different desires and, as I said, when those desires conflict, we conflict with each other. Fear means that we can be attacked and so we feel we must also attack to defend. We feel guilty because we know we are acting against our true nature and throwing away something beyond precious.

These two ideas—born from that original tiny, mad idea—drive this world and ensure that it will continue. As long as we believe in fear and guilt, our belief in them perpetuates the illusion of separation. To protect ourselves from these feelings of fear and guilt, we suppress them, and push them way down into our subconscious minds. We pretend we are not afraid or guilty. The ego hides us from our real feelings because, once again, that's the ego's job. Insanity and denial are our coping mechanisms. As you will see later, this denial is a very powerful force in our lives.

This fear and guilt permeate every aspect of our lives, usually without us even being aware of what is driving us. The fear causes us to go to any extreme to support our bodies, because we have incorrectly identified with them, and they are all we know, and we are responsible for their protection. The fear also causes us to support the ego because the ego wants us to think we are our bodies. When the body is threatened, *we* are threatened.

The guilt has caused us to go into denial about that heinous misdeed of abandoning God and our brothers and sisters, and attacking our siblings out of fear, while living in a false world. Every single human being on this planet is you! That is also an important idea to latch onto. In our deep denial of our own responsibility, we have created a world of other people and things to hide our guilt and project our blame onto. We are here in ego form strictly for the opportunity to blame other egos, so we don't have to acknowledge the guilt of what we really believe about ourselves. We can blame someone else for *everything* and they, in turn, blame us. That's the game here. We are afraid of taking responsibility because we are afraid of really looking at ourselves honestly for what we might find inside. The Course explains that you never did anything, so relax, notice what you've done, take responsibility as its source and you'll see very quickly that you haven't done anything except made a simple error in understanding and you are not in danger of hellfire or any menacing, scaly, soul eating ogres.

Now, of course, because this is only a dream, we did not really separate from God. We are only imagining that we did. But this dream comes with all the reality that the power of the Son of God can muster, because the Son of God has the imagining power of God, and this dream is remarkable. It is beautiful. It is majestic. It is huge and almost inconceivable to the disempowered individuals we have become. It is breathtaking in its scope and complexity. Even though we imagine ourselves as small and disempowered, we still had the power together to create a universe that was enticing and enchanting and awes us every day, but most of all, it is a universe that challenges us and keeps us engaged and distracted from our true purpose and origin. It is so amazing that we really believe that God created it, and in a sense, the power of that immense imagination *did* create it—but not really. We can "make" as God creates, but what distinguishes this universe from God's creation is that it doesn't fit into God's original parameters. It isn't an extension of love, because love is absolute, unconflicted truth and love is the only thing that's real. Therefore, this *can't* exist. It is a temporary illusion, based on a false premise that there is something other than oneness. It is just the result of the goofy Son, playing outside after dark after his Mother has called him to come home.

Inception?

Just to explain things a little more in depth, the larger universe you see in front of you is a huge collective dream of the Son of God, put into place to fully experience the tiny, mad idea. But your personal life is being dreamed by your ego, individually, as one tiny, separated piece of the Son of God; a dream within the dream, based on what your specialness wants you to believe. So, there are billions of ego people, believing they are separate from each other, all dreaming their separate dreams within a larger master dream, living in separate worlds, seeing exactly what they want to see, but believing they are seeing something else. You believe that what you see is outside of you, because that's what your ego tells you to believe. It's hard to conceive of the idea that what is apparently in front of you is not really there, but only a dream you are having, coming from your mind. And yet, as I said, that is exactly what you believe happens in your nighttime dreams, so apply that idea to this so-called waking world. The source is your mind. The result is the world.

The power of the collective dream is much greater than the power of our individual nighttime dreams. When we dream at night, we can have lucid dreams—where we can become aware that we are inside a dream—but in this immense daytime dream, we cannot wake up until we have overcome the power of our collective consciousness. We can intellectually understand that we are dreaming and yet spend years and immense effort to overcome this dream, but we will not break away from this dream created by the immense Son of God, containing the power of all of our souls together, until we can let it go totally. And we can certainly do that; it just means that each of us has to tap into our power and deny the sleeping, collective part of our mind.

Specialness

Not only has the Son of God imagined an amazing world that is beyond our individual ability to create, but in our individual interest to perpetuate it, we use very strange logic to keep ourselves locked into it. We hide inside our egos which are the idols that we have convinced ourselves that we actually are. The false idol of the ego is every bit as fake as the golden calf that Moses sparred with. We believe we are our personalities and our bodies. We believe that the separate "me" is not only real but important to nourish, cherish, protect and above all, to propel to the top of that cow heap that contains all the other egos.

The original purpose of the tiny, mad idea compels us to be special, or different from each other, and to exhibit our unique individuality. Unfortunately, being special is not who we are, because God sees all of us as equal expressions of His love. That seems counterintuitive to the human ego. It seems our entire purpose in life is to outshine everyone else in our own way. Our egos want us to distinguish ourselves from everyone else, to keep us from seeing the importance of rejoining with each other—to keep the ideas of separateness and uniqueness alive. You are not unique but *your path to end the dream is unique*. We have created a very unique ego, who must now take a unique path to freedom. This desire for specialness is very powerful in us.

When God said no to our desire for specialness, we chose to overrule Him and become the father, so to speak, and we created our phony, special ego-selves to sit in as our "children." We have thrown out our own Father so that that we could become the father of our special egos. We really like our special egos. That's why it's so hard to let go of the idea of life on earth, and our individual importance. We truly cherish this idea of being different from each other.

We have often repeated thoughts and phrases that we value:

> *Look what I can do! I will stand out and the world will notice me! I need to express my individuality! You and I are so different! I'm going to take the world by storm! I am so unique! I'm going to make it on my own! I'm standing up for myself! I will prove myself! I am stronger than you! I must dominate! I will show them who I am! I will destroy anyone or anything that gets in my way! I'm so crazy! I have never fit in!*

Our desire for specialness is the only reason for this mess of a world, because as long as we see ourselves as special or different, we *have to* judge each other. Judgment goes hand in hand with specialness. We are used to both of them. When some people or things are different from other people or things, it means we will "naturally" judge some better and some worse. But there can be no love when some are treated differently from others, because love cannot judge. God's nature is that everything is shared equally with everyone. Love is unconditional, and therefore, gets pushed out where there is judgment. How could you judge or hate someone who was exactly like yourself, and made of unconditional love? To single out someone and make him or her better or more important than someone else is an idea that is against love, and against God, because it means that one person must be less than another. It also means that you are seeing people incorrectly.

Pay attention to social media and TV shows and commercials to see how the importance of individual uniqueness is hammered into us over and over again. Uniqueness is quite a selling point, because we are very susceptible to its lure. As the Son of God, we had unlimited power. Now, we have to substitute for our forgotten power by dominating somehow in this world of form by being bigger, more clever, stronger, richer, etc., than others. If our egos can't directly surpass others, then we have to buy stuff that surpasses others. The idea that one of us is better means that everyone else is less than that. The idea of levels of accomplishment is built into the world of form. We strive constantly to climb to the top of the ego heap, to prove to ourselves that we are more important than others by creating pretend power. We have created a huge, complex, remarkable world, and made ourselves small and powerless victims of it, certain to suffer and die, so our only hope is to shine within it for the brief moment we are here. It also goes the other direction, for we also demonstrate our uniqueness with our smallness, our victimhood and our sadness and pain, in our quest for pity and acknowledgement of the cruelty we are suffering.

Every single effort we make alone, without loving our brother, is an effort that is wasted. Every struggle we undertake is a battle that doesn't need to be fought. We must now remember that we are God, and give up everything we tell ourselves is important—this world, this personality, our stuff. Are you willing to give up everything you think you have now and wake up to who you really are? Do you still need to be convinced that what I'm saying is really true, or is there something deep within your own mind telling you that the Course may be on to something? Will you just continue on with the status quo until there is some outside confirmation of this world as dream or do you have the sense to break away from all of your fixed ideas about the world?

Do you see that life on earth, as it is now, is very insane? Do you think it's getting better? Do you think it will someday, in spite of thousands of years of recorded history that denies that possibility? Do you believe that if we keep passing laws and starting community action groups and telling people to be nicer and judging bad behavior that the world will improve? Or do you think that there is something else going on here? Isn't something a little bit wiser needed? Should we continue to try to fix the world using the same tired methods we have used have since mankind appeared on earth, or should we try something radically different instead? Does anger directed at those who cause suffering really help? If you were a perfect, unconditionally loving God, would you design a world this way? Are you happy with the way this world works?

The collective minds of our different societies all have expectations of us and will punish us drastically if we don't conform. We are subject to silly laws, rules that can only be broken by the rich and powerful, power struggles, phony personalities, and ridiculous expectations at every level of our lives. Do you see how we have convinced ourselves that the absolutely insane life we live is not only perfectly OK with us, but required? Why do we do that?

It has been said that *A Course in Miracles* is very simple—but it ain't easy. *A Course in Miracles* is hundreds of pages of wonderful material that all basically says the same thing in many different ways; this world is an illusion. You are not here. You are part of God, and the only way to *know* that is to start living in this world *as if* it were an illusion, by pulling your attention away from this ego world. Make the simple choice to start acknowledging and believing that this isn't real and that you are God—by changing your perspective about it—and soon you will realize that you aren't pretending at all. You really *are* God. And starting with chapter four, I will talk about some wonderful tools and forms of help that the Course lets us know are available to us.

The Purpose

I'm doing my best here with logic to convince you that this is a dream but I know that the only thing that will really convince you is your own heart, and years of disappointment in your investment in a belief that will ultimately let you down. So, at least consider it. And mull it over. If you can accept the idea that this world doesn't exist, can you also imagine how your life is about to change? The hardest part of breaking the spell that hides you from who you are is your desire to find meaning in *this* fake world, and those rigid beliefs in angry gods. Many of us have long-term investments in this world, like children or careers that we can't conceive of letting go.

Many, if not most, spiritual people believe that this world is real and created by God, and therefore, it is of the utmost importance to find meaning here, and also to fix it. They want to find the reasons for their existence by looking at their place in this universe, and understand themselves based on God's beautiful creation. They're here to find *purpose* in this world. They are here to unleash their creativity and use and explore this universe to the fullest extent of their minds and hearts. They call some places more sacred than others, and believe that we can heal ourselves with various natural healing techniques and certain types of food. They constantly look within the dream to solve all of the problems of the world, and many, if not most, spiritual teachers have bought into this earth-centric view hook, line and sinker, and teach it to their students, perpetuating an easy-to-swallow distraction of the ego to keep us firmly off course.

On the other hand, many of those same spiritual seekers also acknowledge that a major goal in spiritual practice is enlightenment, or waking up. Some who become enlightened return for another life, but only as a teacher to help others also find their way out (known as a bodhisattva in Buddhism). But once enlightenment takes place, no one seems to come back. If this world is important, wouldn't experiencing it as an enlightened being of paramount importance? If it's so important, why would you leave, never to return, just when you have reached your highest point of development? I believe you have to choose what you believe about this; is the purpose of life enlightenment, or to find purpose within it? What would the purpose of enlightenment be if it means we don't come back to explore this world in an enlightened way? Why does enlightenment mean we stop coming here? Can you imagine if all of the tens of thousands of enlightened beings stayed here to live out in the open, demonstrating and helping us understand this silly world—playing in its energy, creating all kinds of amazing things, breaking the laws of nature? The only reason they would return is if this world were actually real, or important somehow.

But it isn't. So they don't.

When we become enlightened, we have no desire to come back, because we're now awake, and what we experience when we're awake makes this world absolutely irrelevant. What was once so all encompassing and important is now nothing but a tiny mistake, lost in our memory forever. This world is like an ant you barely noticed on the sidewalk as you focused on your stroll to the Superbowl with the Beatles playing the halftime show the day after you won the lottery. When you're enlightened, you are awake and you not only realize the profound unimportance of the dream, but you experience the truth of God. And that silly notion about finding purpose in this life is just the ego's way of twisting real meaning into another distraction from our taking responsibility for what we're really here to do. Enlightened souls are still available to us all the time to teach us. They are just rarely found in bodily form.

Another reason we don't see thousands of enlightened souls floating in the air, walking through walls and healing all the sick is because it's extremely important for us to find our way out of here on our own; not to be shown the way by overt demonstrations or physically impossible events. We have to come to our own conclusions about ourselves, so we can see our own power naturally. We are too immense for God to step in directly and tell us. He wants us to be the power behind the discovery of what we already know. He does not want to us to feel that we are too weak to do it by ourselves, because we aren't.

A Course in Miracles is a treatise on oneness. It is a description of the idea of oneness and an explanation of the inherent flaws in a world of duality which can never function correctly or even exist. Are we here to find happiness in duality or are we here to find out who we really are? The answer is both, in that order. But the happiness of duality is short-lived, and is the ultimate reason that we eventually look for something better.

Chapter 2 – *A Little Bit More on the Dream*

There is so much mumbo jumbo in the world of the ego. Everything and everyone tells you how important this world is, how important your body is. The ego bombards us with repeated, ridiculous ideas to keep us focused on the world of form and the body. It's terrible when someone "dies," especially if they die before their time, whatever that means. "They were cut down in the prime of life." "You only have one life, so don't waste it." We memorialize the dead and the suffering here ad nauseam and give death and suffering tremendous importance. We just can't give up how important we think this corporeal life is. It is, quite literally, all we know as humans, and it doesn't even enter our minds that the secret to finding God lies in giving up what isn't God. This world isn't God. You are not your body. As long as you believe God created this world, you will never truly be able to find God, because your hatred of Him (for creating this nightmare) will always guide your search in another direction.

Believing that this world isn't real is a monumental problem to overcome—a very difficult concept to understand. And, as I said, we don't have very many teachers telling this to us, because all of us, especially the teachers, believe it to be real. The dream has taken us over with the full strength of the imagining power of the Son of God, and our absolute acceptance of our egos. As the Son of God, the power we have to believe in illusions is just as strong as our power to believe in truth. Whatever the Son of God puts his focus and intention into is what he believes. So, that means it takes tremendous effort to stop believing what you currently believe, that this world isn't real, and also to let it go, along with everything inside it, and to put your focus on the truth of God. The idea that this world is an illusion is made very clear by the Course, by putting the idea into a context that makes incredible sense, but the idea of a dream world is not at all unique to *A Course in Miracles*. As an example:

ॐ

The Om symbol above consists of 5 parts. The large squiggle on the left that looks like a large number 3 represents two parts; the conscious mind and the unconscious mind. The small squiggle at center right represents the subconscious mind. Those three states of mind represent us, as human beings. The crescent at the top represents Maya, the thinnest veil of illusion that separates us from the small dot at the top, which is God. Overall, the symbol is meant to vaguely resemble a human being, or perhaps the Hindu god Ganesha, and represents the idea that we are separated from God by an illusion (Maya) created by our mind. History is filled with many people who have figured out that this is a dream.

The idea that this world is an illusion has been around for thousands of years because there are always individual souls who discover it is true and try to pass it on. It is a concept that is not very appealing to living humans and their fearful egos, and so it is watered down, changed, or ignored by the unenlightened, according to the ego's wishes. Even many who say this is a dream have a tendency to alter that idea by saying it's somehow a real dream, or some other twisted nonsense to make it more palatable to keep their incredulous students from running away. It's a difficult idea to teach because it has a hard time getting any traction with egos that feel threatened by it. Honestly, who wants to give up life on earth? How do you get to that thinking? This is your chance. Please give it a try.

Magic

A strong habit that we all have which compels us to collectively search within this dream world for completion, solutions and happiness, is what *A Course in Miracles* calls **magic**, which is the belief that solutions exist within the dream. Magic is the idea that the things we see in physical form hold some sort of power, like medicine or holy places or guns or fists, or even the actions we take, or anything else, really. If we use *this* thing, then *that* will happen. If we *do* this, then *that* will happen. Magic pulls us out of the real power of our minds, and into the false power of external things. Nothing in this illusory world of form can solve any of your problems because everything that you see in this world stems from your mind and your beliefs. You are creating all of it. So then, it stands to reason that you can't use the stuff inside of the illusion to fix the illusion, including illness, job challenges, stress, poverty, or whatever else may be troubling you.

The objects within this world have become our idols, and we have made them very powerful, in a phony sort of way. As I mentioned, drugs and medicines have no power over your body, which also doesn't exist. The belief in your mind that they do is what causes their effect. And that belief is much more than just the placebo effect because it's one of the collective beliefs of the split mind of the Son of God. Most of our beliefs function at the level of the collective dream, and beyond our own individual dreams. We believe that pills work because we also believe in the body and the diseases they work on. But unless you change the *cause* of the illness, which is only an error in your beliefs, pills can only postpone the illness until another time or another form. You may be "cured" today by magic pills but if the error in your thinking still exists, the cause of the disease also still exists, and will manifest again whenever it's best for you to experience it. It's very possible for the illness to facilitate that necessary change in your thinking, and that is its purpose, but that is also your choice. You don't really need the pills, but we have become so entrenched in the illusion that we have convinced ourselves that they are important and have effect. Of course, as long as you believe that, you *do* need them in a sense, for your own peace of mind.

I do *not* recommend that you stop taking your pills or change the way you do things right now. The point where we can give up illusory methods is a long way from where most of us are right now. We believe in the power of crystals, and rituals, and eating right, and money, exercise and good looks, so stick with them for now. These are all part of the illusion and even though they have absolutely no real power at all, they do have power within the illusion because we believe they do, but so what! On their own, they can do nothing to change your mind and therefore, they can do nothing to change anything real. First, we need to shift the responsibility for what happens to us away from things outside of us, *to* our own mind and beliefs.

That is a profound shift in beliefs. Think about it for a minute, and think about all of the ways in which you give away power to other people by believing they have power over you. We use this belief in external things to gather power from objects for our own purposes, but we also use this same belief to let others take our power from us and make ourselves victims of them. This is just a game of transferring unreal power from one place to another within the dream, using your beliefs. Undoing this world takes an incredible commitment and relinquishment of everything you now believe.

Death, by the way

And, by the way, death of the body is not the end of the illusion and will not help you find yourself or wake up any faster. Death takes us to a different version of the illusion. Death of the physical body is a break from the density of this difficult life, and a chance for you to regroup and prepare for another phase in your growth by returning again to earth under different circumstances in order to learn what you have to learn. Between lives, you still learn but the learning takes on a different form. When you are born into another body, you are able to put into practice the things you've been taught and planned between lives. The way out of this senseless world is not through death but only through accepting the truth of yourself. There are no shortcuts beyond your own understanding. You are here to find out who you are; not to run from it. Let go of the pain, and know that you are God. This world is not the answer to anything. But the answer can be found here, if you know where to look.

This is a Holdup!

How many of you believe you have so much more to offer the world than you have been able to give based on the lack of opportunities you've been given? In other words: how many of you feel held back by circumstances from expressing yourself as magnificently as you would like? Why do you think that is? Where

Chapter 2 – *A Little Bit More on the Dream*

does an idea like that fit into a perfect world created by a loving God who wants everything for you? Why on earth would any one of God's beloved souls be held back by circumstances in any way? If we are here to create and shine and express, then why do we seem to always be led where we don't want to go and feel very uncomfortable going? Doesn't that clearly demonstrate to you that this universe, whether created by God or not, wants something different for you than what you want? Or, it might just mean that this universe has absolutely no meaning.

There really seems to be something going on behind the scenes that keeps many of us from living our dreams. Maybe the problem lies in those hopes and dreams we have for ourselves. I know there are many people out there who are living truly wonderful lives, doing exactly what they love doing, and they get up every morning and can't believe life is so good. But what about the other 99% of us? Where's God for us? To me, there is no greater evidence that either (1) God doesn't exist, or (2) that God is doing something with our lives that we don't understand that seems very random and cruel at times. But looked at from another point of view, God seems very much to be directing us somewhere we would not consciously choose, somewhere that may serve some greater purpose. How do you know what to believe?

The world doesn't seem to be very interested in many of us. No matter how great we may think our gifts to this world may be, they are just not wanted, and therefore, not necessary. Makes you feel great, doesn't it? God must surely appreciate you if He created you with all this creative ability and talent and then makes the universe sit on you like an elephant, unable to get one word out to anyone. For every one of us who breaks through and is successful at sharing our abilities, there are dozens of us, if not hundreds, who don't. Where does that leave you feeling about God? If you are one of the lucky ones, you probably don't think about it too much.

So maybe we're all being redirected for a reason. Maybe there is a purpose behind our lives that is trying to get us to pay attention to something that we don't want to pay attention to. Maybe this world holds a different purpose than we think it does. Maybe we aren't able to create our lives in the direction we would like because that direction isn't the best direction for us, even if we don't know it. Maybe God is trying to get us to see what we refuse to look at. We all want to be ourselves and we want to relentlessly pursue what we want to pursue, and find our purpose as humans, but maybe God sees our desires as counter-productive to *His* desire for us. And so, our life goes in a direction we never expected, and even though we go along with it on the surface, many of us resist it either consciously or subconsciously. If our current way of living and looking at life were in line with God's vision, we would all be joyful at every moment, but we clearly are not. Maybe we have something more to learn about ourselves that we never even thought about. In chapter five, I discuss in greater detail how our lives form around us.

Goal

So, we're living in a confusing world, seemingly created by a confusing god. We have desires on the surface and hidden agendas buried beneath our own awareness. There is so much we don't know. Is that also what a perfect God would create or want for us—confusion? Something is definitely happening here that is either a random, luck-of-the-draw life on earth, or something much more clever that really does make sense on a level of which we are not aware.

There is a goal or a purpose here, but it might not be the goal you thought. If this is a dream, maybe your purpose in this life is to wake up from it; to make this universe meaningless by seeing it for what it really is. In other words, maybe your purpose is to know yourself in a real way. Literally everything you know and are aware of in this life is what you need to give up in every way, in the most profound way, to the smallest detail, including chocolate ice cream, Paris, Ferraris, orgasms, alcohol, crock pots, live concerts, and everything else you think you want or need. That doesn't mean you have to sell all of your things; it just means you have to see them as they really are—unimportant. And, initially, you have to give up all desire for these with nothing but faith that what you are doing is the right thing, because you are hiding your memory of the real world of God.

Chapter 2 – *A Little Bit More on the Dream*

Whatever you feel you own or desire is what you attach to yourself in your mind. It is not you, so your desire for it makes it the baggage you need to jettison.

We have all created a context for this world and the lives we believe we are living. There is no religious context I have found that includes a god and also satisfactorily explains the suffering on earth, or why it all ends in death. If you live within a confusing or contradictory context that doesn't adequately explain this life, you can easily suffer depression and anxiety, or live a sad life without purpose. There is a better context to believe in but only you can decide if it is really better to see this as a dream. Ask yourself what you really believe about this world. If you choose to see this as a dream, then now may be the time to begin undoing it. The secret is in your conscious choices. Whatever you *choose* to believe is what you *will* believe, correct or incorrect. We are here to stop choosing this world, and to start choosing God. Unfortunately, for just about all of us right now, we have drowned out the Voice for God with the loud bellows of the ego, so it's hard to know what it means to choose God, and if we are choosing correctly.

You can relax right now because as you're reading this and examining your life and trying to figure out if you believe what I'm saying, and deciding if you could ever possibly *do* what I'm saying, you can rest assured that there is no hurry for you to choose differently. Time is on your side. However, you also need to know that you will eventually be compelled to make that different choice, and there is a strong possibility that you will go into it kicking and screaming, because God will know you're ready before you do. It will help you tremendously if you have some idea of what you're getting yourself into before that happens, because there may be very little warning, and you won't understand what's happening while it's happening. In the introduction to the Course, it says, "It is a required course. Only the time you take it is voluntary." That doesn't mean that everyone will have to read the book; it just means that everyone will have to learn the real lessons of this world, either on their own through trial and error, or with help from a book or other teachers. What we are all learning is the Truth of this life, in whatever form it comes to us.

Important?

Just like everyone else, I really wanted this life to be important. I wanted this life of mine to mean something. I was invested in every minute I have lived here on earth. It was vital to my mental health that this life mean something to me. I can't imagine that my life and all the work I've done and all the time I have spent on all the various fun, stressful, creative, difficult things here on earth doesn't mean something! This world is absolutely the only thing I was sure of and knew anything about. This is important, dammit! It just is! Even in death, I wanted to believe that I would live on in this world and have an impact on those I left behind. But *A Course in Miracles* has asked me to begin abandoning this thinking.

When you first understand what the Course is really saying, it will scare you out of your wits. It turns all of your beliefs upside down. It seems to negate *you*, but this "you" that it negates is only a shadow of who you really are. And when your fundamental beliefs about yourself and life are challenged, you may run screaming down the block. At that point, you will either abandon the Course or you will stop and think about the unrelenting truth of it. And then you will come back, and the real growth can begin in earnest.

Humanity is collectively making a tremendous error, but it is a mistake beyond the grasp of a quiescent, small, don't-rock-the-boat human being. It requires a bold step from a bold soul. There *is* something out there beyond this life. You have to believe that! There are no steps to take before you accept that idea. There really is a God, beyond what religions can describe, and beyond what our brains can imagine. This world isn't life, or anything resembling life. Changing your life requires a conscious, tenacious effort to change your thinking. When you first earnestly start considering whether this world is a dream, it is natural go back and forth on the idea. You may talk to others about it, consider the pros and cons, the ins and outs, the rationale and the absurdity of the idea. But one thing that will definitely happen is that your ego will tell you very loudly that everything you have invested in this life is absolutely important and *no one is going to tell you any different!* My God, you've got a significant other, kids and a career, money in the bank, loans to pay off, and all those baseball cards or dolls you got as a kid, after all! What about all those immediate obligations and commitments? How would you let go of them even if you wanted to?

You can't just make it unimportant just like that. The immensity of letting go of this life will seem overwhelming, and will cause many of you to put this whole "spiritual growth" thing off until another time. In India, this idea is addressed when the male head of the family retires from his career, and spends the rest of his waning years in devotion to God. For others of you who are able to hear it, the idea that you are living an illusion might start to sound credible. This life is difficult to let go of, because our egos have done so much to make it important. We are deeply dug in. Perhaps you think that the happiness you have found here is real, substantial and lasting. But when you're ready, after the kicking and screaming has subsided, and you have accepted the inevitable and put the subconscious engine in motion, life on earth will slowly begin to withdraw from you, and all of the things you thought made you happy will reveal themselves for the false idols they really are. They will not go quietly, however. The illusions want to be revered and they will bring as much drama into your life as they can, as long as you still hold on to any affection for this life.

But whatever you conclude for the time being, remember that whatever you believe is true for you, and that means everyone on this planet is walking around in a different world and experiencing a different reality; their own dream within the dream. If you can ever get to the belief that this world doesn't exist, except as illusion, then the next step, as I said, is understanding that nothing in this world matters, except what comes out of your mind. That's the only thing you can control, and it's the only thing that's real. If you want to change your life, then you have to change the source, and that is your mind. Even though it appears that we have a lot of overlap in each other's dreams, your collection of beliefs is absolutely unique to you. You have based your current reality on a string of beliefs that no one else even has! This is a very tenuous reason on which to base your entire existence, don't you think? There is a real Truth out there somewhere, but you and I are living a relative truth, a subjective truth, which isn't true at all. There is only what you choose to believe and, as the Son of God, your powerful mind can make anything as real—or unreal—as it wants. Why not choose something better than this to believe in? If only you knew *how*. Hmmm...

Chapter 3 – My Journey

Before I go any further, I have to pause here to explain something. The idea that this world is a dream and doesn't exist at all is quite an over-the-top idea. It is *the* over-the-top idea. It is a laughable idea that couldn't possibly be true. There is no one around to ask to corroborate it. You and I know it can't be true because we are here, seeing and experiencing this life every day, and nothing else. This is all there is. This is what we've been given, randomly or intentionally, and this is what we are hanging our collective hats on. We don't know what happens when we die, if anything, or if there really is a God, whether we think we know or not. Even if we believe in a God, He/She/It is so inaccessible to us that our only hope to understand the Truth will be through our own death. These are the thoughts I had to push through when I was trying to understand this life as a dream. I have to interject my own journey at this point, because seeing it from this perspective may help you can gain a little more understanding.

Atheists

First, I want to share a few kind words about atheists. I have never been an atheist but I have often shared many of the ideas of atheist thinking because they are vital to an understanding of life. To understand God, you have to let go of everything you previously thought about Him, before you can replace those thoughts with ideas that make more sense.

God is not easy to discover from where we stand as a race of humans on earth. As a matter of fact, He is so difficult to find that we have devised hundreds of ways to find Him and describe Him, so naturally, we all have to think of our god as the one, true god. That makes our egos feel justified in their ridiculous belief, and causes endless conflict with everyone else. But buried deep down inside of each of us is the knowledge that we truly are God. That knowledge is extremely threatening to the ego, and so the ego has taken the idea of a god and twisted it into hundreds of confusing, scary, and even contradictory descriptions of Him and of what He wants, to the point that belief in a god has allowed many of us to carry out despicable acts in the name of a flawed and insane version of a god based on our own misunderstanding, confusion and inability to see anything better because of our own flaws. Or perhaps we have used the confusion of others to justify our own cruelty. God is so vague to us that we can easily associate Him with any absolutely ridiculous and insane beliefs which have caused heinous acts to be carried out over the millennia in His name. A job well done by the ego. Create a god that is so confusing with so many negative traits, that we don't respect him enough to even look for him, but if we do find him, he will gladly call on us to do evil, as long as it's for his cause and in his name.

Look at any religion logically, and eventually the silliness of it will make itself plain. In general, religions don't deal in sense; they deal in a strange version of faith alone, without context or substance. Atheists, of course, can't be lumped together to explain their beliefs, but the kind of atheist who really takes the time to think about man's stories about God and endeavors to make sense of them is someone who is really trying to understand a deeper concept about him- or herself. This questioning and doubting is extremely important to every individual's personal growth, and it is a path that we must all eventually take, if we haven't already, before we can move beyond it to something that really does have substance.

Generally, the atheist begins as most of the rest of us, with an IV bag full of the local, prevailing god dripped slowly into his or her psyche from an early age by family and society. That point of view tells us that life on earth owes itself to an invisible, absent, powerful creator who is mysterious but requires us to behave in certain ways, according to whatever our parents or the current religious elders have decided. We learn what we are taught, and we absorb what surrounds us.

There comes a point in most everyone's life where we begin to become curious about all things. For many, this simply means that we ask a lot of questions about everything around us as we grow up, and attempt to understand the answers, no matter how goofy or incomplete they are. When it comes to God, there aren't a lot of very good answers, but that vagueness is also part of the answer; we just can't know yet. Wait until you die. In the meantime, just accept this vague answer as correct because that's the depth (or lack of depth) of our curiosity. For many, if not most, people, the power of the ego limits our searching and curiosity, and this is why religions continue and proliferate. We accept these tepid answers and live our zombie ego lives without any real understanding of God or life's purpose, but that's OK. We still have a lot of human stuff to do here on earth without worrying about a god.

But there are some who are breaking through their ego barriers and continue beyond the incomplete answers to actually begin an active search for meaning. Generally, people who seek meaning stop when they find any meaning that satisfies them, based on their own path and level of understanding, whether it is some version of a god or a scientific understanding or some other answer. Until one finds a personally satisfying answer, one must either continue looking or give up entirely. I believe that most of us become atheists after living many lifetimes of varying religious fervor, trying to find meaning in the accepted structures of society. We seek meaning in religion or other versions of all powerful, mystical beings but finally give up in utter frustration. It seems inevitable. A decent fellow of a God would never have created such a poorly designed world where we can all kill each other. Also, God is not needed here, and He certainly doesn't seem to hang around here much, if at all.

If we look at any and all religions, and we are honest about it, God is not to be found within them. The atheist knows this. If anyone doubts what I say, please consider reading Christopher Hitchens' book, *God is Not Great: How Religion Poisons Everything*. I agree with just about everything he says in this book. It is well-written and irrefutable. Religions are not only universally incorrect about God but they are very bad for society in many ways, simply because they take some truly horrible and incorrect information and impose it on society in a way that is usually very judgmental, controlling, and much more destructive than helpful. Hitchens' book is full of very sad but well-documented examples. Religious opinions are regularly presented as fact by religious leaders and are used to excuse the most egregious moral behavior. An honest look at religion throughout history can easily make you very angry, if anger is your choice. The interesting thing about his book, however, is that the reference to God in the title doesn't reflect what's in the book. Hitchens never directly talks about God or the idea that He does or does not exist. He sticks exclusively to the idiocy of man's interpretations of God.

My Journey

As I said, many, if not most, people come to their understanding of God by their societal environment, and come to accept it, if not weakly and blindly. I came to God from another perspective. For some reason, I *knew* at an early age, about six, that there was a God. When I say I "knew," I didn't know in an arrogant way where I felt the need to impose it on others or to refuse to listen to other points of view. It was not an in-your-face knowledge. Nor was it a specific idea of a well-defined being. It was a quiet knowledge of a shy kid that I never shared with anyone. I didn't get the certainty from my parents or friends. I was just certain that there was a God. I didn't know how I knew, or why I knew. I didn't even question myself about it. But as soon as I began going to Lutheran church as a child, something seemed very wrong with what I was hearing. I didn't do anything about it because I never wanted to make waves or speak up or even ask questions. I just thought it was all silly. There just weren't any explanations or answers that made me feel like there was any truth involved. It just seemed like a bunch of old men standing in front of us in positions of earthly authority, making stuff up. So, I quietly went along with it on the outside, but rejected it soundly on the inside.

My religion, of course, was not all bad. Many religions contain moral codes which, in some cases, can be very helpful. As a Lutheran, I grew up with the Bible, and I always thought the teachings of Jesus were very appealing. But any of the writings on either side of the gospels made me cringe, and I couldn't understand the stories of anger and meanness and people telling each other what to do. God seemed like a mess.

Eventually, after many years of reading and exploring, I concluded without a doubt that religion had nothing to do with God. On the contrary, it seemed that religion was the worst thing that had happened to God. But, instead of rejecting God because of religion, as an atheist might, I pledged to myself to find God *in spite* of religion. If I couldn't find God, then I would accept defeat, but I vowed not to give up as long as I felt there was still a trail to follow.

When I first began my search in earnest after I graduated from college, there were some huge problems I had to overcome. Finding God first meant that there had to be a God worth finding. I was not looking for a god of vengeance. I was looking for a God of love. Of course, this meant that I could be incorrect. Maybe God is a jerk. But I was not looking for a god who is mysterious and wants to hide things from me. I was not interested in a god who punishes us or sends us to an eternity in hell for reading Playboy or eating pork. I wasn't interested in a god who demands that His son or anyone else's be killed as a sacrifice. It all sounded so wrong, but I also didn't want to impose characteristics of my own choosing on God. So, I began to seek out other people to explain their strange versions of God and life, or their wild explanations of real-life experiences that fly in the face of anything I had heard before.

This was in the mid-1970s, and I quickly found some very interesting alternative literature about God. First, I found Edgar Cayce and then Carlos Castaneda and Jane Roberts. I found

Yogananda and Ramakrishna and Gopi Krishna and dozens of others. I was hooked on all of these interesting takes on life. They were all much better than my experience with any religion. They were all about real people living and defining life in very different ways. I became what I would call a New Age, or metaphysical, or spiritual person, whatever that meant. I took all of these versions of life and absorbed them into my being. I saw the similarities in all of them. I understood what they were trying to say. I was able to put it all together in my mind and come to a real and powerful understanding of God.

    Except for one thing.

No matter how hard I tried, no matter what mental hoops I jumped through, I just couldn't reconcile one simple thing about God and all of the teachings I had read; how could a God of unconditional love create a world so absolutely full of countless ways to suffer that ends in certain death? In other words, I never really accepted or understood the purpose of life, as put forth by many of these alternative sources.

As an atheist may say, why do we need a god, and if there is a god, isn't he quite a flawed god to have created such an imperfect world? Even after understanding and accepting the satisfying idea of reincarnation, allowing us to improve ourselves over many lifetimes to supposedly reduce our own suffering, I was still struggling. I was trying so hard to learn and understand, and yet my life was so miserable. I wasn't physically suffering but I was in constant mental anguish over romantic relationships and friendships and financial issues and career issues and just general meaning in life. I was a serious student of God, yet my life seemed a never-ending mess. What was wrong with this picture?

I was a firm seeker of God, and yet this life didn't work according to any of the spiritual material I was reading. I was constantly angry at God for being so hard on me, and for being so hard to understand. I never stopped believing in God, yet I also never stopped doubting what I learned, and continued to question more and more. I was still certain the answers were out there somewhere. Atheists, in general, don't believe in God because religions don't make any sense, and

Chapter 3 – *My Journey*

because they can't find a definition of God that makes any sense in the context of this flawed universe. Not only is a god not needed here, especially in light of the scientific explanations that keep getting better, but if there is a god, he must be quite psychotic to have created this universe.

I immediately went out and bought a copy of the *A Course in Miracles* in the early 1990s, just after Marianne Williamson published *A Return to Love*. But, I couldn't read it somehow. After all the countless spiritual books I had read up until that point, it just didn't resonate with me. I didn't like the language and it bored me to tears. I picked it up again a few more times within the next 20 years or so, but it still never worked for me.

Then I read *The Disappearance of the Universe* by Gary Renard when it first came out. I quickly realized that this was a powerful book but it said something about the Course that I had not noticed before in my half-hearted attempts to understand it. It said that this life and this universe didn't exist. At all. It's all a dream. That idea not only didn't sit right with me, it made me angry. The more I thought about it, the more angry I got. Really angry. This was turning everything upside down, and asking me to throw out my life. It invalidated me and you and this entire world at a deep level and I resented it in a big way.

Loathing in Las Vegas

I had just moved to Las Vegas in 2008 and Mr. Renard was speaking there at a Hay House Conference in the late spring of that year. I specifically went to see his talk so that when he asked for questions at the end, I could rant at him in an angry tirade about this being a dream. "If God is everything, then this universe has to be part of God!" and such. But after he finished speaking, he didn't take any questions. Even though I was disappointed, I was also a little relieved. It was just as well. I wasn't mad at *him*, I was mad at the Course but I felt he represented it, so ranting at him was the best I could do. This apparently was also the conference where he met his wife Cindy, the Arten to his Pursah (or is it the Pursah to this Arten?) Because of my biting wit and unassailable logic, I'm glad I didn't get a chance to express my justifiable anger and thus force him to prematurely run up to his hotel room in tears and miss meeting his soul mate.

Anyway, no matter how angry I was at what the Course said, I had vowed from the beginning of my search for God that I would never stop my searching and questioning. I knew a lot about man's theories about God and spiritual matters, having studied earnestly for over 35 years, but I also knew that I was missing something from my understanding. There was something incomplete that wouldn't let me go. So, in spite of the anger I felt, I never stopped wondering if what the Course said could be true. Could this be a dream? This struck me as something important to consider. It was so outrageous that there had to be a reason behind it. I had heard of this idea for many years, with the Om symbol representing the idea of Maya, the illusion, the thinnest of veils, separating us from God, so I was aware that this was not an idea unique to the Course. But I also knew that there *was* something different here. There was something that intrigued me and scared me at the same time. I thought about it a lot.

I thought about it for five years.

The main reason I had difficulty seeing this world as a dream was that I believed, as I said, that I had already come to the understanding that there could be absolutely nothing that was not part of God. That had to mean that this world had to be part of God and that meant, in turn, that God must have created it. There could be no other way to look at this world if I wanted to continue to believe that God is everything.

Now, along comes the Course and says that this world is, indeed, nothing. How can that be? I had absolutely convinced myself, as I'm sure you did, that this world and life is real and important and substantial. So, the only question I had to sincerely understand was this: What is real?

So even though I rejected the idea, I still kept thinking about it. While trying to understand that this world might be a dream, I also maintained the idea that this world as real, but as I was switching from one side to the other, the idea that this world is real began to lose the battle. When I compared the two ideas—dream or not dream—I eventually realized, very slowly over five years, that the only belief that made sense was that this is a dream. If this world is a dream, then I also had to figure out why it was so different from the dreams I had at night.

From the time I was small, I was never satisfied with this life. It *never* made sense to me. Never. There was no way for me to justify a belief in the God I always hoped for with a belief in this world that admittedly contained quite a bit of good—but so much suffering! There were so many people who treated others so poorly, and so few who stood up for the mistreated. There was so much struggle and pain and injustice, even if we brought it all on ourselves. There was always good, but it was always overshadowed by the bad that never seemed to go away. Why is there a world where anything bad can even happen? Everyone goes through hardship of some sort. Everyone gets sick and everyone dies. It just seems to have nothing to do with God, no matter what I heard in church, or how majestic and grand and enticing and beautiful it seems.

For many people who struggle with the idea of God, we have to reluctantly accept that any god who created this world must be extremely flawed. This world is such a mess that any explanation of this world must take into account that who or whatever created it must take responsibility for that mess. In order to try to keep God a fairly decent guy, we have to invent amazing scenarios for what God is, or we have to create a God who is mysterious, who won't tell us why He did this awful thing.

Reality

The biggest hurdle I had to jump in order to get to the mindset of accepting this world as a dream, was that I had to decide if this world lived up to a logical idea of reality. How could it not be real? It has so much, well, substance, and reality. What is reality? Who decides?

The second hurdle was, if I have, and am, the mind of God, and thoughts are real, according to the Course, then how can it be that the thoughts that I think that made this world have no meaning or reality? Am I less important than God? If we share the same mind and thoughts, and God created me as His equal, why does it seem that God's thoughts are more real than mine?

As I discovered later, the answers are not complicated. I was just asking the wrong question. God has created the Truth, and the Truth is that God created us as His Son or Child. We are His Son, and that is simply true. The problem with *our* "truth" is obvious if you think about it. It isn't true. We currently believe that we are *not* the Child of God. Therefore, we have made up a lie about ourselves. We have decided, without anything to support it other than our desire, that we are humans. And in order to make this lie believable to ourselves, we had to make a new world in which it *is* true. We had to give our lies credibility by forgetting the Truth about ourselves and separating ourselves from each other and God. With those parameters set, we can easily believe that something that is not true *is* true. We made this entire universe for the sole purpose of supporting an idea that is not true. We can't be humans if we were not created humans, no matter how hard we try. The real question I should have been asking is not What is Real? but What is True?

Our thoughts are as powerful as they need to be to *believe* whatever we want to believe. This world did not *happen* to you. It's a *choice* we are all making. The Son of God is currently living a lie within that tiny, mad idea out of choice. It is an idea that does not exist outside of itself, and we have conveniently hidden the exits. God's idea of the Truth is the same as love. Truth must extend itself, which is its nature. This world does not extend. It is an enclosed loop of hidden ideas and separation. It does not include everyone; it excludes at will. God's Truth does not change, but truth for the ego is different and changeable for each of us here on earth. Each of the separated pieces of God can choose to believe whatever they want; truth or not. We can choose beliefs that are at odds with other people, as well as ideas that conflict within our own minds. There is no "truth" within this world; there is only an individual's choice to make his or her own world of subjective truth that has nothing to do with the bigger Truth.

If we are part of God, then it is simply true that we are. Of course, if you don't believe or understand what the Course is saying, then this may be irrelevant to you. If you don't subscribe to the idea that this world doesn't exist, then you must somehow justify the suffering. If you do believe in the reality of this world of separation, then what you will never possess is the opportunity to know yourself beyond that of a separated being, struggling to understand the unending conflicts and confusion, constantly looking for meaning in a meaningless context.

We have used the power of our incredible minds to make up something that wasn't true based on that original desire we had to be special. What's very interesting to think about is that, from where we stand, we have no idea if the Son of God does this on a regular basis. How many other worlds or "realities" are out there that are just unreal musings of the mind of God's Son based on other fantastic thoughts that have no basis in Truth? Are we just tiny thoughts of God's Son that are merely going through a mental exercise to play with ideas that aren't true? Does God's Son make thousands of temporary worlds of unreal possibilities in an attempt to amuse or understand Himself? Does it matter?

It is no small thing to believe that this is a dream, that it doesn't exist, that it's a figment of my imagination, just like my nighttime dreams, and that everything I've done for the last 65 years or so has meant absolutely nothing, except maybe for the good thoughts I've thought. Do you *really* expect me to acknowledge that? Come on! This *me* that I supposedly am doesn't even exist? Wow.

In spite of my anger and doubts, the more I thought about this life as a dream, the more credible it sounded. The more I thought about it, the more it started to sound like something that was about to change everything I had ever thought about myself, life and God. It scared me more and more as the enormity of it started to sink in. It scared the ever-loving crap out of me. I kept trying to understand that this life was real, as I had always done, but that idea was losing the battle in my head. The dream was becoming more and more understandable, and the idea that whatever was *really* real, was beyond my current horizon.

Then a remarkable moment in my understanding took place. One day, I realized that I had finally crossed that line. I had not only come to fully accept that this was a dream, at least intellectually, but I also realized, much to my absolute shock, that this new belief was also the final solution to all of my previous questions about life and God. I had to cross the line to really understand this. It was the final piece of the puzzle to truly understanding what this life is all about. It was precisely what I had always been looking for! It was the game changer. It wasn't just a difficult idea, it was the single most *important* idea I had ever come across, and the idea that allowed everything to fall into place. The dream that I had so soundly rejected was the answer to my dreams. God can very much exist and also be unconditional love because He didn't create this world of suffering! *We* made it. He didn't kill his Son for our sins! He isn't vengeful. He isn't mysterious. He isn't absent. We just don't want Him around. We designed this world so *we* could live without *Him*! It's *our* decision! God *is* love! A God of love *can* exist in a real way that makes sense!

The ego is profoundly attached to the dream of this world, and letting it go in the deepest part of your soul is a powerfully meaningful event. The dream contains suffering and conflict and struggle and attack and death. Not only is it a perverse upside-down realm, this world is also the argument *against* God. How can a god have created this? There certainly can't be a god worth believing in if this is all he came up with. The dream is a self-fulfilling prophecy. If you believe in the reality of this world, obviously, it's real and God isn't.

I have spent my life reading hundreds of spiritual books. I have read everything I could get my hands on, all in my search for meaning. When I finally decided, after five years of contemplation, that I was ready to say out loud to myself that this world is a dream, I started reading the Course again. This time, something else profound happened. From the first sentence I read, I got it. I was hooked. Every word made perfect sense in a substantial way. Well, not every word, but almost. I was absorbed with it and began to read it as fast as I could comprehend it, which wasn't really that fast. I cried through most of it because it seemed there was something on every page that touched my soul. I felt as if the world had changed forever. And it had. So, after all of those books and decades of searching for the God I knew must exist, I finally found Him, and I finally found myself.

A few weeks after I started reading the Course, I had a dream. I was standing outside on a sidewalk, and from my right side, a hand extended the blue Course book to me, and a voice said, "This is the last book you'll ever need." And that was that. These are just words on a page in a book, so I don't know if you who read this can understand the immense effect that dream had on me when I woke up, tears streaming down my cheeks. You'll just have to take my word for it when I tell you it was a profound and life-changing event.

After starting to read the Course, another thing that happened was that my daily meditations took a sudden and dramatic turn for the better. My meditations have always been good, and I have gone through some remarkable periods. But when I accepted this new world view, I started having meditations that were exponentially deeper and more wonderful than I have ever had. It was as if a wall had been knocked down. And they just keep getting better. Before the Course, it was as if my meditations were slowly leading me as I walked along the correct, peaceful path through a beautiful forest, and then when I found the Course, I was suddenly picked up by someone who looks a lot like Jesus in a Lamborghini.

Over the course of the past few years, the most remarkable change I have noticed in myself is that I go through long stretches of my life without thinking, unless I need to. It is quite a wonderful feeling to experience, without any ability on my part to explain it further, except to say this: because my mind feels extraordinarily empty much of the time, the only thing left within it is the experience of an incredibly deep peace and calmness. It is something I regularly experience in my meditations and often during my waking hours. This is not a calm that I have felt before, and it does not resemble any previous human definitions of the words "peace" or "calm." It is a profound peace that envelopes me in a permanent embrace that is impossible to describe because there is nothing in this world to compare it to. I am not awake, as the Course defines it. I know that. But I also know now that I will be eventually, whether it takes another week or six more lifetimes. It is inevitable.

So, the problem for me and all of the atheists out there isn't that God doesn't exist; it's that He's very difficult to find because of all of the obstacles we have put in place to keep Him hidden or distasteful. All of the gods created by religion are ridiculous. I don't mean that in an insulting way. I mean that from a logical point of view. They are nonsensical concepts. They are shadows, created by the ego, in the image of the ego, in the service of the ego. God is difficult to find because the ego has made Him hard to find on purpose. God has been reduced to a comic book character; humanoid and flawed, with superpowers that he uses to unremarkable effect.

All religions are ego distractions to keep us off course while we still think we are on course. So, the first step in finding God is to reject these distractions purporting to be God. That's hard enough and may cause many who are reading this to feel anger. That's OK. Many atheists focus on attacking God through religion, without realizing religion has nothing to do with the real God. If we can all stop believing that some sort of man-made religion is the only way to explain a deity, then maybe it would be possible to find a God Who is worth believing in and one Who makes sense in spite of the insanity of this world.

The second step, after giving up the idea that God can be found within any religion, is to then come to some understanding that **there still may be a God**, in spite of all of the ego evidence to the contrary. Even outside of religion, bad ideas about God abound. That doesn't mean there isn't a God! It just means that you have to have the courage to let go of the bad ideas. Everyone has an opinion, and just about all of them are ego-based distractions. The ego has made this search for God as hard a task as there could possibly be. Finding God is the ego's ultimate threat, and so the ego employs the ultimate weapons to thwart any real search. What kind of a God could possibly exist? He doesn't exist within religion and, besides that, He seems quite absent in every other way, especially if you aren't looking for Him with any passion. It's quite easy to believe that we made Him up. It's just as easy to understand that we destroyed Him by negating Him. He will exist in any way that your thoughts want Him to exist. He didn't create this world, according to atheists, and they would be correct. What do you need Him for anyway?

The Path

So, after you have passed through the phase of blind acceptance of a politically correct, nonsensical God, and then through another phase of rejection of God and religion and straight into existential angst, then you have to somehow get back to thinking that there might still possibly be a God. And from my perspective, there is only one way to get to that place, and that is to live your life and enjoy it and hate it and explore it and immerse yourself in it until it stops working for you. There must come a time when all of us will say to ourselves that we don't want this life anymore, that there has to be something more; there has to be a better way. The only way to get us to stop focusing on this life is for it to lose its appeal. It has to drop away, and it *will* drop away because it is false and temporary and shallow. It's the only way to get us to think about something else, and to pull us away from the enjoyment of our bodies, and all of the drama and conflict. We have to go through the withdrawal of this drug called the "illusion." You can try to convince yourself that you don't need to go that far, but we have designed this world to draw our attention away from who we really are and keep us focused on something false. The only way to withdraw your attention from this life is to feel in the deepest part of your being that you have given yourself to it as much as you could, it doesn't work, this isn't what you want, and this human is not who you feel yourself to be.

That moment will be different for each one of us and it will come extremely quickly for some and slowly for others. That doesn't matter at all. But then, when you have decided that this life isn't working, you will face a crisis of existence. There must be answers out there somewhere, and so you must once again ask yourself all of the big questions about life. If this life doesn't hold the answers, then what else is there and who are you? Who is God and where is He and what does He want from us? And then, after that long and confusing road the ego has laid out for you, the final step is to understand that there is only one possible, very narrow and specific explanation for the existence of that God and of understanding yourself. There is a very tiny window to escape from this world that the ego has painted over and grown heavy bushes in front of and does not want you to discover.

That obscure explanation is the most difficult idea you will ever hear, and accepting it will force you to discard your humanity, and everything you have ever believed about yourself or done here on earth. That explanation is that God did not create this world, it doesn't exist, and neither do you. There are no such things as humans. This is a dream. We have made up this universe to experience ourselves as something other than God. You must finally realize that the only acceptable result is for this life to evaporate into the nothingness that it is, like a wisp of smoke from an extinguished candle. You are something much more incredible.

How does a normal Joe or Jane, standing in line at Starbucks before work, get from their current thinking down this incredibly convoluted, confusing, life-changing path to that bit of radical thinking? The final step requires that you throw out everything you thought you knew about yourself and everyone and everything else, and give in to the idea that this world doesn't exist by overcoming your deepest, ingrained beliefs that it is absolutely real and true. This is the scariest step of all because it requires that you first become one of "those people," who seem obsessed with God and uninterested in this life. Then you have to throw out your self. This is the inevitable result of finding your true Self, and discarding your ego self. Who you are now does not exist; your personality, your quirks, your likes and dislikes. None of it is true, and so it must go. All of your ideas about yourself must go. If it's hard to understand this world as a dream, it is even harder to understand yourself as a dream. The idea is not that Joe and Jane must work on themselves to gain entrance into heaven: the true idea is that the Son of God must stop believing he is Joe and Jane so he can awaken and realize that he's never left it.

Most of us get to these beliefs slowly over time. How long do you have to hang on to yourself before you can begin to let it all go? How many days will you awaken from sleep each morning and give your energy and time and effort and focus and drama to this non-existent world and your fake body and personality in your search for money, fame, orgasms, alcohol and the completion of all the tasks of daily life? It is a very narrow window to find God. It is also a window that you must find on your own, through trial and error, lifetime after lifetime of learning and unlearning, of suffering and pain, joy and ecstasy, frustration and anguish, hope and despair. How does one find it? How can one travel to that narrow pathway that leads away from an all-encompassing, magnificent dream to a tiny, hidden exit that holds only the timid hope that there's something more?

I am still not awake, and my search so far is only intellectual. All I know is how I got to where I am, just as so many others have done. I understand that even though I feel my searching for God is over, now I have the tremendous task of doing something about it. Now, I have to wake up from the dream. I can only do that by withdrawing from it, by not giving it importance or energy or reality, by changing my mind about myself and everything else through forgiveness, which is explained in the next chapter.

So now the work begins. I will always keep an open mind to any possibilities that I might have missed, but after all of the paths I have pursued, and all of the doubts I have felt through decades and even lifetimes, I finally feel I *know* what to do. *A Course in Miracles* is the last book I'll ever need. Everything I thought I was supposed to do turned out to be false and misleading, but it has all led me to where I am now. Now I know about the power of forgiveness and the purpose of my life here on fake earth. I understand *why* forgiveness works, and why it is my only purpose. Even if, for some strange reason, forgiveness turns out to be the wrong path, it still seems like it's quite a good direction to go in for a few decades, and I know I will feel better about myself for having pursued it. Now I know where to find God, on that tiny pathway in that obscure corner in the recesses of my mind. And I understand why it's so hard for so many to find Him. I hope I can help a few others as I walk in that direction.

Chapter 4 – The Solution

Your Role

If I have worked verbal magic and convinced you that this life is an illusion, then I hope you don't think there's no point to anything and assume that nothing we do here matters. If you believe that, then your only viable options are probably extreme depression or suicide. Well, cut it out! It may be that nothing matters but *how* it doesn't matter matters. Don't give up on life, give up the dream! You have a purpose, whether you admit it or not. That purpose is to remember who you are by waking up.

You also have a *special* purpose, which is a unique, natural talent we have all been given that can help you discover who you are. Like Jake and Elwood, we are all on a mission from God, whether we are aware of it or not. You cannot remember who you are by not participating in your current experience, whatever that may be. This world is not important, but *you* are. And if you can muster up the strength to give up this world, your greatest human challenge lies just head of you, and it requires your complete dedication and concentration. If you really begin to believe you're living in a dream, then it will serve you well to spend as much time as you can reminding yourself of that fact. It will give you tremendous power over yourself, and it will change your perspective on this life. It takes time and practice, but it is worth it. As a matter of fact, it is the only thing that has any value at all.

The Answers

The greatest teacher of all is inside you. The only question is, how much are you willing to learn from that inner teacher? How much of your suffering do you want to stop? *A Course in Miracles* is a self-study course, including some very powerful daily lessons and was written for the sole purpose of helping us understand more quickly what we are doing to ourselves so that we spend less time suffering on this fake planet. You will get to the understanding you need no matter what path you follow, but the Course, and other teaching methods, can speed up the whole process. In very general terms, the Course consists of two different types of discussions. They are blended seamlessly, but simply put, they are the **Problem** and the **Solution**.

It explains, in extreme detail, the **Problem**, which is the context of this life; the idea that we are living in a dream but we don't know it, and all of the mental/ego/psychological games we play to keep this dream world in place, as well as the idea that we are creating this entire world based on our beliefs; both conscious and subconscious. I have rambled on about this problem of our life on earth in the first three chapters, and now the mood lightens just a tad and we come to the solution. The **Solution** consists of the help that has been given to us to get us to break the spell of the dream and wake up.

If you don't acknowledge the problem—the dream—and if you don't understand that larger context of this life, you probably don't see a need for the solution. If you really believe this world is real, there is obviously no need for you to figure out how to let it go, or think too much about it, which is where most people are today. This would be a good time to pick up a different book about trout fishing or textile manufacturing.

This one solution, which is really a bunch of solutions, that God offered to this inane idea of separation is extraordinary and awe-inspiring. In combination, these solutions fit right into life on earth without the smallest indication that they are there, without any intrusion on our mistaken thinking and without forcing any agenda on our egos. Yet, at the same time, they are powerful and unstoppable teaching devices quietly at work in everyone's life, slowly helping us to accomplish one simple task: that we remember Who we really are.

The Atonement—The Master Plan

As I said, the truth of what's going on here is remarkable, yet very few people are even aware of it. Even if you are a student of the Course, this may come as a complete surprise. As the Course has stated in no uncertain terms, a deep sleep fell over us (the Son of God), as we made a world of chaos and separation to experience ourselves as something that we were not—something that was not love. God noticed that there was a breakdown in communication with His Son, so He immediately made a plan to correct the problem. The plan He created is so simple and elegant that just to know it exists can be immediately life changing. It is His Master Plan with a few beautiful pieces built into it. Most earthlings have made sure that we will not see or acknowledge this plan in the near future because our egos are firmly committed to this fake external life we have made. It doesn't matter at all, for the moment. The entire purpose of *A Course in Miracles* is to tell us about this plan, and explain its beauty and simplicity, because the acceptance of this plan's existence will change your life.

As we made a world of dreams, God immediately responded with His plan called the Atonement, and laid it like a comforting blanket over the entire universe of chaos that we made. This Master Plan includes the Holy Spirit—Who was created to carry out the plan—forgiveness, which is how we implement our part of the plan, and the real world. It contains other pieces as well, and I will talk about them throughout the book. This Atonement is no small thing, and even though it is mentioned throughout the Course, I'm not sure how seriously most Course readers take it or understand how truly important it is. Once again, and I can't stress this enough: **This world is not what you think it is.** There is a remarkable and massive plan happening here, just under the surface of our awareness, and it is time for us to begin to notice it. It is vital to life here on earth.

The Holy Spirit, as the Master Engineer, implements the plan, and it runs quietly in the background of our lives every second of every day, whether we notice it or not, or choose to actively participate in it. And you *are* participating anyway, aware of it or not, even as it operates gently and quietly. It is not meant to interfere with our choices but to show them to us from another perspective that helps us reevaluate them. When we become aware of the plan and choose to actively participate, the Holy Spirit can then more easily lead us back to God. But before we become aware of the plan, life will go on as the world does now for most people, full of seeming chaos, randomness and needless suffering. We will live our lives in ignorance, by our own choice, as the Holy Spirit slowly but surely tries to help us become aware of this plan, never interfering with our decision that this insane world makes sense, in spite of the obvious imperfections and anguish here.

When we first came up with the tiny, mad idea, our goal was to experience, to the fullest extent possible, specialness and separation and its ensuing chaos in a world without God. But God's Atonement plan changed this dream instantly and permanently. The Holy Spirit's mission was simply to take the mess we created and co-opt it and turn it into a process that focused on the correction of our thinking. This world of chaos made by the ego has been totally restructured and redefined under the guidance of the Holy Spirit to help us end it, based on God's will. In short, the Holy Spirit is helping us correct our incorrect beliefs. His task is to show us that there is something better; that we are something better. And He uses the Atonement in every moment of our lives. But as I said, we can choose to ignore it and continue to live as if it doesn't exist.

The very rich process that the Holy Spirit put in place is perfect and beautiful. It does not interfere or demand or attack. It just notices that we need help and offers it all the time, to constantly remind us that we are God, and love. The Atonement happened instantaneously to God, but to the beings living in the 3-D world of form, it may have taken place over time. In one of the most significant but overlooked passages in the book, it states:

> *T-19.IV.A.7. ²As you look upon the world, this little wish, uprooted and floating aimlessly, can land and settle briefly upon anything, for it has no purpose now.* **³Before the Holy Spirit entered to abide with you it seemed to have a mighty purpose; the fixed and unchangeable dedication to sin and its results.** *⁴Now it is aimless, wandering pointlessly, causing no more than tiny interruptions in love's appeal.*
>
> *T-19.IV.A.8. This feather of a wish, this tiny illusion, this microscopic remnant of the belief in sin, is all that remains of what once seemed to be the world.* **²It is no longer an unrelenting barrier to peace.**

This is the moment the world we made changed forever. It is the moment the Atonement plan blew like a gentle breeze over all of creation. The Holy Spirit, an extension of God, as we are, has one foot in God and one foot in the illusion, so to speak, and whose sole purpose is to assist us in bringing this world of error back to truth through the elegant Atonement plan. Because God doesn't acknowledge this world, He created the Holy Spirit to act as liaison between us and Himself. It became the Holy Spirit's job to be our guide and help us find our way back home in a very gentle, quiet, loving way. His purpose is to remind us who we are, but *how* He does that requires some understanding.

Note: Now, this may sound a little wacky, and it's certainly not in the Course, but I believe that this incredible moment, when God appointed the Holy Spirit to take over this world behind the scenes, could be the moment when the asteroid or comet destroyed the dinosaurs 66 million years ago. It states in that short paragraph that there was a time of chaos on earth, an unrelenting barrier to peace, before the Holy Spirit was given the Atonement task and God implemented His plan. In the physical world, billions of years of random chaos could have passed, but to God, each moment in time is the same as every other. The chaotic reign of animals without conscience or understanding did not allow for any substantial learning by the Son of God. The only way for the Son of God to correct his thinking about this separated world was to allow an animal with a complex brain and nervous system to evolve, thereby allowing the Son of God to enter into it more fully and personally experience this plane of separation with the ability to evaluate it and respond to it in a new and much more substantial way, in order to learn why this separation thingy wasn't such a good idea, and in a way that could allow the Holy Spirit to implement His teaching plan. This complex animal body allowed us to see and experience the results of our actions much more directly. The problem with this theory, as I see it, is that I am only considering earth and not the many other possible planets or dimensions where life might be. Maybe the Holy Spirit only takes over a planet when chaos reaches a certain point? In any event, this is just a thought, and just a possibility to think about . . .

This is a powerful message that the world that we live in is not the world we think. It is overseen by God's Teacher at every instant, watching, helping, encouraging from behind the scenes. We are not alone. We have not been abandoned or forgotten. And what you see in front of your eyes every day is not the truth of us. When the Holy Spirit took over this world, He made every second on earth a beautiful, non-stop training session. Every complaint you make in your head about what's going on around you is an opportunity you have missed—at least for the moment. Every imperfection you see in anyone's behavior, including your own, is an error in your thinking that you can still go back to correct. There is a profound love engaging with us at every moment, not intruding upon our mistaken choices, not interfering with what we think life is, but helping us to see things a different way, waiting for us to notice this extraordinary plan, and coaxing us softly to turn our heads in another direction, away from judgment, so that the real learning and healing can begin.

Communication Breakdown

When that tiny, mad idea arose, and God noticed there was a disturbance in the force, He reacted to the sudden shutdown of our communication with Him. Now think in these terms: everything God creates is an extension of Himself. Everything God creates contains the mind of God, and the totality of God. Everything God creates is life. The Holy Spirit is the *totality* of God in this world. But God does not have anything to do with our dream, so God made the Holy Spirit His proxy here; a rich, living benefactor, helping us from the wings of the theater, doing everything possible to bring us home. The Holy Spirit has been given the duty by God to be in charge of and take over this world—totally. God the Father, the one we pray to and worship and hope is really there, is unaware of our problems because He does not understand them. We have disconnected ourselves from Him and He does not acknowledge this untrue world. So, God made a complete stand-in for Himself in the image of Himself who does understand us and listens to us and works with us, exactly in the way we would want God to. *The Holy Spirit is God, as we understand Him, with all the power and love.*

He is God's vast and quiet temporary replacement for what God cannot participate in. He is all of those things you have ever understood about God in your life and what goes on behind the scenes in every aspect of your life. The Holy Spirit is responsible for your guides, your intuition and hunches, your guardian angels, hearing your prayers, your special function or talent, your nighttime dreams, and miracles manifesting in whatever way you need them at the moment. The Holy Spirit is the Universal Mind. He plans your life and all your lessons. He *is* you, and everything He decides for you is what you are deciding *with* Him. The *you* that is deciding with Him is the part of you that is still aware of What it is. It is the part of you that agreed to this process and agreed to the teachings of the Holy Spirit. What we understand to be the path our lives are taking is created by the Holy Spirit, along with our Higher Self.

Every prayer you pray goes through the Holy Spirit. Every manifestation of God in this three-dimensional world is of the Holy Spirit. Every bit of help and support, every coincidence, every vision, absolutely everything you now believe to be from God, and much more, is actually from the Holy Spirit, acting on God's behalf.

The phrase "Holy Spirit" may come from traditional

Christian-speak, but if that's a problem for you, look beyond that and just try to understand the idea of what it means. He is the Spirit of God; the means for us to end a silly, temporary dream; something to stand in for God and intervene for His sleeping children. Call It whatever you like.

Eliminating Conflict

For those on the planet who have not yet gotten to the point of accepting the Atonement, the Holy Spirit is left with only one choice; He must keep trying to get their attention. But He has to do it in a way that will not interfere with the freedom to choose. For those who are not aware of the Atonement plan, life looks like a lot of randomness and suffering and effects appearing without cause. The Course states that the Holy Spirit is not concerned with form, which simply means that he doesn't care what happens in this world because He knows that it doesn't matter, except as a means of bringing us closer to God. The Holy Spirit operates on the level of thought, or content, because thoughts are the source of everything.

The way he gently inserts Himself into our lives is by seeing conflict and attempting to eliminate it. There is no conflict in the mind of God, so if we are God, in truth, there can be no conflict in our minds either. This world is dysfunctional simply because our thoughts conflict with God's will and each other's. Consider how vast is mankind's conflict with nature, or your own conflicts with your family and friends, or how you disagree with politicians or corporations. Our egos are just our own wills that are separate from God's will. Each situation in which we find ourselves (and that word "situation" covers a lot of territory) is a relationship, because a situation is anything we are relating to at the moment. More on the Holy Spirit later.

Forgiveness

After the Holy Spirit, the second big piece of the Atonement plan is forgiveness. The overwhelming message of *A Course in Miracles* is forgiveness because while the Holy Spirit has His job to do, forgiveness is ours. We have all heard the word forgiveness from the time we were small, but the odds are that you have never experienced the profound power of it. Forgiveness is no small thing, but it will not work its magic unless you unravel the ego's version of it, which is the version we all know. Forgiveness is not only a method for undoing the dream, it is the *only* method that will undo the dream, no matter what name you give it. Because of the way the Course defines it and has us apply it, it takes forgiveness to a new level. Forgiveness is the most powerful solution offered by the Course because it represents your personal commitment to ending the dream.

The ego has created many so-called methods within the world to make us believe that they are the answers to our problems, but most of them don't help at all, but they sound great! We use religions and objects, like crystals or pendulums, sacred places, sacred words, psychotherapy, medicine, planning, analysis, research, history, mathematics, and everything else you can think of here on planet earth to which we give our problems in search of solutions. They are all superficial solutions and they support the world of the ego. These methods are just ego distractions designed to keep us exactly where we are and help us all feel better when we employ them.

Forgiveness is the only method that works, but as I said, it is not the forgiveness that you are probably used to. It is a new understanding of forgiveness because it is the change of thought behind it that generates it and makes the difference. The act of forgiveness is the act of eliminating "sin" and practicing to become who you really are, and it is the **only thing you can do** that will make any positive difference at all in the world. Forgiveness is your only purpose! I kid you not, but I'll explain that later. This is powerful stuff.

We tend to think that we need to learn how to love each other more, but the Course reminds us that love cannot be taught. The problem isn't that we need to learn to love, because love is simply what we already are. The problem is removing the incorrect thinking that blocks that love, so that we can begin to recognize it in ourselves and our brothers. It will appear naturally as we clear away the debris through forgiveness.

Attack!

As we go through life, and we observe the actions of our "brothers" (which is the non-gender specific term the Course uses to describe all other people on the planet), our first reaction is to judge them. We do this because they are different from us, so we need to put them into a familiar box to understand them better (tall, dumpy, rich, poor, nice perfume, ugly shoes, funny eyes, ethnic of some sort, etc.) Then, we assign our past associations to them, and decide, based on this silly, superficial information, whether or not they are acceptable to us. This judgment is so automatic and swift and subtle that we are barely aware we are even doing it. It is the immediate and very constant pattern of our thinking. It is our current, habitual mode of reacting to the life we see in front of our eyes, based on living within a three-dimensional world of separation.

Even if we are paying attention to our role in the bigger picture, we judge everything we come into contact with. These judgmental thoughts are your thoughts in the dream world, and they aren't your real thoughts. They are what people do. Too bad you're not a people. The problem with judgment is that it's always wrong. Always! That's a bold statement but true, nonetheless. The reason judgment is always wrong is because you and I are living within a context that doesn't even exist! There are no such things as opposites or differences or degrees of any kind, and therefore, there is nothing to judge. Breaking this pattern is vital to breaking the dream.

There is a subtlety and great depth to our thoughts that needs to be emphasized. This is a very important concept; if you are angry in any way, at anyone, for any reason, you are thinking incorrectly. If you think or say anything that ridicules anyone in the *smallest* way, you are thinking incorrectly. If you judge anyone for any reason or become angry, you are always making yourself or someone else a victim of something that you wish to correct in them. Since you cannot be a victim and nothing outside of your own thinking needs correction, any anger is a certain sign that your thinking needs adjustment. This is always true. How many times each day in your life do you act the victim, because someone is "making" you do something you don't want to do, expressing an opinion you don't agree with, or laying some small or large burden on you that you don't want? And how many times each day do you victimize others with those same demands and burdens?

The Course calls these **attack thoughts**. Attack thoughts are the tiniest of judgments, and the largest of tantrums, arguments of any size, including genocide and world wars. They are the subtle thoughts behind every roll of the eyes, small jokes at someone's expense, heaves of frustration, a sigh, or hundreds of other unspoken thoughts that don't even reveal themselves. These can be so subtle and part of our makeup, we aren't aware we are even thinking them, or what they indicate about our state of mind. These are all of the things we do to keep ourselves separated from our brothers.

Each thought of judgment on any level is a statement that there is a gap between you and your brother because he or she isn't living up to your expectations, and they are therefore, apart from you. It is a gap that restates the tiny, mad idea on a second-by-second basis. We are saying that there is something missing in our brother. Something is wrong with the current situation. Something is wrong with him or her. You see something that you wish would change. Something is lacking. There is conflict of some sort.

That is the gap that must be closed. It is the smallest gap, but we are all scared out of our wits to step over it and go past it because it would negate our current reality. These tiny thoughts are pervasive in our lives and by their repetition, represent what we believe, and they all point to the same conclusion—we are not our bothers. These thoughts of attack and judgment represent our newly acquired habit of separation.

Is It Real?

You may have a great deal of difficulty forgiving people, especially if they really did something to you. But there is a problem with that statement. They didn't do anything. We are unquestioning in our belief that we are really here on earth, either living a life that God gave us, or a life that arose from primordial soup. It's real. We're real. Stuff that happens really happens, and what really happens has a life of its own, beyond the present moment. It *really* happened! You can't undo something that really happened. The idea that this life might not be real has never really crossed our minds. Remember when I said the consistency of this universe convinces us that this is a dream? That's the reality we give to the past. If it happened, then it always remains, consistent and real.

True forgiveness, according to Course's explanation, ***is absolutely dependent on the fact that this world doesn't exist.*** If this world were real, true forgiveness would be impossible, and that's why the way we currently forgive doesn't work. We have tacitly given everything that happens in this world our acknowledgement of its truth because our memory of all that has happened is so obviously real, especially if you believe this world was created by God. You can't say that something God created or allowed isn't real. If God created this world, that means God created all of the good and all of the bad, which then would also really exist. Even if you don't believe in God, you still believe in the reality of this world. If someone does something rotten to you, then that action, in a real world, really exists, and has a permanence to it. All of those rotten things that other people do to us are absolutely real, just because they are. We saw them all happen! Our *belief* that they are real has made them real to us. They have life everlasting because we *believe* they do.

The Course differentiates between the terms sin and error. It refers to sin as the human belief that what happened is real and therefore, permanent and uncorrectable. Error, on the other hand, is the acknowledgment that every negative event that we see here as humans is all simply the result of our own incorrect perception and can be corrected by changing our thinking about it. The incorrect thinking exists now—not in the past—but only as an illusion. There is no past connected to it, because there is no past. Simply changing your thinking will correct the error. The incorrect thoughts that caused these events are the thoughts of the ego, and they, and the ego, do not exist. Making these thoughts real makes this world real. Correcting them through forgiveness begins the process of making the world go away.

> *T-26.V.6. Forgiveness is the great release from time. ²It is the key to learning that the past is over. ³Madness speaks no more. ⁴There is no other teacher and no other way. ⁵For what has been undone no longer is.*

Another way to see your life is to understand it this way: the Course says that everything you see is either *an expression of love* or *a call for love*, and the only appropriate response to either of those possibilities—is love. That narrows it down quite a bit, don't you think?

When we think about God, we have accepted the idea that He can somehow be unconditionally loving and vengeful at the same time, along with many other strange flaws, like demanding sacrifice. We have done this because this is how we view ourselves. We have taken our flawed and confusing character traits and applied them to our idea of God, instead of seeing His perfection and applying it to our idea of ourselves. We are fatally flawed because we believe that all of the sins we have committed are real. They really exist in the past, which cannot be changed, and because we were made in the image of God, He must also have these characteristics.

Hanging onto the past and those rotten "sins" makes forgiveness incomplete or impossible because even if we *say* we forgive them, even if we really believe it, those rotten things still have their own existence apart from what we do with them, and we can never make them go away. The reason for this is quite simple; we believe that the past exists and also that the past can't be changed. Our sins are as real as the lamp post on the corner that has stood for 90 years. We believe that what we hold in our memories is the truth, no matter how distorted our perception of it might be.

> *T-13.IV.5. "Now" has no meaning to the ego. ²The present merely reminds it of past hurts, and it reacts to the present as if it were the past. ³The ego cannot tolerate release from the past, and although the past is*

> over, the ego tries to preserve its image by responding as if it were present. ⁴It dictates your reactions to those you meet in the present from a past reference point, obscuring their present reality. ⁵In effect, if you follow the ego's dictates you will react to your brother as though he were someone else, and this will surely prevent you from recognizing him as he is. ⁶And you will receive messages from him out of your own past because, by making it real in the present, you are forbidding yourself to let it go. ⁷You thus deny yourself the message of release that every brother offers you now.
> T-13.IV.6. The shadowy figures from the past are precisely what you must escape. ²They are not real, and have no hold over you unless you bring them with you. ³They carry the spots of pain in your mind, directing you to attack in the present in retaliation for a past that is no more. ⁴And this decision is one of future pain. ⁵Unless you learn that past pain is an illusion, you are choosing a future of illusions and losing the many opportunities you could find for release in the present. ⁶The ego would preserve your nightmares, and prevent you from awakening and understanding they are past.

The Course is telling us that we can make evil deeds go away by forgiving them because they never happened! They aren't real because this world isn't real, there is no past, and your evil brother isn't evil; he's just caught up in an illusion, like you.

The ego has also done something remarkable to undermine our ability to forgive. We believe that if something bad really happened to us, then if we forgive it, we are just trying to cover up something that happened, and pretend we are good and kind, and even superior, for doing so. The ego has turned forgiveness into a lie. If the event is real, then our egos convince us that real forgiveness of it cannot be possible and, therefore, forgiveness is just one more lie we are using in this world to deceive ourselves. So, when we forgive, we feel bad about ourselves for playing the game of lies. In this sense, forgiveness for something that really happened just makes the whole situation worse. When we forgive something real, we are weak for doing so. This cannot be true if the events never happened.

The consistency of this dream means that everything in the past carries over into the present. The consistency is just the trick we are playing on ourselves to convince us this dream is real. The past can be erased, not just symbolically, but truthfully, if you believe it can be, just as everything else is subject to your beliefs. And that's because the past doesn't exist. The idea that the past can be erased sounds like an impossible scenario, because our memories have embedded themselves into our brains. The past is part of who we are. But that's exactly what we are trying to undo—who we are.

When you change your thinking, you can make events from the past lose all meaning and drama. The only reason we hold onto the past is because of the importance it holds for us. It contains our treasures; all of the evil things people have done to us that we cherish because we can call on them anytime to justify our anger or rotten acts against them. It doesn't have to be that way. Giving the past reality is only a choice you are making.

Forgiveness to Destroy

The Course teaches that there are some fundamental ways that we now forgive that simply don't work. They are called **forgiveness to destroy** (insert minor chord on Hammond organ here).

These are the three basic ways most of us forgive today; bringing no real closure, hanging onto the event in the back of our minds; saying over and over that we forgive but we still see that person as "the one who did that awful thing," in spite of our best efforts. Most importantly, we cut ourselves off from any real change and perpetuate our views.

The first type of incomplete forgiveness is to forgive from a superior position. That is, we say that the person who wronged us did it because they are inferior, didn't know any better, are morally bankrupt, etc., and we, on the other hand, will overlook their nastiness because we are better than they are. We look down on them with superior pity, patting their little heads and muttering, "There, there. We forgive you." This is not forgiveness at all, but merely condescending showmanship.

Another way we forgive incorrectly is by saying, "There, but for the grace of God, go I." In other words, we look at what someone has done and feel that we are very similar to that person, and under the same circumstances, we probably would have done the same thing, or else we already have done the same thing previously. And so, we forgive by "understanding" why they did it and that we are all weak and subject to these temptations of nastiness. We're all in this mess together! Instead of forgiving by becoming the Son of God, this is an attempt at forgiveness by lowering ourselves to the basest level.

The third way we forgive in error is by bargaining. We promise to forgive if only the person who did the nasty deed will agree to our terms. "Buy me dinner and I'll forgive you." "I'll forgive you if you promise never to do it again." Forgiveness must be earned somehow. This is a perfect representation of the ego's games; the only way to receive forgiveness is by paying for it. This is, of course, because we believe that they have taken something from us by doing the nasty thing they did, and now we need to get something back in payment. It is merely an opportunity to blackmail.

The first type of incomplete forgiveness above is just about the same as a misguided idea that has currently become very common among the spiritual community. It is the "forgive but don't forget" or "no pain, no gain" idea, with the belief that it's easier to forgive if you remain "strong" by giving yourself permission to remember that you were hurt by someone, yet humble enough to forgive the event. Somehow, the bigger the hurt, the stronger you are by forgiving it. So, hang onto the hurt to feel good about how strong you are. If you let go of what happened, then you are weak or in denial.

You may immediately see why these forms of forgiveness don't work at all. Even if you never thought about them, they just don't feel right. If you *have* thought about them, then you may realize that they all keep the sin real. They acknowledge, first and foremost, that whatever the sin was, it really occurred, and that forgiveness is just a little mind game. If the sin is real, then the world, as well as the past in which it exists, must also be real. These forms of forgiveness to destroy do not reflect who you are. They are just the ego's way of forgiving without really forgiving, making you think you're moving forward, when you're just treading water.

This is just another way the ego takes a great idea and twists it until it really means nothing but still makes us think it does. The ego has us believing that forgiveness is weakness. It is giving in. If we forgive, we are really saying the other person has won, and we have lost. They have gotten away with their rotten behavior, and we have allowed it. Then we feel more guilt for letting them do that to us, and we look on them as guilty as well. This is the perfect excuse for the ego to hold on to the anger and judgment and guilt it needs to survive.

Also, understand this; we don't want to forgive in a meaningful way because we feel we deserve whatever happens to us. There is a part of us that wants to feel bad all the time because of that guilt. We *want* to be the victim, and feel we deserve it because we believe in our own evil past. Why should we forgive anyone if we deserve what comes our way, in spite of our loud screaming about the injustice? And so, we sabotage forgiveness because we deserved that bad thing on some level, and we know that what's done is done, no matter what we may think about it afterward.

Real Forgiveness

So, how do you really forgive? You are God! God sees all of us as His perfect children, beyond this world of form, beyond these bodies, beyond our flawed personalities. We are not this human form, full of imperfections and desires, looking for satisfaction in an imperfect world. The only way to forgive is if you become the God you are and see your brother as perfect, as yourself, as God. You overlook the evil by overlooking the dream, just as you would see the evil done to you in a nighttime dream as nothing.

All of the evil that is ever done to us is by dream figures within a dream. If you dream that Mother Teresa is chasing you with a machete, when you wake up, you know that wasn't the real Mother Teresa, and so you will hold nothing against her. Look at all of us that same way. We are just dreamlike characters, chasing each other around with machetes. But that is not who we really are. We are just desperately trying to survive in our own silly ways within a dream that we don't know is a dream. And when we all wake up, we will see each other as we really are. Start doing that now while you're still within the dream, by practicing forgiveness.

What you are seeing when you look out from your human eyeballs, without realizing it, is that you are a character in your own stage play, where none of the actors, including yourself, are who they really are. Everyone is playing a role based on the fact that they truly believe they are the characters they are portraying. Their appearance in the play comes from a collective script they have all agreed to, which they believe to be the truth about themselves. All have agreed on a very deep level to forget they are actors for the purpose of this experimental play. To *really* become the character they are portraying as someone who has turned away from God, this experiment requires that they disconnect themselves their true natures. The stage is the known universe. So, when one of the other actors cuts you off on the freeway, and you judge him angrily, is that judgment correct? It *can't* be. There is no real car, no real freeway, no real person. It's only pretend. There is only a dream constructed by the theater director of your mind, based on your belief that you are now a separate being, and seeing others in the same imaginary position, cut off from their memory of who they are. Your character is programmed by your own choice to react in the accepted way to the situation and get angry.

Your forgiveness should be unconditional and based on the fact that no one has done anything to you at all, because **this isn't really happening!** The Course contains an oft-quoted line that says, "Be willing to forgive the Son of God for what he did not do." (T-17.III.5) The only thing you are really forgiving is yourself, for your error in thinking. That dream was a product of *your* thoughts and fears, not the reality of the other person. And just so you know, if you haven't already guessed, ultimately, forgiveness is absolutely unnecessary. It is only useful for humans and practiced for the purpose of helping you remember who you are, and that this isn't real. Once you remember who you are, forgiveness is not needed, like the rope you need to climb out of a well. Once you're out, you don't need it anymore. But don't allow that to let you underestimate the power of forgiveness. Right now, practiced correctly, forgiveness is the only thing that will correct your thinking and it is extremely powerful and extremely necessary to us all.

Guilt

Forgiveness is one of the most eye-opening concepts in the Course. But the real culprit, the big enchilada to the entire Course, is the idea of guilt. I have mentioned guilt slightly so far, but now it's time to understand the gravity, the pervasiveness and importance of it. Guilt is what keeps you and me in this world. It is the one thing we all have deeply buried within ourselves that is the engine of this illusory world. Guilt drives us and makes this world almost impossible to escape. It is hidden for the most part, and immense. We attempt to dispense it to others with our blame. Blame is also called judgment, projection, anger and fear.

Our ego's need to blame someone else for our own dream is just our ego's way of hiding Who we really are. Blame and judgment are the tools of the ego to maintain this illusion. They are the ego's self-protection game of not taking responsibility for our own thinking and beliefs, by keeping everyone else's thoughts and actions apart from our own.

We are projecting our denial of the Truth—our suppressed incorrect thinking—to create all events around us but we are very afraid to look at our thinking process honestly because that would reveal our own responsibility for our lives. And so, we store the tremendous subconscious guilt that we have created within ourselves in an effort to make sure that the status quo is maintained, and that we don't disturb our external lives.

There is one very important idea to understand about this guilt stuff; every judgment, every bit of blame, anger and fear you feel and constantly hand over to others, is guilt you are adding to yourself. If you think about this for a few seconds, you may begin to realize the amount of guilt you carry subconsciously within your own mind, and what a tremendous amount of baggage you are here to undo.

We all think of ourselves as a fairly nice, or fairly decent person. And we certainly aren't all that bad. But there is so much in our egos that is just plain dishonest. We can do a tremendous amount of judging without one other person being aware of it. We don't think much of it when we casually judge an action, an outfit, a behavior, or an event in a negative way. It is the habit of our egos. It is why there are so many people you have known or been aware of who suddenly seem to have a tremendous fall from grace. "I always thought he/she was such a nice person." It turns out that it just had come time for that person to face some of their hidden, incorrect thoughts, fueled by guilt, in a much more open and dramatic way. Thoughts that we all harbor.

Guilt is one thought. It is the idea that other people are somehow different from us. We might believe they are inferior or superior to us. Either way, this is just simply not true. Guilt is the idea of separation. They are different. They are doing or saying or demonstrating something in some way that deserves our subtle or not-so-subtle anger and judgment. Guilt is the root of the idea of separation. It carries with it the ego's entire agenda. You can only keep what you give away.

> T-7.VIII. ⁵*Using its own warped version of the laws of God, the ego utilizes the power of the mind only to defeat the mind's real purpose.* ⁶**It projects conflict from your mind to other minds, in an attempt to persuade you that you have gotten rid of the problem.**
>
> T-7.VIII.3. *There are two major errors involved in this attempt.* ²*First, strictly speaking, conflict cannot be projected because it cannot be shared.* ³*Any attempt to keep part of it and get rid of another part does not really mean anything.* ⁴*Remember that a conflicted teacher is a poor teacher and a poor learner.* ⁵*His lessons are confused, and their transfer value is limited by his*

> confusion. ⁶**The second error is the idea that you can get rid of something you do not want by giving it away.** ⁷**Giving it is how you keep it.** ⁸*The belief that by seeing it outside you have excluded it from within is a complete distortion of the power of extension.* ⁹*That is why those who project are vigilant for their own safety.* ¹⁰*They are afraid that their projections will return and hurt them.* ¹¹*Believing they have blotted their projections from their own minds, they also believe their projections are trying to creep back in.* ¹²*Since the projections have not left their minds, they are forced to engage in constant activity in order not to recognize this.*

Guilt is so central to the Course's teaching that it makes a rather dramatic statement:

> T-5.V.5. *The guiltless mind cannot suffer.*

Ridding yourself of guilt through forgiveness means you are at the end of the journey. Our human condition simply means that we do not like ourselves at all, if we are honest about it. That's because, even though the guilt is subconscious, that feeling of self-loathing, caused by our guilt, is always just below the surface of our thinking, and it certainly drives much of our conscious thinking and behavior. The more arrogant the ego, the more in denial he/she is about the guilt. That is why we associate arrogance with a big ego. They are simply people more desperate to hide their true feelings of self-hatred from themselves.

We have been conditioned by our egos to avoid at all costs looking deeply or honestly at ourselves so we can spin our beliefs about ourselves into justifiable deniability. The only way to make your incorrect thinking go away is to see it honestly, and the only way to do that is to take responsibility for everything that comes into your life as your own, and then forgive it and forgive yourself. That scares us because we are so afraid of what we will find (because of the guilt we feel). We have created a separate, physical world outside of ourselves solely for the purpose of separating our incorrect thoughts from ourselves, seeing the source of our problems as outside ourselves and projecting the fault and blame away from us.

Forgiving ourselves is all about letting go of that deep subconscious guilt we feel for believing what our egos have constructed, for denying our responsibility, for believing that something outside of us did something to us, and for giving it importance.

We are deathly afraid of looking deeply into our own psyches because we are afraid of discovering how terrible we really are. We are afraid of what others will think about us if we admit what we did. We deny because we are trying to avoid punishment. But the Course reminds us that we're making up all of this stuff about ourselves as well. If you look into yourself honestly, you will see nothing but the face of God. You will see love so pure and perfect that it will make you never want to give it up again. But the only way to see that is to first see through all of the crap you believe about yourself. It's not there. They're not doing anything to you, you're not doing anything to them, and you're not doing anything to yourself. You aren't guilty!

The only reason anything negative comes into your life, is because you have invited it in, with the Holy Spirit's assistance, solely for the purpose of giving yourself the opportunity to forgive it and let it go! Did you really hear that? Everything negative that comes into your life appears because you are giving yourself the chance to let it go forever! Bad things don't happen to you because you are a victim, or unlucky, or deserving of bad things, or in the wrong place at the wrong time! You are giving yourself an incredible, wonderful opportunity to forgive! Take it! Wipe away the guilt. If you don't forgive what happens to you, it will return again and again in another form, over many years or lifetimes, as long as it takes for you to see it as a shadow of nothing at all, because it will belong to you until you stop owning it.

Chapter 4 – *The Solution*

Subtlety

As you practice forgiveness, you will naturally get better at seeing your reactions more easily and quickly. You will also begin to notice something quite remarkable; you will see in yourself more and more the extremely subtle judgments you make on a regular basis. You will see exactly how judgmental you are, how pervasive those judgments are, and how they are the basis for all human life on earth. Just about all of our thoughts are based on comparisons and judgments and fears. That's who we are as humans, and the energy that causes them is part of you. These tiny judgments and the residue they leave behind are our almost unnoticeable grievances. They are the things that we create and hold against someone after we leave their presence.

It's easy to notice our judgmental nature when it comes to the big and dramatic events of our lives, but it's really eye-opening when you begin to notice the small judgments that run through most thoughts. Virtually every contact you have with another human being brings in a judgment that you never let go of, because you think it's real. They are the things that don't make you necessarily feel anger, and so they are more easily ignored. They include those quick thoughts of correction for anything your brothers and sisters do. They may fall more into the category of mild cynicism, or even just putting people into your pre-defined boxes. They might not even feel like judgment if you become consciously aware of them.

As you see yourself more and more clearly, you can see the very subtle thinking patterns we have all created, and as I said, these patterns appear in most every interaction we have with each other; a car driving too slowly when you're trying to cross the street, a bagger at the grocery store who puts your gallon of almond milk on top of your quail eggs, someone walking down the street toward you, everyone else in a restaurant, your coworkers, your family members, etc. These feelings can be extremely fleeting and unnoticeable. The more you pay attention to your thinking, the more quickly you can forgive yourself for these unimportant judgments. This should happen naturally as you become more aware of yourself in each moment. It is helpful to get into the habit of asking yourself, whenever you are leaving the presence of another human, "Am I OK with him or her?" Any subtle judgment you may have made toward that person will slip away as you say yes to yourself by forgiving everything, acknowledging that you hold no grievances. You have made the world in front of you unimportant.

Whenever you don't feel good at all, on any mental level, it is because there is some thought or attitude you hold that is causing it. If you can't figure it out, don't worry about it, because it might be something deeply buried. Just ask for help and you will see it clearly when you are able, and forgive yourself for the thought. All you have to do is forgive! Remind yourself that this isn't real and keep your mind as focused as much as you can on that simple idea. Being vigilant for God and His Kingdom means remembering unceasingly that this is a dream and being aware of the things that your mind is focusing on that are keeping you from waking up. Paying attention to all of those small judgments requires a level of awareness that may take a lot of practice and persistence. Don't focus on the substance of the judgments; merely focus only on being aware of them so you can let them go. You are using the power of your mind, along with help from the Holy Spirit, to undo the entire universe. When we can all let go of our ego thinking, the only thinking left will be the ecstasy of God's mind.

Looking Within

When I said not to focus on the substance of your judgments, I mean that the form doesn't matter. What someone actually did to you doesn't matter, as powerful as it may seem at the moment it occurs. It's not time to analyze the details; it's time to take responsibility for them because you are bringing them into your life. Everything you see external to yourself is coming from inside you. You are bringing events into your life so you can see what you are holding onto. If you can understand that, it will be a major revelation.

Pay attention to the anger and judgment you feel and understand that this is what you must let go. Simply say to yourself, "OK, I see that I am holding onto jealousy," or impatience, or intolerance, or any one of a billion other ideas. These are nothing more than your attempts to make this dream real. The ego defines your strength by the "justifiable anger" you hold. Holding anger is easy for us to do. God's strength comes from letting go, and it is much more difficult—at first. You need to acknowledge the existence of your grievances within yourself and give them to the Holy Spirit. See them, acknowledge yourself as their source, and give them away because they are not serving you.

This is a profoundly powerful way to participate in this wonderful process you are living through. It sounds simple, but it takes constant awareness and observation and practice. Don't go any deeper than acknowledging what you notice about yourself, and give it away. Don't beat yourself up or look at specific events from your past. Just see it and give it away to the Holy Spirit.

Miracles

Another solution, and part of the Atonement plan, is the miracle. An important piece of creating your life is understanding miracles. *A Course in Miracles* is a course in forgiveness because, as you read it, you will begin to understand that forgiveness and miracles are the same thing. A miracle occurs when you forgive. Forgiveness is responsible for all miracles, and miracles change your world. This sums up the Course pretty well. When you forgive, you see an event differently and you reinforce a better view of the world, and if you forgive enough, the world you live in will begin to transform into something beautiful.

Some of these miracles will be very noticeable to you but most will not be. That doesn't mean they aren't happening. Every time you are able to truly forgive in a way that eliminates your negative thinking toward yourself and the event or the other people involved, is a time when you create a miracle. It is called a miracle because you have caused a change in the space/time continuum. Something has occurred that is beyond the laws of the egoverse. You have changed your trajectory in time and space, and you have become, however immensely or subtly, a different person. You have changed yourself and therefore, you have rewritten the script of your life.

The Course says that when a miracle occurs, there is a collapse of time. An event which used to exist, a "sin," no longer does, because it does not exist in your life any longer. That doesn't mean you won't remember it; it just means it won't mean anything to you anymore. It turns out it was only an error that has now been corrected. Every "sin" you forgive changes your life, puts you on a new path, and eliminates the need for that issue to enter your life again. You have slowly begun to open the door to another world.

Every miracle affects everyone of us. Granted, your forgiveness of Uncle Louie might not be noticeable to him or anyone else but you, but it is a small and necessary step to eliminating this dream world and all of the thoughts we hold of past sins that never really happened.

> *T-1.I.37. A miracle is a correction introduced into false thinking by me. ²It acts as a catalyst, breaking up erroneous perception and reorganizing it properly. ³This places you under the Atonement principle, where perception is healed. ⁴Until this has occurred, knowledge of the Divine Order is impossible.*

Eliminate the Past

The Course is very clear that living in the present moment is quite an important idea, because quite simply, there are no such things as the past or the future, and that if you were to truly live in the present, you would see your brothers as they truly are in God—not as they were in your memory or as you hope them to be someday. It appears that we are living in the moment right now. Where else could we be? But truly living in the present moment is not a simple intellectual exercise, even though it may be a new age platitude. It is a fundamental change in the way you view life. It isn't something you can try for a day or two. It will not even occur without a change at the deepest level of your being.

As a matter of fact, we are now living in the present but we are completely unaware of it because we are so preoccupied with the past and future of our ego minds. Our investment in the past and the future is as pervasive and as subtle as our thoughts of judgment. Many lessons in the Course workbook are devoted to undoing the past. Every second of every day, you have convinced yourself that what you see in this world is based solely on your past understanding of it. Our engagement in our humanness is really just our engagement in the past. Time is part of this world; not of God.

When you live in the present, it means simply that every moment of every day, you look at people as if you don't know anything about their human past, because they have no human past. That includes all of those rotten things they've done that only exist in your idea of a past. You look at them as they really are; perfect and right here and now. Just as we learn to love by eliminating the barriers to its natural expression, learning to live in the present requires eliminating the past and future.

The Course first requests that you change your mind about the context of this life by understanding it is a dream. That change of mind can be a long and difficult process, as I have already mentioned. Accepting this world as a dream is a change of mind in the *long-term*, general beliefs you have. The second change of mind that the Course asks is that you forgive, which is a change in the immediate, *short-term*, real-world sense. Forgiveness is something you practice on real events, right now. Intellectually accepting the idea that this world is a dream will change your greater understanding of life, but forgiveness penetrates directly into the fabric of the dream.

The cause of your life comes from inside of you, so when we forgive, we can mentally disconnect the person in front of us from being the source of the so-called evil things they have done to us. At the same time, we are also reconnecting those "evil things" back to ourselves as the source. Notice how quickly you react when someone does something negative to you. Your built-in ego reaction is to immediately associate that person with their action, and to then get angry, become a victim, and blame them for it and make them guilty. But because *you* have subconsciously created the situation by inviting them into your life as a reflection of what *you* believe, they are merely playing a role that is only possible because of *your* beliefs and *your* invitation. When you see yourself as the source of the event, you are right there with it, able to see it as merely a mistake in thinking, and change your mind about it and yourself. You are not evil; you are just allowing your ego to make your choices for you. Take back your power and let go of the error.

When I was first beginning the Course, and I realized that forgiveness was something I needed to practice and learn, I began doing it every night before I went to bed. I would spend as much time as I felt I needed to forgive the events of the day, and then the events and people of the past. I tried to remember everything I could, going back as far as I could. It was a little difficult at first, but I was able to eventually put every event into a different context as I saw all of these evil people as only doing what I asked of them, as part of a bigger picture.

The most amazing thing about it was that very soon, after only a few days, I felt like I had a shift in consciousness. This was not a small thing. I felt as if I awakened to a different life, as if I had crossed into an alternate reality that looked the same but was subtly different. All the same people were there, but it didn't feel as if they were really the same people, and I certainly wasn't the same guy.

This shift didn't make my life any easier; as a matter of fact, it made life more difficult for a while, as if I had to prove to myself that this was really a path I wanted to go down by pushing away the obstacles that appeared at every step. But after a few short weeks of determined practice, my life started to lighten up considerably. My life blended back into something that seemed normal again. I still had to constantly go back and re-forgive the same people and events over and over as my attachment to the past kept creeping back in. The most difficult task I found was to forgive myself, which is the ultimate goal. It was difficult to not feel guilt, and to let myself off the hook for all of the things I could remember doing and saying. I felt so responsible. I had to convince myself firmly that none of my guilt was real, just as no one else's guilt was real.

That was the beginning of what has been a consistent uphill walk from that time on. My life still has difficulties, but with practice, I can now see them more quickly and clearly and trace back them to myself, and forgive myself and others for believing in the nonsense of it all. Problems slip away, as promised by the Course, as I give them away with the certainty that they will be handled well and positively for all concerned. I still have subtle fears of the future, and I still hold onto things I shouldn't, but I feel that forgiveness is truly working in a very effective way in my life. Forgiveness starts out being about simple individual acts that must be swept away, but ultimately, forgiveness is not about those acts we forgive but about the entire context in which we view life, ourselves and this universe. It's about changing your idea of who you are.

The Real Purpose of Forgiveness

The Course can be summed up like this; we are dreaming. Our only purpose here is to wake up. We do that through forgiveness.

We are creating this dream with our minds by giving it drama, attention, importance, focus and reality. The only way to wake up from the dream is to stop feeding it. We have to stop believing in it. Forgiveness pulls us out of the dream by putting us into a different frame of mind that reminds us that we and our brothers are God, and not this.

The real purpose of forgiveness is to shift your focus from this phony world you are making to seeing yourself and your brothers as they really are. The purpose of forgiveness is to minimize this world and eliminate a past that doesn't exist. It's to help you shift your focus in a way that lets you see this world as unimportant and not real. It's to remind you of who you really are.

Before we can see or know anything about a better world beyond this one, we must first let go of this one. If you believe that another human being did something negative to you, then you are seeing this world upside down. Forgiveness can turn it right side up. Letting go of the evil act through forgiveness is the same as letting go of collective humanity, because humans cannot exist without the idea of separation. When you see beyond the body, knowing that fleshy, annoying blob that appears to have wronged you isn't really there, you will begin to change your thinking. When you do it enough, it starts to become a habit.

In chapter one, I mentioned that this life is like a video game, and that the third step to end the game was to take action to end it. That action we must take is forgiveness. When you remember that one word, ***forgive***, in every challenging moment, it will come to represent the entire context of your new life. It will immediately send you on a quick mental journey to remind you that you're not here, that they aren't doing anything and that you aren't either. When you say that one word to yourself, you can look at your brother, whatever they may have done in form, and smile and see them with the love of God that is in your heart. From a strictly human point of view, forgiveness has nothing to do with the person you are forgiving. It is only about you, changing your mind about a world that doesn't exist and something that never happened. The other person doesn't need to be aware of your forgiveness at all, and usually isn't. From God's point of view, when you heal your own mind, you are healing the mind of the Son of God, which includes the person who "did" something to you, by removing one more speck of your own guilt. This may also help you understand the energy you give off that is part of everything, at every moment.

If you are having any difficulty forgiving, or even understanding how you could possibly forgive someone for what they have done, or forgive yourself for what you have done, try to talk yourself through the process. Whenever you are in a position to forgive, either at the moment something is happening or later, tap into the real idea behind forgiveness. Begin by telling yourself that you are a Son of God. Remind yourself that this is not really happening. It's a dream. You are making it all up. There is no one here, including you. No one is doing anything to you and you are not doing anything to anyone else. The person you think you see in front of you is also the Son of God. The only reason they did what they did, was because you needed to be there to see it, so you could forgive it. They are doing your bidding, because that person is your mirror and your savior. They are merely playing their part in the Holy Spirit's Atonement plan. They are giving you the opportunity to make a different choice and to become someone new. Don't just say the

Chapter 4 – *The Solution*

words but feel these ideas deeply. I will expand on this idea in the coming chapters.

Judgment

Your self-discovery will happen in stages. When you begin to notice more and more the way life is structured, you will see the level of judgment you cast against everyone you see. You may go through long periods when you don't notice, then suddenly, you will finally see that almost every thought you think is a judgment, putting yourself and your brother in a cage of your own construction. Forgiveness at this point is vital, but it can also be very disheartening.

The judgment you will feel against yourself may be overwhelming, because you are working so hard to overcome your negative thoughts, and you are now feeling that your ability to forgive is impossible, and that all of your work has been frustrating and for nothing. This is the overwhelming signature of guilt. This is the time to pick yourself up from your bootstraps and focus all of your attention to forgiving *yourself*. Every time you forgive another, you must also forgive yourself for the judgment you felt in the first place. They go hand in hand. We cannot forgive our brothers if we do not forgive ourselves, and vice versa. We are a package deal. You only keep what you give away. All of the things you must learn to look past in others, you must also look past in yourself. The only reason you even see anything wrong with anyone else is because you are projecting what you feel about yourself, from deep in your subconscious, onto them. Pull yourself away from this world and what you think about yourself.

It's not easy to change your habitual reaction to the things that come into your life from outside of you. Forgiveness also isn't natural to us. It's not in our deepest nature, which is God. In God, there is no such thing as forgiveness because, to God, no one can ever do anything that needs to be forgiven. Forgiveness is part of the ego's world, and it is the only tool that we are able to use to get beyond it. It has to be learned and practiced.

There is also good news in all of this. You will begin to notice something rather startling when you learn to forgive. You will begin to see yourself differently. You are becoming someone new. You are not reacting to the world in the same way you used to react, so that means you are not the same person you used to be. The changes will be most noticeable when you are able to forgive the things that are the most difficult for you. Those things represent the ideas in you that you most fiercely cling to, so when you are able to begin to let them go, you will begin to see that you are becoming unrecognizable to yourself. You are becoming, slowly but surely, Who you really are.

When you begin to forgive on a regular basis because you see and feel and understand the value of it, it will also have the added side effect of changing the world around you in a number of ways. You may first start to notice that all of the events of your life seem to have a much higher purpose. You will see that things are happening to you to tug at certain parts of your personality and beliefs. You will begin to understand how it is all beginning to fall into place. Not all of it will be easy. In fact, after you start to forgive, it may be like pulling your finger out a dike that holds back the water of your deepest fears. Some very difficult challenges may come your way because you have demonstrated that you are now willing to see them. These are the more difficult things your ego and mine just don't want to release, like fear of death and the unimportance of the body.

You may also experience feeling more and more cut off from people in your circle. Friends may drift away, relationships may fail, the things you once loved will hold less and less appeal. As you forgive more and more, you will play the game of human less and less, and you will find yourself looking for more real experiences with people who feel and think more like you, and less like your old circle. You are separating yourself from the ego, so those who demonstrate the ego more will be less likely to end up in your life. As your ego fades, you will depend less and less on others to approve of you and give you external self-worth. This may sound scary now, but once you begin to do it, you will understand that it is the right and necessary thing to do. You are dying to be who you really are. It might be better to know about this ahead of time. It will all work itself out, because God is with you for the entire journey.

> *W62.1. It is your forgiveness that will bring the world of darkness to the light. ²It is your forgiveness that lets you recognize the light in which you see. ³Forgiveness is the demonstration that you are the light of the world.* ***⁴Through your forgiveness does the truth about yourself return to your memory. ⁵Therefore, in your forgiveness lies your salvation.***
>
> *2. Illusions about yourself and the world are one. ²That is why all forgiveness is a gift to yourself.* ***³Your goal is to find out who you are, having denied your Identity by attacking creation and its Creator.*** *⁴Now you are learning how to remember the truth. ⁵For this attack must be replaced by forgiveness, so that thoughts of life may replace thoughts of death.*
>
> ***3. Remember that in every attack you call upon your own weakness, while each time you forgive you call upon the strength of Christ in you.*** *²Do you not then begin to understand what forgiveness will do for you? ³It will remove all sense of weakness, strain and fatigue from your mind. ⁴It will take away all fear and guilt and pain. ⁵It will restore the invulnerability and power God gave His Son to your awareness.*

So, here's what you do. You ***forgive. Everyone. Everything. All the time. Again and again. Until you get it right. Forgive yourself for needing to forgive***. And be extremely patient with yourself. This does not mean you are getting it wrong now. It just means that it takes a lot of practice to forgive someone because you are practicing creating an entirely different reality from this fake universe. You must put yourself into a frame of mind that sees this world as a dream that is not happening. You are eliminating the guilt that holds you here. That's a hard thing to do and it's also why I have spent so much time talking about this world being a dream. *It's hard to do!*

Forgiveness is an opportunity to replace what you currently think with something better. If you find it difficult to forgive, then keep talking to yourself. Tell yourself who you really are and who your brother really is. You are both the Son of God, living in a made-up world that is not really here. Both you and he are not bodies but sparks of divine light. What you believe he just did to you did not really happen. He is you and you are him. He is showing this to you as a gift because it represents an incorrect thought of yours, so you can let it go forever.

You may also realize when you start forgiving that it's not really sticking very well. You may have to forgive someone dozens of times for the same thing before you feel it's really starting to take effect. Then again, I could be wrong. Maybe that's just me. You might nail it the first time. It's up to you. I thought I was able to forgive fairly easily when I started. But then after some weeks, I noticed that I was still feeling resentment toward a particular person or event I thought I had forgiven and needed to start over. It gets better and easier the more you do it. You're not really just practicing forgiveness; you're throwing out your old life. You are not just eliminating bad feelings about others; you are changing them into Sons of God.

Timing

Especially at the beginning of your forgiveness practice, it can be difficult to forgive people at the precise moment they do something to you. Usually, you have to wait for the anger, overreaction, argument, and swearing to stop, the blood to clot, and then count to some large number, and then finally remember that forgiveness is an option. This is not a problem. You will get better at learning to forgive as it's happening. In the meantime, forgive those people later. Forgiveness exists outside of time, and therefore, the moment in time you forgive them is not important when you first start to do it. When you don't forgive immediately, don't feel guilty about it. That's just another game of the ego to use this wonderful tool against you and to increase your guilt. True forgiveness is always liberating and it carries no baggage of any kind. If you feel any negative thoughts associated with your forgiveness, you must forgive again.

We have taken something indescribably beautiful and given it up for a life of struggle and suffering that our egos have convinced us is a good idea. This fake world definitely has its moments, but the most amazing feelings of joy we feel here on earth pale to the ecstasy we will feel again when we rejoin God. We are aware of that fact somewhere inside ourselves, and the wrong turn we have made to get here makes us feel terrible about ourselves. We have turned our backs on God and our true nature. God doesn't hold anything against us for it. We hold it against ourselves. All the pain we feel is the pain of the guilt we feel for what we have done.

Forgiveness is the solution that God has given you to see your brothers for who they really are, so you can see yourself as you really are and let go of the guilt. There is nothing wrong, nothing lacking, nothing to fix. There is only for us all to see the truth. Forgive.

Your Brother

There are so many people on this planet who are sincerely trying to be good and kind, yet they are struggling to use their frozen grins to suppress their tremendous anger and frustration at this cruel world that seems so heartless. It's hard to forgive when you seem to be surrounded by so many who won't. In fact, forgiveness of others is the most difficult challenge we face as humans, because our judgment of others represents everything the ego stands for. Forgiveness is pretty much the opposite of humanness, because it supports the idea that we are all the same spirit, and that this life, world and universe just don't matter at all because they aren't real. Behaving differently, seeing others differently, taking personal responsibility for everything that comes into our lives goes against everything we want and believe. They are real! They are jerks! They deserve pain! What if we're wrong about all of that? What if this *is* a just a dream? Now that this has been presented to you, can you continue to live your life the same way?

Forgiveness is much more than the ideas I have stated so far. Forgiveness is the most life-changing action you can take. It is not a vague, intellectual concept. It is a clear, active strategy that you can begin right now. You will become a different person when you learn to forgive in a real way. You will not react to the world you see in the same way. The world will quite literally change before your eyes. It won't matter who is president or what bills congress passes, or what the governor said. You will not see injustice, or victims, and the events of the world will recede in importance as you realize that everything is happening as it must, without judgment, and there is no need for you to do anything but forgive and be of help in whatever way you feel called to help.

Chapter 5 – Your Mind, Your Life

The Mind

If you are not entirely aware of it at this point, I just want to state the obvious right now. The Course is about the mind and nothing but the mind. There is no world and there are no people. Everything that happens to you, all the time, is happening in your mind, which happens to be the most powerful thing in the universe and beyond. This life, this world you see in front of you every day when you open your eyes, is a reflection of you. You are making it up and you are populating it with the people and things you expect to see because of what you *want* to see. No one enters your life unless they are a witness to your mind, and you are a witness to theirs. You must be willing to accept that you are here on earth because it is your choice and desire to be here. You can't be saved from the nightmare unless you make the choice to stop being here. Nothing is punishing you; nothing is holding you here except your desire to remain. As a matter of fact, you and I aren't here at all; we are just imagining we are.

"Witness" is a word used by religions to refer to people who can confirm your faith. The Course uses the word to describe the idea that absolutely everything that appears in your life is a witness to what you believe. Every person and event that comes into your life is testifying under oath that they were called by you specifically to do exactly as you requested. The people, things and events you experience all prove that what you believe is true. They confirm your thoughts without fail, good or bad. And just as importantly, no one comes in *unless* they were called.

The mind is all there is and it's the only thing you have to deal with, worry about, and change. It is where everything else comes from. It is the source of your life and within it is the solution to all of your problems. It is the most powerful thing in all of creation because it made all of creation. All of the drama and stress and hurrying around and pain and fear and missed appointments and traffic jams and arguments and disappointments are all in your mind. They are not happening to you at all from the outside where they appear to be, and there is not one thing you can do about them, not one thing that will make them lessen or go away, except changing your mind about them.

At some point, you must learn to accept the unbelievable; that your mind is powerful enough to manifest your thoughts in solid form right in front of your eyes. This is what it is doing at every moment to make this world of yours. It does this so easily without your conscious awareness that it appears that these things you see were somehow created by something else and came into your life randomly or accidentally.

It is very difficult to convince anyone that the thoughts they are thinking with their tiny, little brains, putting out these tiny, little electrical impulses could in any way affect the external world to such an extent that they are actually manifesting the entire world. Especially since there are seven billion other tiny, little brains doing the same thing. If you feel you have to understand everything according to the laws of the physical universe, it will be difficult to comprehend something so obviously impossible. But this world is not created according to those laws. It's happening according to God's law, which I speak about later, and it is far beyond the possibilities of physical laws. Besides, it feels so good to be a victim of others. It is so relaxing to accept within your mind the idea that you are in a bad way because others have put you there, or that you are in a good way because of your hard work and talent. It absolves you of any responsibility for anything bad that happens to you or the world at large, and explains everything neatly and finally. It is an idea supported by the vast majority of humans and requires nothing of you.

But you are behind all of it, having a dream and seeing your deepest beliefs and absolutely nothing more than that. We must undo the programming we have been fed from the time we are born that makes the mind less important than the external world. It's hard to imagine that thinking simple thoughts that come and go as wisps can be powerful enough to create mountain ranges and steel girders and all the events of our lives. We simply don't believe we have that power, and it is also very difficult to see the connection between our thoughts and the confusing results of those thoughts in our lives because the physical world we see is not necessarily what we would directly expect from what we are thinking.

Most of us believe that we create our own lives but we also understand that we can't instantly create what we think, so there is a disconnect between thinking and manifesting. We just don't know how it works. We don't really understand the power of the mind. We would rather believe in the power of the body and the actions we take to cause change in this world. It's easy to perform an action and watch it succeed or fall apart. It seems to make so much sense.

We believe in the system of the physical, which is clunky and imperfect, with time relentlessly pushing things forward, where people and things bump into each other and create endless conflicts. But the world that's going on behind the scenes is a world of thought, which is perfect and unaffected by time or conflict. Thoughts flow perfectly and endlessly from each of us. They don't get in each other's way and they always work exactly as we instruct them.

For most of us, the power and depth of the mind is beyond our ability to fathom. We are aware of, and use, a tiny part of it that is engaged solely with life in front of us as our conscious mind. It is only the tiny tip of an immense iceberg. We are devastatingly unaware of the part of our mind that is beneath our conscious awareness. The information that we carry subconsciously should astound and flabbergast us with its immensity and power. The engine that drives your life is what you have stored and forgotten or denied and stuffed deep down, out of your conscious reach. These are the beliefs and thoughts you hold onto. This is what creates the world you see in front of you.

Tiny and Mad

I have put forth the Course's idea that this life and world are nothing more than a dream. I have also related the importance of forgiveness in life. It is vital to understand the context of this life as a dream and the role of forgiveness, but now it's time to understand the manifestation process that's taking place here without our awareness. This includes the process of creating our lives, because it is a very common concern and one that has bred a great deal of misunderstanding.

How does what we see in front of us make it into manifestation? It's not a difficult process to understand, but it probably does mean letting go of what you currently believe. The spiritual community has bought into some very distorted ideas about creating your life. They are ideas the ego made and loves, but it is time to let those ideas go.

The Holy Spirit is intimately involved with the creation of our lives, and that process is fairly simple, but it's not a sound bite concept, so understanding it in a real way will change the way you look at your life in every moment. The Course's version of creating your life is the only one I have ever read that makes perfect sense. You have to decide if it makes sense to you.

The Course also does not lay out its description about how we create our lives in one simple-to-understand section. The concept is more like a jigsaw puzzle that can only be pieced together after multiple readings of the book. This is how the Course works, encouraging us to see a bigger picture by understanding, not bits and pieces, but the entire concept of the world by looking at it from different angles and at different times. Every time you read the Course you will come away with a broader understanding of its true meaning. This life is simple but it is not easy, and the Course is the same. Every time around, it will reveal more and more of its open secrets to you, and there will be many moments of exhilaration as the pieces begin to weave themselves together into a beautiful fabric.

Send in the Clowns

You and I are here on earth because of a single incorrect thought. That curious thought is the basis for this entire universe. Real change within yourself can only come from a change in what you believe yourself to be, and what you believe the purpose of life to be. Because mind is the source of everything, if we don't change what we fundamentally believe about why we're here and who we are, then nothing new can really stick, and the predetermined course of our lives cannot change. We have to let go of the accepted ideas of science and religion and philosophy that describe this universe. Those ideas coddle us and keep us warm and fuzzy and powerless and asleep.

If we can come to accept that we are much more than human beings, then we must think outside of the current, accepted box of global society to experience that immensity. We must undo the curious idea that created this universe by harnessing our own inner power and thinking bigger than the idea that created it. If you believe that you were created as a human by God, then your goal will most likely be to find a purpose for your humanness—to create a more glorified ego—and therefore, you will never be more than that. That just isn't enough for the Course—or for me.

Together as the human race, we have accepted a very strange way of living life on earth in three dimensions, designed by our egos who don't want us to know very much, and certainly not enough to disrupt the status quo. Directed by our egos, we spend our lives pursuing the useless, absolutely convinced we are pursuing the useful. Not only do our egos try to keep the truth from us, they are even more clever than that: they convince us that the truth we are looking for can be found in the ridiculous. Our egos go out of their way to convince us that silly things are important and real and true, so we will stop searching beyond them for the truth, because we may stumble upon something *really* true, and that would be the end of the ego.

Think of yourself wandering in a labyrinth looking for meaning, but you don't know what that might look like. You turn down a lane, and at the end of a long corridor is large painting of a clown, with bright spotlights and giant arrows pointing to it. So you say, "OK, I've found it. The search is over." The ego has shown you its prize in a loud attention-getting way, so that you didn't notice that the real goal was through the small, hidden pathway behind the painting that leads you out of the labyrinth.

Your ego is just your personal collection of distracting thoughts that are a front for the tiny, mad idea, and those thoughts conspire to support this world, and keep you from any truth that would end up compromising life on earth, as it is now firmly established by the ego. As a race, we are obsessed with entertaining clowns instead of exits. We like the clowns—for now. Our awareness has been carefully constricted to include only the three-dimensional world. There is no more difficult task in this life than overcoming the tricks of the ego to convince you that your false self is real.

Always keep in mind the way in which your nighttime dreams work. They put you into a world that comes entirely from your mind as a strange reflection of your daily mental gyrations. Every night, the world is different, and every night, you create a universe and everything in it. Nothing in the dream is real or important or warrants your anger or fear, and when you wake up, it is over forever. Our waking life works in exactly the same way.

This is a world that seems self-contained and perfectly functional all by itself. We have five senses that tell us what's happening, and we respond to this world around us by reacting with our thoughts and actions. We don't even question the obvious idea that our *actions* make everything happen, as incorrect as that may be. We have decided that the physical world perpetuates the physical world, so the only way to change the world or your life is to take an action in the physical world. "What should I do now?"

This physical world seems to be the source of all that happens. We work hard to get rich. We study hard so we will be able to get a good job. We practice hard to get better at what we do. We hurry to be there on time, and yell at our kids for doing something wrong. We define our lives in terms of the actions we take in reaction to what the physical world throws at us because there seems to be so much evidence to corroborate normal ideas of cause and effect—that what you do and what happens all around you causes your life.

We have fallen into an absolutely mind-boggling pattern of life in which we wake up in the morning and go about our day doing one thing after another, acting to make things happen, and reacting to what comes our way, not connecting our thinking or our beliefs in any way with our external lives, focusing instead on what we should do next.

The Source

The Course—and the Course is certainly not alone in this—reminds us that cause and effect are the opposite of what we now believe. The outer world, including our actions, doesn't cause anything. But the Course tells us *why* in a very profound way. From the Course's perspective, if we accept that this is a dream, and that your body and sensory organs do not actually exist, then you may be able to see that your mind is truly the cause of *everything*, and what you see in front of you is the effect, coming from your mind, all the time, for every second of your life, in every circumstance. Your life as you know it is the *effect* of your conscious and subconscious beliefs. *Everything* that happens is the direct result of the thoughts you think and the ideas you hold.

You may have worked hard, practiced hard, and done all of the things that were required of you, but for some reason it didn't work out the way you thought it would. But still, you hang onto the belief that the idea of trying harder or maybe trying something different, based on frustration or impatience or outside pressure, is the way it to go. And since it doesn't seem to be working that way in our lives, we either must be doing something wrong, or someone else is doing something to hold us back, like Wall Street, or the government, or our uncaring boss, or the devil, or just bad luck. So, we choose to either feel bad about ourselves for not doing it right, or we declare ourselves victims of someone or something else—or both. But maybe there is another way to look at life that will require us to totally discard what we believe today.

Take a step back and look at the big picture and be honest with yourself. How many people are you aware of who work as hard as you, but they're much, much richer than you, or much, much poorer than you? Why does it work so differently for everyone? How many people seem to take the same, or similar, actions but have such different results? How many of you are frustrated because you thought you would have a much better life by now because you've played the goofy, little game that society asked of you?

Believing this is a dream is a large leap for most people, no matter who you are or what you have believed in the past. When you attempt to resolve a problem from the superficial level of the world of form, you are merely moving around images in a dream with no real consequence. By taking action to manipulate the world in front of you, no matter what happens, you are not addressing the *source* of the problem. This is what the ego dearly wants, to keep you firmly on its harebrained circular path.

But *thoughts* must be addressed, and any action taken must instead be based on your inner guidance and your desire to change your thinking and give your life to the Holy Spirit. This is another difficult concept because, as I said earlier, our actions seem to be wholly consistent within themselves, not to mention the fact that there are seven billion others with whom we interact every day who also believe this world is real and who also live by their actions. Also, who is this Holy Spirit guy and why should I trust Him with something as important as my life?

Projection

The Course describes the manifestation of our hidden thoughts as *projection*. You are projecting everything you believe and deny about yourself directly from your mind into a phony external world about you, just like a film projector. Our projections are merely confirmation of our beliefs about life. Projected thoughts are thoughts that we have held long enough to become part of us. They are the patterns of our egos. We do not like many of these beliefs, and so we deny them in ourselves, and we project them away from our bodies to separate them from ourselves and disconnect ourselves from our responsibility for their existence. These subconscious thoughts are the important ones to understand.

> T-6.II.2. **What you project you disown**, *and therefore do not believe is yours.* ²*You are excluding yourself by the very judgment that you are different from the one on whom you project.* ³*Since you have also judged against what you project, you continue to attack it because you continue to keep it separated.* ⁴*By doing this unconsciously, you try to keep the fact that you attacked yourself out of awareness, and thus imagine that you have made yourself safe.*

This world represents our sorrows, regrets and fears but mostly our guilt, even if it doesn't feel that way all of the time. We have come to think, as a matter of habit, that what happens in the external world is not our responsibility. We see other people doing things, causing things to happen, changing things and causing all of that external strife, just so we can blame them for all of the problems we see in our lives that we have projected! We really believe that our eyes are seeing what is external to us because this dream is absolutely convincing, and our minds are so powerful that we can believe anything we want and project anything we want. We believe that what we see exists on its own, separate from us, outside of us, apart from us.

This is the first part of understanding how we do and do not create our lives. You create your life with your thoughts. You are not aware of your subconscious thoughts, but they manifest in your life and represent the things you fear and deny. Read on for the real difference that the Course brings to the idea of creating your life.

The Old Ideas

Until I read the Course, I could not find a description of the process in any other source that felt accurate and that I could demonstrate in my own life, even though, admittedly, I bought into the currently accepted views taught by most spiritual teachers. I am sure all books and teachers that describe the process of creating our lives mean well, but I always had the sense that most all of these teachers were likely describing the process from their own life experience.

No one will write a book or speak about how we create our lives unless they already have a life worth creating, and are reasonably successful, as far as the world of prosperity or fame or contentment is concerned. Therefore, the way they have lived their lives so far must be the way everyone else can employ to become like them. Every single person on earth takes full responsibility for creating their own successes. How could they not?

But that's only anecdotal evidence, and simply not a good reason to think it's true. And if things are going well for you, it's very hard to think that you aren't directly responsible for your prosperity. It's easy to believe that you are the poster child for achieving what you have achieved. "Just do it this way, because that's what I did, and it worked for me!" The ego loves to do that sort of thing. But there seem to be few teachers of the process of creating your life who are able to take a big step back from their own lives and examine the process for what it really is.

My life

As it stands now, I have no particular victories or losses in my life that stand out. I am the poster child for the average life of modest successes and failures. Financially speaking, I have always had either very little, or just a modest amount, of money. I am neither rich nor poor. I have used sincere, thoughtful visualizations for decades with almost no results. As everyone else, I thought that every one of the countless decisions I have made throughout my entire life would lead to something better for me. All I have to show for all of my attempts to control the direction of my life is a modest existence along with a tremendous amount of personal growth, and that's only because I believe that I have kept an open mind to the path that was laid out before me, and it is a powerful, driving force deep in my soul. But very little in my external life has gone in any direction I would have consciously chosen, in spite of my sincere attempts to control and improve my circumstances. My most passionate decision has been to let go of any frustration with my external life because, deep down, I have always known that, surprisingly, I was exactly where I was meant to be, no matter how intensely I focused on another path or how fervently I believed that something else would have been truly better for me.

My life has always led me forward to the next place, and always in ways I could never have chosen or foreseen. I have always tried to pay close attention to my own role in creating my life so that I could understand it. I have also tried to understand the lives of my friends and family, spiritual and not, and how their lives have unfolded according to their desires and their personal attempts at control. I have also listened to the stories of well-known people as they relate how they came to be where they are in life. Sometimes, especially for the rich and/or famous, it seems that efforts to create their professional success and prosperity work easily and effortlessly—at least it appears that way from the outside. For most of us, those same efforts don't work at all. Nothing I have observed correlates with the generally accepted spiritual belief that we can create our lives beginning with any degree of conscious control by practicing any particular intentional method that I have read about.

Most people in happier circumstances think they are consciously in charge of the direction their lives take, while people who lead miserable lives seem to be victims of something outside of them. What a surprise! We take personal responsibility when things are going well, but not when they aren't. There's that denial thing again. We love to take responsibility for the good stuff, but the bad stuff must have been made by someone else.

Along came *A Course in Miracles* and the explanation it provided finally made perfect sense to me. It fits in nicely with everything else the Course says, and it also explains everything I have seen and heard in the lives of all of the people I am aware of. It may also be a little difficult to accept, because the ego will take it as an attack on one of its core beliefs. Because of that, there may be lots of resistance to the idea, but I ask once again, please keep an open mind. It's a beautiful idea.

The Law of Creation

First, we need to understand some of our current misconceptions about life and the false ideas that need to be undone by the spiritual community.

Your thoughts manifest in your life. In fact, they *are* your life. This has been noticed by many seekers for thousands of years, and those who noticed it attempted to describe it the best way they could. They called it karma. Karma is the idea that what goes around comes around, and it is based on action; that you get what you give to others. It is a vague concept that seems to happen somewhat mysteriously, with "good karma" and "bad karma" being used to explain, many times in a joking manner, what happens in one's life, and what punishments or rewards await. The law of attraction, on the other hand, is a law that says we can focus our thinking on what we want in order to get it. Karma is about the past; more about our previous actions coming back to us, while the law of attraction is more about the future; using your conscious thoughts in various ways to control and direct your life. They are two sides of the same coin. Actions and thoughts, past and future.

Both of these ideas contain partial truth, but both also fall far short of helping us understand how or why life really works, especially since the past and future don't exist. Karma and the law of attraction are currently the cause of tremendous confusion. These simple ideas are the most misunderstood in all of alternative thinking because of all the baggage we have attached to them. They are overused and misapplied. Real meaning has been watered down in yet another ego-takeover in order to ensure we don't really learn anything important. Karma and the law of attraction have become pale descriptions of the true process that occurs. So, throw them out. They are not relevant anymore.

The Course describes these processes in a deeply powerful way, much more than both karma and the law of attraction together. It is called God's law of creation, working in your life through the Holy Spirit. It was God's law before we made this world, so the Holy Spirit has adapted this world of ours to reflect His law, as part of the Atonement plan, and that is the Holy Spirit's ongoing task. God's law of creation simply states that thoughts never leave their source and whatever thoughts you are holding onto are the thoughts that are making your life. Because we hold so many thoughts that aren't true, we can only eliminate them by changing them to the truth. This has nothing to do with the past or the future. It is about the thoughts you hold Now.

God's law is not merely some law on a piece of paper that sits on top of creation like the U.S. Constitution that we can choose to use or not. It is alive and part of us and we function according to it, like gravity. So, try to get this—the Holy Spirit *is* the law of creation in this world. The Holy Spirit is the manifestation and agent of God's law of creation while karma and the law of attraction are both just very limited and incomplete descriptions of the vastness of this law, and of the Holy Spirit and His role. The Holy Spirit is our guide behind the scenes in every possible way. He is the living voice inside of us that keeps alive the idea that we are God.

The first important concept to understand is that everything that comes into your life is from your own mind. Because this is your dream, your mind is creating your life 100% of the time. You attract into your life exactly what you believe. In other words, you manifest 100% of your life with the thoughts and beliefs that you have made into the pattern of your being. You do not create merely a portion of your life, but *all* of it. **Nothing happens that you do not want, and nothing you want can be prevented from happening.** Your life is a perfect reflection of who you believe yourself to be. One of the biggest steps you can take in your personal development is to accept total responsibility for everything that happens to you, not as punishment but as a reflection of what you are thinking. Stop looking outside yourself for the source of your circumstances. It is coming from your mind! And as I stated before, another way of understanding the law of creation (or the law of cause and effect) is just this: **you only get to keep what you give away.**

There are two very important ideas to understand about God's law of creation. The first idea is that the only things that manifest in our lives are made by thoughts that we hold so dear that we have made them a part of us. They are the deep thoughts we are giving out to the world, thoughts that are mostly beneath our own level of awareness. You can only manifest what you already have, and so, because you are seeing what comes from your mind, you must be seeing what you already believe, what you already *have* in your mind. Every person, event and object in your life comes from what you expect the world to give you, based on what you believe life to be.

The second idea is that we have very little understanding of what is in our subconscious minds, what we truly believe, or how to change it. We really don't want to know. I can't stress this enough; **we don't know our own egos and we are in firm denial of what we are hiding about ourselves.** We do not understand that our conscious desires might not be the same as our subconscious desires, and are often completely opposite. We are very casual about thinking that we know ourselves and our thoughts very well, and we know we could never be responsible for thoughts that are powerful enough to translate into such misery as our homes being destroyed in a flood or getting a fatal illness. Yet that's exactly why those thoughts are subconscious. Your conscious mind and your subconscious mind rarely, if ever, want the same thing. When your conscious, positive thoughts conflict with your subconscious beliefs, it is your subconscious thoughts that manifest. It requires a great deal of honest introspection to understand your own motivations and deeply held beliefs. You must realize that at a profound and fundamental level, you think you're a human being, so everything that goes with that belief must be undone. Think about that. This is no small task.

The reason we even have a subconscious mind is because we are trying to hide our true beliefs from our conscious awareness. What is so powerful and shameful or just plain difficult that we would try to hide it? Why would our minds be divided unless we were trying to separate some hidden thoughts or protect ourselves from something? What is the purpose of a subconscious mind other than to hide something away from our conscious minds?

All of our judgments and fears are our deepest desires. These are the things we believe, yet deny. For example, if you believe people should be punished on any level, then you believe in the validity of physical punishment. We are quietly happy when a criminal on the news gets caught or sentenced. We cringe when we hear about crimes in our neighborhood. This is the world you are giving away, so this is the world you receive. If you believe you need money, then you believe you lack it and that you are incomplete. These thoughts are what you must eventually experience from another perspective by seeing them manifest in your life so you can re-evaluate those beliefs and choose again. Our lives appear from this hidden level, because we very much want to deny some of the strange and unkind things we believe, and we need to separate ourselves from them. We don't want to really know ourselves! These hidden beliefs are part of us, so they *must* manifest. The following paragraph talks about the struggle between our conscious and subconscious minds.

> T-24.I.2. *Beliefs will never openly attack each other because conflicting outcomes are impossible.* ²*But an unrecognized belief is a decision to war in secret, where the results of conflict are kept unknown and never brought to reason, to be considered sensible or not.* ³**And many senseless outcomes have been reached, and meaningless decisions have been made and kept hidden, to become beliefs now given power to direct all subsequent decisions.** ⁴**Mistake you not the power of these hidden warriors to disrupt your peace.** ⁵**For it is at their mercy while you decide to leave it there.** ⁶*The secret enemies of peace, your least decision to choose attack instead of love, unrecognized and swift to challenge you to combat and to violence far more inclusive than you think, are there by your election.* ⁷**Do not deny their presence nor their**

> ***terrible results. ⁸All that can be denied is their reality, but not their outcome.***

We are seeing (or receiving into our lives) exactly what we are giving out with our thoughts about each other and the world in general. This get-what-we-give idea applies from the shallowest to the deepest hidden thoughts we have. And the corollary to it is that it is impossible to receive what you have *not* given. Consider that carefully. You can never see anything that you don't truly believe. The bottom line is that the law of creation is real, but it was created by God, and therefore, created for God's purposes; not human/ego purposes. God does not even acknowledge this dream and the meaningless stuff that we want. Therefore, we cannot consciously use the law of attraction to create "stuff" in the dream world of form, and karma doesn't punish us for past actions. These are two firmly held beliefs we must let go of before we can understand how our lives manifest.

God's law is universal but it can only be used for God's purposes, and God's purpose, our true purpose, is to return home—to return to God—to undo the world we live in by waking up. God's law gives us what we need for that purpose, whether it's all that precious "stuff" or circumstances or people. It was not created to support the ego or the dream world in any sense, other than for us to use this world and the events in it to return to our real home. In other words, you don't get what you want when you want it; you get what you need, according to the Holy Spirit and Mick Jagger. And what you need is to learn who you really are in order to facilitate your exit from this dream. You will get what you want; but what you want may not be what you want *consciously*. What you really get is a day-by-day lesson to see your hidden beliefs and to learn to let them go.

God's law of creation has always been a part of God, implemented by God, and it will always reflect what we are to all of our brothers, and to confirm the idea that we *are* each other. It supports love and denies illusions. In this dream world, it shows us the good and the bad we are creating with our beliefs so we can learn to support correct thinking and undo our incorrect thinking. It will always remind us that we are God.

This law of creation is not about acquiring anything except what is helpful to us, and we usually don't know what that is. Although we will all have lots of things in this world that we temporarily need, it is ultimately about letting it all go. The world is merely a mirror of our deepest thoughts, held up to us so we can look at ourselves and consider what we are seeing. This law of God is always active, second by second, and reflects back to us who we are now, at the deepest core of our being, hidden by lifetimes of denial. Used by the Holy Spirit, you will never be forced to learn what you are not ready to face.

I spoke of our hidden beliefs, but we also have many beliefs that we are aware of in our *conscious* minds that are judgmental or negative thoughts. These firmly held thoughts also reflect subconscious beliefs and will also manifest in our lives in whatever way we need to see them. You may not be in denial of this conscious negativity, but the denial that you cling to, in this case, is not the denial that the thought exists; it is the denial that the thought is incorrect, and the denial that you need to do something about it.

But this has been only the first part of understanding how our lives manifest and it reflects current spiritual understanding. The next part is the hook.

Hold Onto Your Horses

The Holy Spirit is mentioned hundreds of times in the Course, and the role He plays in our lives is huge, because it is the role of God. When God noticed that something was really wonky in creation, His reaction to our untidy dream was to create the Atonement and the Holy Spirit, Who is a bridge between us and Himself, Who took over the world entirely. He uses the law of creation to demonstrate to us the idea that we are seeing ourselves in everything that manifests in our lives, and also to demonstrate to us that everything we do, we do to ourselves, because there is only one of us. The Holy Spirit took our out-of-control dedication to sin and imposed a change in the way everything works here on earth, so that we could take the opportunity to undo the errors we have made. He also took over time to use it for our benefit, instead of letting us continue to use it for our own self-destruction. He uses God's law of creation exactly as God designed it, with one huge difference; in the 3-dimensional world, He uses it in time.

> T-2.V.A.17. (7) *⁵**Time is under my direction**, but timelessness belongs to God. ⁶In time we exist for and with each other. ⁷In timelessness we coexist with God.*

God's law of creation states that everything you think and believe, and *only* what you think and believe, will appear in your life because you have drawn these things to yourself with your thinking. They must appear to you because you believe in them and you affirm their existence. There is absolutely no way for you to know *when* those things will come into your life. They come in when they are perfectly directed to.

> *We decide **what** we think and believe. The Holy Spirit decides **when** those thoughts and beliefs manifest in our lives.*

So, after all that set-up, this is the bombshell about how we truly create our lives. This is how all of our lives unfold all of the time, every moment of every day. Nothing happens that you do not personally create. **All of it!** There is no randomness or chance or luck here on earth. There are no coincidences, no happenstance, no victims, no accidents, no special privileges, and no injustice or unfairness. Everything that happens to you is happening for a profound personal reason at a very specific time, determined by the Holy Spirit working with your Higher Self. Timing is everything.

Accepting how this profound teaching of the Course works will change everything you believe about life. Have you ever thought about the mysterious force that is behind the scenes deciding *when* everything happens? Why are some people held back and others blessed with easy luck? Do you think you decide when you get what you get? Do you believe as most people, whether they admit it or

Chapter 5 – *Your Mind, Your Life*

not, that life's events are random or, is there some disembodied law, like a computer program, that inexplicably doles out your life to you?

Or could there be an intelligence beyond measure? Could God actually be that personally and directly engaged in our lives without us even knowing it? Could it all be coming from a deeper part of you, behind the scenes, that knows exactly when to manifest events and bring people into your life?

The often-used phrase that "everything happens for a reason" takes on a whole new meaning. Do you understand the power and implications of that belief, or is it just another casual phrase that's thrown around? Do you really believe that everything has an intention and purpose behind it? Do you believe there could be any accidents here? Now you must go back again and reexamine your definition of God. If you believe that events occur accidentally, then you either believe that God is not powerful enough to prevent accidents, or He doesn't care enough to prevent them? Which is it? Either way, you are creating a small god, more likely based on your beliefs in limits and human traits. Your life can only go as far as your view of God goes. Your life will always be as limited or as immense as your personal definition of God.

When God created the Atonement plan, He gave the Holy Spirit the power to use absolutely everything here for His purpose. He transformed this world from one of chaos into one of incredible order and love. God gave over all duties and communication to the Holy Spirit as His intermediary, and placed Him into your mind, as a thought that we all share, whose sole purpose is to heal our incorrect thinking and bring us back to the awareness of Who we really are. He is the one, as God and as your Higher Self, who decides when everything happens.

> *W 135 L 19.* **What could you not accept, if you but knew that everything that happens, all events, past, present and to come, are gently planned by One Whose only purpose is your good?** *²Perhaps you have misunderstood His plan, for He would never offer pain to you. ³But your defenses did not let you see His*

loving blessing shine in every step you ever took. ⁴While you made plans for death, He led you gently to eternal life.

L 312 1. **Perception follows judgment. ²Having judged, we therefore see what we would look upon. ³For sight can merely serve to offer us what we would have. ⁴It is impossible to overlook what we would see, and fail to see what we have chosen to behold.** *⁵How surely, therefore, must the real world come to greet the holy sight of anyone who takes the Holy Spirit's purpose as his goal for seeing. ⁶And he cannot fail to look upon what Christ would have him see, and share Christ's Love for what he looks upon.*

The Holy Spirit knows exactly when each belief or idea (that *you* have created by what *you* believe) needs to appear in your life for optimum value. It can be seconds or lifetimes before any particular thought may manifest. Because our egos are full of conflict, the Holy Spirit sees those thoughts that conflict with God's will, and He decides, along with your Higher Self, when you will be ready to see one particular conflicting thought manifest in your life. He does this by setting a goal of holiness for it, which means that He joins it with an opposing thought so they can cancel each other out. It is a thought you believe and hold dear, and have decided it represents who you are, but because it is in conflict with God's will, it is incorrect, so the Holy Spirit merely lets it manifest in conjunction with the people and events around you. In other words, He finds a person or event with the opposite thought—probably the person or situation you have had this conflict with before—and joins you together in a way that allows the thought to manifest in some form, which is a symbol of the problem; a representation of the thought. This is how He makes your brother your Savior. I write more extensively about symbols in the next chapter. This is how He symbolically presents your thought to you.

> *T-5.I.4. The Holy Spirit is the only part of the Holy Trinity that has a symbolic function. ²He is referred to as the Healer, the Comforter and the Guide. ³He is also described as something "separate," apart from the Father and from the Son. ⁴I myself said, "If I go I will send you another Comforter and he will abide with you." ⁵His symbolic function makes the Holy Spirit difficult to understand, because symbolism is open to different interpretations.*

The brilliance of this is that the other person or situation represents the opposite your idea, and therefore lets you see your thinking from another point of view, giving both of you the opportunity to balance out your thinking at the same time. If any of the people involved don't get the message and learn the lesson, it simply means they are hanging onto the original incorrect thought in their mind. In that case, the lesson is simply repeated at another time for them, whenever the Holy Spirit again decides with that person when it will occur. He will create another symbolic situation with people or situations that are a perfect opposing match, presenting another opportunity to accomplish the solution again.

Conflict is dominant in our thoughts. Our minds are a constant maze of conflict on many levels: all judgment, all anger, all frustration and stress, all illness. Any time you are not perfectly at peace is a time when your will is in conflict with God's. All of these conflicting thoughts, once again, merely represent that original conflicting thought called the tiny, mad idea of separation and specialness.

Our subconscious minds are constantly churning with our hidden thoughts as they try to manifest the chaos and the fear they hold. The Holy Spirit works with our higher selves to allow these terrible, incorrect thoughts to appear at a time that is best for us, in a way that will hurt us the least, or not at all, and give us the best opportunity to release them forever.

We do have some conscious control over the timing of events in our lives. The Course teaches that we can set the tone for our day and decide what kind of a day we would like to have. This process works exactly the same way. The thought to set the tone must be a thought that you have made firm and real and a part of you. If you are casual about it, or lack faith in it, it just won't work.

The Holy Spirit cannot stop our thoughts from manifesting through our projection of them, because He will not interfere with our choices, but He can and does control the timing of their appearance. We control what we see; He controls when we see it. Our thoughts are intentions. The form they take before they appear comes into focus as the Holy Spirit puts all of the pieces of the puzzle together for an optimal result. It is always as gentle as the Holy Spirit can make it, but as you know from seeing the events of the world around you, we have some pretty nasty things hidden away, and they can make for some seriously painful manifestations. But that's what we believe and want. That pain is our subconscious choice. Our beliefs will always manifest at the precise time we need to see them. As I said, it may be immediate or it may take lifetimes. And understand, we usually do not recognize that the people and events that enter our lives represent our thoughts because the Holy Spirit works symbolically.

> T-31.5.9. *Thus are the Holy Spirit's lesson plans arranged in easy steps, that though there be some lack of ease at times and some distress, there is no shattering of what was learned, but just a re-translation of what seems to be the evidence on its behalf.*

The Holy Spirit is doing this for seven billion people at once, arranging and coordinating all events and situations, every encounter everyone has with every other person, and every seeming coincidence. This life is a rich tapestry at every moment, orchestrated by God's stand-in in a beautiful and loving and helpful way. Can we even conceive of such a thing? The lives of seven billion people at once? And that's not even counting the other possible planets or dimensions with sentient life. Would you rather stick to the belief that if you just concentrate hard enough on what you want in the illusion while squinting, without a desire to change yourself, you can make money or romance appear? This idea of the Holy Spirit endlessly weaving a beautiful fabric of interconnecting symbolic manifestations over many apparent lifetimes is as difficult to accept as the concept that this life is a dream. But nothing is beyond God, and nothing is beyond you. As long as we think ourselves small and disconnected, we will never understand the immensity and power of God and ourselves. Release that small, linear, action-based thinking we have all lived with for far too long. The power of God is impossible for the finite mind to grasp. We will bring into our earthly lives all we have hidden in our subconscious minds until it is all cleared away. And that is our only purpose.

Chapter 6 – Problem Solving

Quiet, We're Taping

Think of yourself as a brightly burning light bulb, with God as your source of electricity. We are pieces of God, and we are perfect. We are made of love, and we know everything. With a small portion of our infinite mind, we have made a choice to forget all that by thinking one tiny, incorrect thought, which is represented in trillions of ways by smaller incorrect thoughts, each one conflicting with God's will. They can be thought of as layers and layers of small pieces of black electrician's tape that we have stuck onto the light bulb of our true nature, obscuring our light. We have to remove that tape that represents our incorrect thoughts, to let the light of our God-selves shine through. That black tape is all of the thoughts you and I hold in our subconscious minds. They are things we now think are true about us:

> *Of course I am human. I am my body. Life is cruel. I get sick. I must fight to survive. I wish I had ____ (fill in the blank). If I could get those things, I would be happy. If someone takes anything from me, I won't have it anymore. I must protect what's mine. We are all going to die. Sin is real. God will punish me for my sins. I am small and helpless. I deserve to be punished. I am better*

than everyone else. I am worthless. It's a dog-eat-dog world. Suffering is cleansing. We must all sacrifice to get anything. I must work hard to succeed. If I don't get caught, I will get away with it. I am alone. I am on my own. I am in charge of my life. I must be in control. I feel guilty all the time.

This is thick, sticky, nasty, black tape. Of course, this is only a small sample of the millions of silly things we think. We have been piling it on for centuries, lifetime after lifetime, suppressing the things we don't want to see, and stuffing them down into the depths of our psyches, lying to ourselves about who we really are, afraid to see who we have become, until our light bulb is covered with enough obscuring tape to make it the size of a basketball.

In addition to the hidden thoughts we hold, we also openly glorify the incorrect thoughts we are proud of, no matter how silly they may be to others, and use them to hide all those other fearful thoughts. We have hidden *a lot* of stuff. We have suppressed garbage heaps of fears and guilt and regret and anger over many lifetimes. There is so much of it that if you were allowed to see all at once, you would be overwhelmed and probably have to sit in a corner and drool for a few decades. What we believe is so far from the truth of who we really are that we are unrecognizable to ourselves. We are absolutely blind to our true natures. We have become solidified as human beings, and nothing but an act of God can undo this predicament we're in and of which we aren't even aware.

The first step to clearing off the black tape is to admit it's there. Because we are in denial of those incorrect thoughts, the Holy Spirit comes to us on a constant basis and says to us gently, "You are now ready to look at this particular belief you have and let it go. Remember Who you are." Because God will not coerce us to clean up our incorrect thinking, the only way for that cleansing to happen must be our choice. If something negative is presented to you, you may not see how you created the situation because the thoughts that caused it may be buried deeply within you, or the event may be the result of thoughts you haven't felt for a while. There is *no* way I am really thinking this! This is not my thought! This is coming from outside of me and happening *to* me! Forgiving the person or event is the way you can make that connection and bring the responsibility for everything in your life back to you, its source. You don't need to know the specific thought that caused it. You just need to forgive what is happening right now, symbolically, right in front of you.

Solutions

Now, let's take it to another level. There is something much more remarkable going on that makes the Holy Spirit's use of God's law of creation much more real and alive than the stale ideas of karma and the law of attraction. Know this without question: **Every negative event appears in your life only when the Holy Spirit has also created a solution for it.** A solution is built into every problem and is an undivided part of it.

> *W-90.3.2. I seem to have problems only because I am misusing time. ³I believe that the problem comes first, and time must elapse before it can be worked out. ⁴I do not see the problem and the answer as simultaneous in their occurrence. ⁵That is because I do not yet realize that God has placed the answer together with the problem, so that they cannot be separated by time. ⁶The Holy Spirit will teach me this, if I will let Him. ⁷And I will understand it is impossible that I could have a problem which has not been solved already.*

This means that the Holy Spirit is arranging everything that happens on this planet to make sure every problem that is ever presented to you can be solved. In fact, that is the entire purpose of all conflict. Each problem may also include many other people and the coordination of their lives with yours. This is the other major idea the Holy Spirit brought to our fixed and unchangeable dedication to sin and its results. Not one event will cause you any pain, *if you see it correctly*, and give it to the Holy Spirit through your forgiveness. Every solution the Holy Spirit offers is perfect for all involved. The way we live now makes this idea seem almost impossible in a world where there must always be suffering with winners and losers.

> *T-25.IX.3. Be certain any answer to a problem the Holy Spirit solves will always be one in which no one loses. ²And this must be true, because He asks no sacrifice of anyone. ³An answer which demands the slightest loss to anyone has not resolved the problem, but has added to it and made it greater, harder to resolve and more unfair. ⁴It is impossible the Holy Spirit could see unfairness as a resolution. ⁵To Him, what is unfair must be corrected because it is unfair. ⁶And every error is a perception in which one, at least, is seen unfairly. ⁷Thus is justice not accorded to the Son of God. ⁸When anyone is seen as losing, he has been condemned. ⁹And punishment becomes his due instead of justice.*

In order for the Holy Spirit's solution to be accessed, you *must* acknowledge and accept how the process works. This is the Atonement; the blanket of love God laid over the earth. It is our gift to use. This is the unseen level on which all lives operate. This idea is restated in different ways on virtually every page of the text and it cannot be overstated. It is the most profound and powerful concept in all the Course. You *must* see the world differently, acknowledge what this world really is and the process that's happening here. Accept the reality of the Atonement plan. Forgive everything and everyone without limit or end. Change your mind from the ego's point of view to the Holy Spirit's point of view and resolve all of your conflicts effortlessly. The ego is incapable of recognizing this process.

Problems exist in *this* world, so in order to eliminate the problem, you must go to another world, to a world of peace where they do not exist. Use your perception to go deep inside yourself to a place where there are no problems, to that world of peace, forgive the situation, and give the problem to the Holy Spirit to solve permanently, because in truth, they are already solved.

Chapter 6 – *Problem Solving*

> *T-19.I.2. Every situation, properly perceived, becomes an opportunity to heal the Son of God.*

This is all that is asked of you and the only way to escape the dream, yet it is the most difficult idea in the world of the ego because the ego doesn't want to give up its petty, backstabbing, stubborn, vengeful, cruel reactions. If you are unwilling to first see the problem as your own, as something you have created with your mind, the Holy Spirit cannot take it from you and solve it for you because, ***if you don't believe the problem is your creation and owned by you, you will not believe it is yours to give away***. You must understand that you cannot blame anyone else for what comes into your life. Giving any problem to someone else, to blame them and make them feel guilty and to deny your own responsibility, is the ego's method.

You must make a conscious choice to forgive. But most importantly, this is asking us to understand the idea of faith; faith in the existence and efficacy of a process that is beyond our ability to sense. Acknowledge the problem as yours and then let it go to the Holy Spirit by forgiving it. Letting it go means that you have perfect trust in the Holy Spirit to solve the problem for you, that you have withdrawn your own mind and thinking from the problem through forgiveness of yourself and any others involved, and that you are willing to see God's will as your own will. There *is* no problem. Understand and accept the idea that this is a dream, and that there is an unseen, loving being out there somewhere in the ether whose sole purpose is to help you, and that His help is real and consequential. When you do this, you will see every event differently and it will literally transform your world.

> *T-25.III.6. ⁵And when he chooses to avail himself of what is given him, then will he see each situation that he thought before was means to justify his anger turned to an event which justifies his love. ⁶He will hear plainly that the calls to war he heard before are really calls to peace. ⁷He will perceive that where he gave attack is*

but another altar where he can, with equal ease and far more happiness, bestow forgiveness. ⁸And he will reinterpret all temptation as just another chance to bring him joy.

Give It Away

For the Holy Spirit to solve your problem, you must give the problem to Him. When I say *give*, I mean *give totally*. You must trust the Holy Spirit to solve it. If you give your problem to Holy Spirit, it means that you absolutely trust that the Holy Spirit will handle it, give you the answers you need, and lead you out of harm's way in the best way possible.

However, it is the nature of the ego to want to get its own answers and solve its own problems. Our entire purpose for creating the ego was to deny God's presence, power and control in our life, so letting go of your problems is a 180° shift in thinking. The way you take back your question or problem, and yank it back out of the hands of the Holy Spirit, is simple; you continue to think about it. If, for any reason, after you give the problem to God, you feel stress about it, or continue to mull over possible solutions, your ego has taken the problem back, because you are demonstrating that you don't quite trust God without your assistance, because you still believe somehow that human problems require human solutions and human thinking and human problem-solving, and you are still afraid.

The Holy Spirit will take your problems and solve them for you, if you give them to him, and *leave* them with him. It requires your conviction and your trust and faith in who you really are. Forgive the problem and trust in the correct answer by making it unimportant, and know that the solution is at hand. Give up your worries about life, not in a way that you have in the past, but in a much more complete way that requires you to let go of who you are, and to let go of the results. If your ego still can't do that, the Holy Spirit will respectfully back away and let you take your problems back. Once again, what I am saying is no small idea, and requires a radical shift in your belief system.

When you continue to think about a problem, you are telling the

Holy Spirit that you still want to be in charge of it, no matter what you may have said to Him earlier, because you still have fear about it. He will politely oblige you. You may also be angry because He didn't seem to give you a solution when in fact, you told Him unwittingly that you didn't want His help anymore. When you realize that you have taken your problem back, simply start over, and give it again. Ask for help in giving it away. Acknowledge your difficulty in giving it away. Get to a place where you feel total trust that your problem will be resolved by God or the Holy Spirit, and where you feel no stress or fear at all about the problem. Then, go about your life. Whenever you feel the problem coming back, smile and say, "No thanks. You're not my problem anymore." You can do this over and over again for the same problem.

Time and Space

Time and space are the parameters of this fake world, and they are two different representations of the idea of separation. We use them to keep ourselves separate from each other, and to support the tiny, mad idea. If you walk away from another person you are having difficulty with, you are putting space between the two of you, and putting space between you and the problem. If you decide not to think about a problem for the moment because it's too painful, you are using time to remove yourself in exactly the same way. These are two ways of separating the problem from the solution. The problem and the solution always, always, always go together, so when you decide to separate them, you cause yourself pain. **All suffering exists between the moment a conflict arises and the moment you forgive it.**

It is also important to note that even if you are not able to forgive instantly, the solution that was created for the problem does not go away. As long as the problem exists, the solution exists. Forgiveness will still reveal it, as it merely waits patiently for you to get to it. You can go back right now and begin to heal everything that still brings you pain and eliminate it forever.

Your Brother

Now, let's take it up even one more notch. The Course also states that when you acknowledge your ownership of the events of your life, and you forgive them, you not only access the solution to the problem, but **you also heal your brother!** Forgiveness of your brother connects him or her with healing. You are sending healing, because you have acknowledged the truth that he or she did not do anything to you, because the body you see in front of you is not who they really are. When we blame someone for something they did, we are attempting to place a dollop of guilt in their souls. When we forgive them, we are reaching back into their souls and pulling out the guilt, which is the source of our separation from each other. This can be a good way of forgiving. Imagine yourself removing the guilt from someone you believe did you wrong. When you can forgive to the point where you believe they did nothing to you, then the Holy Spirit will place you in a world where they really did nothing.

The person you forgive may not feel the healing in themselves or demonstrate it right away, but the seed is planted and it will one day sprout. That person is not a human, and if you can forgive him or her, then you are able to see them as perfect souls, beyond anything resembling a human.

Your healing heals the whole Sonship—all of us, including the entire physical world and universe—because we are all in this together, and there is no way to separate yourself or to exclude your brothers when you embark on your path to awakening. This is a group effort, and this is a vital part of the process. Every thought of forgiveness and love is a thought you think with God, and therefore, a thought you think with all of your brothers. Those thoughts are part of each of us because our minds are not separate, except in the ego's world. Forgiveness is the manifestation of God's law of creation here in three dimensions. It shows us that what we give is truly ours and it is what we receive. Forgive, and you will be forgiven. Forgive, and you will begin to see that you have already been forgiven. Forgive, and you will see that you have never done anything that needs to be forgiven. Forgive, and soon forgiveness will become unnecessary as this world becomes unnecessary.

To me, the way problems are handled in the Atonement plan is nothing less than a revelation and it adds a whole new dimension to this dysfunctional life. It is not at all obvious that all negative situations have solutions built into them. Every single negative event can be resolved instantly, *if* you see its true purpose. The real reason events come to us is not obvious because we usually don't apply true forgiveness to those negative situations to reveal that solution, *because we don't acknowledge our ownership and responsibility for them*. This is a hidden treasure that has been right in front of all of humanity for lifetimes, and most of us don't even know it's there. It is the beneficence of the Atonement plan.

As you read this, you might even be very skeptical that this is possible, but I found out that it is true in my own life. It may be anecdotal evidence but the more I am able to use forgiveness, the more I can see that there is, indeed, an easy solution to what I'm facing, no matter how impossible the problem may have seemed. I am finding that negative circumstances melt away into nothingness as I see them as they really are and give them to the Holy Spirit, and remind myself this life isn't real and I am merely dreaming all of it up. It is a truly humbling experience to watch this process working in my life: a process that I didn't even know existed until I discovered it in the Course.

Bigger Still

Now take a step back from this view of creating your life that I have just explained. There is another and more powerful way to see this life that is mind-blowing in its scope. God is creation and He created us. Just like God, when we hold a thought, it will manifest. That's basically all there is to creation. When God holds a thought, it has no choice but to instantly become actual and real. It unfolds naturally and beautifully, unstoppable because there is nothing to stop it.

Now look at your life. The thoughts you hold will unfold and manifest naturally and beautifully. What God has done here is simply to have the Holy Spirit take over time, so that your thoughts manifest in this clunky, three-dimensional world when they are most helpful to your awakening. All thoughts manifest. They *must* manifest. There is a tremendous cloud of thoughts that is owned by each of us individually. All of those thoughts are potential. All of them must manifest unless you remove them before they get a chance. The universe will unfold as it is meant to do. All potential; anger, fear, love, intolerance, joy, hate, gratitude, will all come into your life, whether it is a conscious thought or a subconscious thought. It will manifest perfectly, according to your needs, in a symbolic way that is the perfect scenario for you to learn.

Just as God's creations unfold, the universe we have made is now under the guidance of the Holy Spirit, Who is a huge, impersonal, non-judgmental, loving creation engine who knows exactly how to let you see each thought you think come into your life as a manifestation. He is doing this for every creature in existence, because that is the only way it could possibly happen. He has taken all of our thoughts, whether or not they conflict with God's will, and naturally lets them unfold into our lives as they are needed and most helpful.

The only difference between our thoughts and God's thoughts is that ours exist in time, which is under the guidance of the Holy Spirit. Those that conflict with God's will must be revealed so they can be eliminated. God is incomprehensibly powerful and immense and this capacity and power is so far beyond our ability to grasp that it takes a lot of rethinking to even get close to the idea. Start doing that. Know that God's power is your power. Know that your thoughts will all manifest. Know that they *must* manifest.

The Holy Spirit has a plan for your life. That plan is not in your control. It overrides your personal, conscious plan, even if seven billion people are unaware of it. That plan does not exist as a fixed "script" even though it begins to unfold well in advance. It will change in an instant the moment you change your thinking. That's called a miracle. The Holy Spirit's plan for you exists on a second-by-second basis with Him presenting you with manifestations of your thoughts as they are needed for your optimal progress. It is a plan you cannot fight or change at all with your conscious desires. Your

Chapter 6 – *Problem Solving*

life is planned based on your beliefs. It unfolds from the potential to the actual, naturally and perfectly. If you want a better plan, begin forgiving.

> *T-7.3.4. That is why you need to demonstrate the obvious to yourself. ²It is not obvious to you. ³**You believe that doing the opposite of God's Will can be better for you. ⁴You also believe that it is possible to do the opposite of God's Will. ⁵Therefore, you believe that an impossible choice is open to you, and one which is both fearful and desirable.** ⁶Yet God wills. ⁷He does not wish. ⁸Your will is as powerful as His because it is His. ⁹The ego's wishes do not mean anything, because the ego wishes for the impossible. ¹⁰You can wish for the impossible, but you can will only with God. ¹¹This is the ego's weakness and your strength.*

Accept His plan because you can't fight it. Accept the world as it is. Accept what comes your way. Stop making your own plans. They don't work. His do.

Ego

Giving up the ego means giving up this universe. That will happen when you don't see it as a sacrifice because you are beginning to see that it just doesn't work for you anymore. The plan of Atonement that God has put in place takes care of this problem in the most non-invasive way possible. The deeper part of "You" is your Higher Self, the part that has agreed with the Holy Spirit to undo this error in thinking. It is the part of you that decides, with the Holy Spirit, when to see which of your hidden beliefs manifest in your life. You are working with the Holy Spirit every moment of your life to construct an incredibly appropriate series of circumstances designed specifically for you. Every event that occurs, every person you encounter is perfect for you. As I stated earlier, there are no accidents and there is no chance. You are doing this along with God through the Holy Spirit. Nothing you can do can bring anything into your life unless it is something you need, to remember Who you are. Your only function, your only purpose, the Holy Spirit's only task, is for you to return to God, no matter how much you want something of this world.

It doesn't matter who you are as an ego; you are still the Son of God and, behind-the-scenes, that Son of God still is aware of the process that is occurring. The Course states that the Holy Spirit always sides with the Son of God because the Son of God is the will of God within your human form. If you are not ready for something to appear, the Holy Spirit will delay it. This choice you make is not made on the conscious level, but on the depth of your readiness at a soul level.

> *T-24.VI.4. Forget not that the healing of God's Son is all the world is for. ²That is the only purpose the Holy Spirit sees in it, and thus the only one it has. ³Until you see the healing of the Son as all you wish to be accomplished by the world, by time and all appearances, you will not know the Father nor yourself. ⁴For you will use the world for what is not its purpose, and will not escape its laws of violence and death.*

There are many lines and phrases and paragraphs in the Course that hit me dynamically, but as I reread the book, this one never seems to fade in importance for me. If we could keep this thought in our minds and truly believe it, the world would change in an instant. This world is an entirely different animal than any of us see as we engage in the bustle of our normal human lives. This world is not what we think it is. Our striving for material things is pointless. At every moment of every day, the Holy Spirit is giving you the opportunity to see what you believe and correct the things that need to be corrected through forgiveness. No two people share the same path.

Chapter 6 – *Problem Solving*

> *T-27.VIII.10. The **secret of salvation is but this: that you are doing this unto yourself.** ²No matter what the form of the attack, this still is true. ³Whoever takes the role of enemy and of attacker, still is this the truth. ⁴Whatever seems to be the cause of any pain and suffering you feel, this is still true. ⁵For you would not react at all to figures in a dream you knew that you were dreaming. ⁶Let them be as hateful and as vicious as they may, they could have no effect on you unless you failed to recognize it is your dream.*
>
> *T-27.VIII.11. **This single lesson learned will set you free from suffering, whatever form it takes.** ²The Holy Spirit will repeat this one inclusive lesson of deliverance until it has been learned, regardless of **the form of suffering that brings you pain.** ³Whatever hurt you bring to Him He will make answer with this very simple truth. ⁴For this one answer takes away the cause of every form of sorrow and of pain. ⁵The form affects His answer not at all, for He would teach you but the single cause of all of them, no matter what their form. ⁶And you will understand that miracles reflect the simple statement, "I have done this thing, and it is this I would undo."*

Choice

You have the power to do only one thing here on earth. You have the ability to choose. It may be the only thing you can do, but it is also the most powerful tool there is. It is the one thing that the Holy Spirit will never interfere with. It is your free will. Choice is the mind powerfully making its own course and deciding its own nature.

But we have a problem. When we think of choosing, we generally think that a situation is presented to us consciously, in an obvious way, and then we choose what to do about it by rubbing our chin and contemplating for a while. But the power of choice is much more subtle and pervasive. You are using it on a constant basis. You never stop choosing because most of our choices happen on a subconscious level. With every moment, with every single situation in your life, you are making subconscious choices about who you are and what you believe. These choices make your life. They literally make the entire world you live in and we are extremely unaware that we are even making them.

Every person you see is provoking you to choose what you think about them. Every tiny delay or upset is another judgment made beneath our conscious awareness. Every interaction you have with another person or your current situation is compelling you to choose. These constant judgments build up and form a powerful belief system that becomes what we are as egos. This belief system becomes your personality, as well as your hidden beliefs, and ultimately, all of your circumstances and the world you live in. The connection between the power of your choices and how you create your life cannot be understated. Your mind is powerfully and subtly deciding who you are and what you believe every second of every day.

So, this is how we create our lives. As we go through our life and our days, we are continually building up a reservoir of thoughts through our conscious and unconscious choices that we don't want to acknowledge because we feel guilty that we have them. Even if they are thoughts of love, we feel uncomfortable with them. That reservoir must be illuminated because we cannot understand ourselves until everything behind the curtain is brought to light and dealt with. The Holy Spirit sets an agenda for us that allows everything we subconsciously believe to appear symbolically when we are ready for it in a way that only He understands.

He takes each incorrect, angry, subconscious thought of ours that represents our separation from each other and turns it into a gift. He shows us what we need to see at the perfect time, when we are most open to its impact. Each projection we see at every moment comes with all the support we need to see it for what is really is and heal it. You are here to heal the world. **Your entire life is nothing more than this.** This is the most profound idea in the Course. The Holy Spirit has taken over this fake life on earth so that we can understand that we are here for the single purpose of returning to God.

Most likely, you now believe that you wake up every morning and time passes. The world presents its daily rewards and challenges and you react to them by taking action. What happened in the past truly happened, and the past extends endlessly behind you. It is solid and real. Time passes inexorably as the days repeat themselves. Your struggle is for a "better life," which consists of material comfort and relationships. You will experience joy and pain and then, one day, you will die.

This is what we call life. Can you now possibly accept that what you have believed your entire life is not at all true? There is no past. Your struggles for anything in this dream world do not matter. Your actions make no difference if they are not based on the decisions you make with the Holy Spirit. Your entire unseen goal is to let all of that go and understand that you are here only for the purpose of returning to your Source, returning to God.

So Easy

The ego sees life as linear but life flows in a beautiful way. Creation answers to your every whim as your thoughts flow out as potential, gaining strength in time as you support them with your continued belief in them, and the Holy Spirit allows them to take form at the precise time you need them. It is a natural and effortless process, and serves only to help you, no matter how beautiful or ugly your thoughts may appear. Your thoughts *must* appear. No matter how much your ego believes that it is creating your life consciously and creating your successes and opportunities, it is just desperate to prove its own worth, power and control.

It's very difficult to make the decision to turn cause and effect upside down and then to consistently live inside of that decision. What you see in front of you seems tremendously solid and important and, by contrast, what goes on in your head seems to be invisible and fleeting and to have very little effect. When God handed over this dream to the Holy Spirit, He wanted to make certain that we had everything we needed to end it, without any of His interference at all in our free will. This gave rise to the elegant idea of an ongoing personal psychotherapist.

Here is yet another way to understand cause and effect and how the world really works. This world is an illusion that was made by us but controlled by God through the Holy Spirit. ***Your entire life is a video of your subconscious thinking, projected in front of you for the purpose of letting it all go!*** Every second, you are watching a video of your beliefs. It appears to be an external series of events outside of you, but it is just your dream. That video script was written by you but directed and edited by the Holy Spirit. You are responsible for all of the content. The Holy Spirit decides when each scene will appear. It's your biopic, showing you the story you believe about yourself. It is giving you the opportunity to change that story into a much, much better one. Every time something comes into your video that has any negativity to it, it is because you subconsciously believe in that negativity. You created it, and now the Holy Spirit is showing it to you and asking you to respond differently to your own beliefs. Forgive! This life isn't what happens to you. It's how you react to it. It is trying to undo your habitual negative reactions and judgments. It's trying to get you to forgive your brother for doing nothing, and help you understand that both of you are pieces of God.

At the beginning of our journey, we don't need to go hunting for all that negative garbage stashed away in our subconscious minds, because it is easily and effortlessly being handed to us on a platter! If you want to psychoanalyze yourself and understand what you think about life and what you are hiding from yourself, don't work too hard, just look around you! It's right in front of your fake face! You are working behind the scenes with the Holy Spirit to constantly see small pieces of your subconscious mind appear in front of you exactly when you need to see them, in exactly the right amount for you to handle, and each piece has the solution built into it, so that you can learn from it, right now! No one could ever have a better psychotherapist! God is doing it all for you! It is a remarkable and elegant plan! This paragraph has way too many exclamation points!

See it, change your reaction, and forgive it! Do you understand how simply beautiful—or beautifully simple—this is? God and the

Holy Spirit have taken all of the work out of what you need to do in this world of healing. Your part is to accept the plan and participate in it. This life has been redesigned to be nothing more than a school of forgiveness. This is so easy it's not even funny, as long as you get on board with it. He is your analyst. He shows you what you need to work on and He presents it directly and gently to you, when you need to see it, more kindly and beautifully than you would choose if it were up to you.

> T-20.IV.2. Sin has no place in Heaven, where its results are alien and can no more enter than can their source. **²And therein lies your need to see your brother sinless. ³In him is Heaven. ⁴See sin in him instead, and Heaven is lost to you. ⁵But see him as he is, and what is yours shines from him to you.** ⁶Your savior gives you only love, but what you would receive of him is up to you. ⁷It lies in him to overlook all your mistakes, and therein lies his own salvation. ⁸And so it is with yours. ⁹Salvation is a lesson in giving, as the Holy Spirit interprets it. ¹⁰It is the reawakening of the laws of God in minds that have established other laws, and given them power to enforce what God created not.

So, here is your glorious opportunity! The choice is yours. Will you continue to see events as opportunities to control with earthly power, physical force, strength of will and timely decisions, or are they merely chances to change your mind? Will you react to life as a victim or creator? Will you react to events in the short term with dramatic actions and hysteria, or will you merely observe and withdraw your power from them? Do you want to acquire wealth or become someone better? Are you able to see that this world is not at all what we think it is?

See the world as perfect! Let go of your judgment. React to the world as if it is perfect because, no matter what you think you see in front of you, it *is* perfect! By perfect, I don't mean you should go into denial. I mean that you must acknowledge that any imperfections you see are perfect projections of your own mind and they are not true. Forgive yourself to transform them.

When your conscious reactions change, your subconscious beliefs will slowly follow, and then the video that appears in front of you, which is your life and your world, will also change. See your brothers as perfect, no matter what they appear to do to you or others. See past their bodies and their actions. Practice seeing your personal dream as perfect over and over again, until it starts to sink in that the way you react to your life is your opportunity to change your life. You need perseverance and belief in what you are doing. Vigilance for God and His kingdom. Forgive everything you see, unremittingly.

If you don't see the elegance of this plan, and if you don't forgive, and if you continue to support the ego, then you are a normal human and all negative events that come into your life will cause you the usual pain and suffering. If you don't see life's events as gifts from the Holy Spirit, you will be causing yourself all the pain you believe is possible. Whatever suffering you tacitly accept for others is the suffering you will experience yourself, to confirm your beliefs.

And, if you do see all events as coming from yourself, your life has already changed dramatically, because now, the Holy Spirit can change how He deals with you. He now has a learner who is conscious of the plan and willing to change and understand and grow into something bigger. Now, He can bring your thoughts to you in a different way that will be much more efficient and meaningful to your progress. As you accept the Atonement plan and look more honestly at yourself and your responsibility for your life, you will start giving your problems directly to Him to solve and He will accept them easily and instantly. You will speak to Him regularly about your life and your problems and you will see how you make problems out of nothing in a convoluted tangle of ego madness. That tangle will begin to unravel, and you will start to feel the relief from your self-imposed stranglehold.

We strive after all of the things the ego wants that we firmly believe we need, and we think we are in control. We see suffering and wish it upon ourselves and our brothers, because we believe in sacrifice and strife, illness and death. Open your eyes to an absolutely different world of truth that is right in front of you, hidden by the ego. The Holy Spirit can only remove your negativity if you give it to Him. The only way the healing process works is for you to admit that what you see is being created by you. Forgiveness makes that happen.

God will not interfere with the choices you make, so if you believe you are in charge, your life will go on as if you need to be charge. You will work and stress and worry, because you think you have to, because you do not trust that all of the things you think you need will show up by themselves, like money, relationships, chili cheese dogs, etc. If you trust only yourself to manifest them, you are thinking incorrectly. All you have to do to make your life easier is to understand that God is happy to take over any time you decide, and what God wants for you is far better than anything you could ever hope or wish or provide for yourself.

Chapter 7 – Symbols and a Bigger Picture

More on Symbols

I mentioned previously that the Course says that the Holy Spirit uses symbols, saying among other things, that words are "symbols of symbols." Most people seem to think that this line is talking about the inadequacy of words because they are only symbols. But the deeper meaning to this phrase is the idea that *everything* is a symbol of something else, because there is nothing real here. Words represent something else; objects, events, actions, etc. Those actual objects, events, actions, etc. also represent something else. In other words, everything you see in front of you at every moment is a symbolic representation of your beliefs, in solid form, and neither words nor those things they represent should be taken literally.

There are many seekers of truth who believe that the only way to forgive yourself or others for what happens in your life is to thoroughly examine the problem in front of you (your boss's goofy demands, getting honked at, financial problems, your partner's look, etc.) in great detail, represented by these symbols, because you have to understand *why* you are seeing it and where in your psyche it comes from. In other words, we have to become our own shrink, go back to our childhood trauma, hidden fears and angers, and dredge up all kinds of the darkest stuff we can find. We need to know about our about broken boundaries, our daddy or mommy issues, etc.

But the symbols are not real, and a single thought may be represented by many different symbols at different times, just as a single word can have many meanings. You can't get to the source of your problems by examining a symbolic representation of it, because you probably won't know what the symbol represents. The reason the Holy Spirit uses symbolism to present our thoughts to us is that there are usually many people involved in all situations, even if they join the situation at a later time. There are situations that may be personal to you alone or situations that involve the people of an entire country or even the world. The Holy Spirit creates richly complex symbols so that the appearance of each event resonates equally in meaning to everyone involved. The Holy Spirit's meaning is always the same; there is one purpose to all perception, and that is bringing all errors to correction.

All conflict comes when we continue to see a meaning different from the Holy Spirit's in these symbols, these events of our lives. When we see attack or personal threat in any event, we are not seeing symbols accurately. We must only see the opportunity to heal. Putting emphasis on the symbols causes people to fear the Holy Spirit, because their inability to correctly understand the events of their lives causes them to direct their anger toward God for situations they cannot comprehend.

In all situations, you should only see that it causes you to judge or to feel fear and anger. And that's where your focus should be—letting go of the judgment and fear and anger with forgiveness, and not focusing on the actual situation. To analyze each event of your life is to make the symbol real and important, when you should only be concerned with the feelings you need to release.

> T-2.V.8. *The fear of healing arises in the end from an unwillingness to accept unequivocally that healing is necessary.* ²*What the physical eye sees is not corrective, nor can error be corrected by any device that*

> can be seen physically. ³As long as you believe in what your physical sight tells you, your attempts at correction will be misdirected. ⁴The real vision is obscured, because you cannot endure to see your own defiled altar. ⁵But since the altar has been defiled, your state becomes doubly dangerous unless it is perceived.

The Course clearly says not to look at the symbols at all, neither in yourself nor your brother, because the symbol is not the actual problem. We are to *overlook* the symbols. If you examine a problem, based on the form of it, you are just giving life to the illusory symbols. You are focusing your incredibly powerful mind on something that doesn't exist and making it real to yourself. No matter what happens to you, the Holy Spirit is trying to get you to see that the purpose of life is to correct your perception. As long as you see the physical problem, you are looking in the wrong place. There is only one real problem behind all of it.

> T-9.IV.4. The ego, too, has a plan of forgiveness because you are asking for one, though not of the right teacher. ²**The ego's plan, of course, makes no sense and will not work. ³By following its plan you will merely place yourself in an impossible situation, to which the ego always leads you.** ⁴The ego's plan is to have you see error clearly first, and then overlook it. ⁵Yet how can you overlook what you have made real? ⁶**By seeing it clearly, you have made it real and cannot overlook it.** ⁷This is where the ego is forced to appeal to "mysteries," insisting that you must accept the meaningless to save yourself.

The problem isn't how life appears at any moment; the problem is what you are thinking about it. Analysis is just a mind game, and what we see as a problem is merely a result, or effect—a symbol—of our incorrect thinking. Analysis is of the ego, because analysis is the act of chopping the problems up into tinier pieces and separating them even more. When you do that, you're just spinning your ego wheels. Our one problem is that we are the Son of God who is trying very hard to justify this dream world and deny who he really is. Problems are not real, because they are not thoughts that are shared with God.

Remember that you are seeing a scenario in front of you that is never real, and every time you forgive, you are forgiving the whole dream for trying to take your attention away from who you really are. These are all just pictures in a dream. Also we, as humans, are not able to correct the problem. Only the Holy Spirit can do that. Your focus on and attention to everything is what makes this life and those problems real—at least to yourself. When you perceive someone as doing something wrong or hurtful, you are making something true that simply isn't, no matter what it may look like, whether it's genocide or wearing a torn shirt. What needs to change is your judgment of what you are seeing, not *what* they're doing.

The symbols in and of themselves are unimportant. They represent content that you may not understand because it's difficult to connect the events of your life with specific thoughts you have. The Holy Spirit is using our world of form to try to get you to understand what you believe about yourself and life in a way that is much bigger than the small event that is currently in front of you. Your emotional reaction is the key. It just doesn't matter what the circumstances are. Focus on your own *reaction* to the circumstances. It is not the form your thoughts take in this fake world that matters; only the content and correction of your thoughts. The Holy Spirit uses your emotions to get you to notice what you are holding onto.

We know these symbols as "life." The many forms that our thoughts take may seem very scary or unsettling, because some nasty things happen here on earth, but it's all illusion to the Holy Spirit. This life is not real, and if we change the way we see it, no form can harm us in any way. **We must change our perspective about why things happen!** The Course says to *notice the anger or judgment* you feel, as well as any other accompanying emotions, to recognize your discomfort, and the moment you feel it, *change your mind!* Let go of the form. Get out of that drama that makes it real, and remember who you are! What you must focus on is simply trying to change your reactions to your life.

The Holy Spirit can only teach us by transforming the incorrect ideas we believe here on earth, which means letting us see very real (to us) representations of our thinking, so that we can move past them.

> T-25.I.7. *4Yet must It use the language that this mind can understand, in the condition in which it thinks it is. 5And It must use all learning to transfer illusions to the truth, taking all false ideas of what you are, and leading you beyond them to the truth that is beyond them.*

In other words, we are unaware of what our life is representing to us on any level that has meaning to the ego. We see effects, yet we discern their source as randomness, chance and chaos. What appears in our lives is always a representation of incorrect thinking we share that will manifest in billions of ways, in billions of circumstances, in billions of symbols. It isn't necessary to trace what appears in your life to its origin; it is only necessary to notice your own reactions and change them. All things that happen to you are attempts to get you to look at this world in a different way. Our goal is merely to change our minds through forgiveness. It is only necessary to understand that you have caused your life, and now it's time to change it.

We are the Sons and Daughters of God. This isn't real. Nothing can harm you at all. You have never been in danger and you never will be. If you see each negative event without the negative judgment, there can be no pain, whatever form it takes.

Emotional Response

You are not trying to become a psychoanalyst. When you feel anger or fear or any strong emotion, you are allowing the dream to be your reality. The Holy Spirit will use your attempt to change your mind to begin to correct the thinking that is at the root of your feelings.

> T-9.IV.1. Atonement is for all, because it is the way to undo the belief that anything is for you alone. ²**To forgive is to overlook.** ³**Look, then, beyond error and do not let your perception rest upon it, for you will believe what your perception holds.** ⁴Accept as true only what your brother is, if you would know yourself. ⁵Perceive what he is not and you cannot know what you are, because you see him falsely. ⁶Remember always that your Identity is shared, and that Its sharing is Its reality.

Let's say you dislike being tailgated by other drivers and when you are driving, someone begins tailgating you. Your emotional reaction may be to get quietly angry, or gesture inappropriately, slow down, speed up, swear, etc. You may try to psychologically analyze *why* you hate tailgaters so much. Analysis may make you think that this person is really attacking your control issues. He's trying to make you go faster, and you don't like being told what to do, so that makes you feel he wants power over you. He's just sticking his nose into your driving habits. Or he's judging your driving, and saying that you are driving slower than conditions call for, and he wants you to drive faster. Or he's driving dangerously close, and that makes you feel like you or your passengers are in harm's way. There may be any number of other personal feelings that you may keep buried.

This detailed analysis will make the ego feel like it's getting to an understanding of your hidden motivations. But if you understand what the Course says, none of this analysis amounts to anything. When you notice your emotional response,—anger, swearing, and gesturing—catch yourself and know that you are the source of this situation somehow, beneath your awareness, because of some deep fears or guilt you hold, and that this situation has been presented to you to show you that you are making the world real. The anger has gotten you to see the separation between you and your brother, and this is all you need to notice. This is one small piece of black tape on your light bulb, and the Holy Spirit has arranged for your brother, your savior, to come into your life to help you notice how you are making this dream real with your drama and your reaction. So, to help you undo it, He has planned for your savior to drive closely behind you, because that brother also needs to experience something from his perspective to help him learn something about himself. Maybe he will notice for the first time in his life that his actions are adversely affecting someone else, and make him rethink his tailgating habit. Maybe not.

This experience has appeared to both of you to give you the option to let it go, and that the solution to it, of which you are totally unaware, will appear to either one or both of you if you are able to forgive the other and yourself. It only matters that this particular symbolic event reminds you that you think you are an ego, struggling in the world against all of the other separate egos. Give the problem to the Holy Spirit, and have the unquestionable faith that you are safe in His hands. Don't worry about the solution showing up because that's just wishing for a particular outcome, over which you have no control. It will appear.

You will notice that the Holy Spirit is not only presenting you with your beliefs in this world of form, but He is also the one you must make your decisions with, because only He can steer you in the right direction. He knows exactly why these things appear and wants you to consult him for your reaction to all events. He is showing you your thoughts and helping you correct them at the same time, if you would only stop trying to make your own decisions.

When you forgive the event that appears in front of you, you are also forgiving the source of the event, or at least part of it. You are removing the guilt from yourself and your brother. You are able to let go of the anger through forgiveness, and are therefore letting go of whatever triggered the anger, even though you may not be sure of what that is. It may require more similar events and more forgiveness, but the healing has begun.

Creating Lack

Your life flows out effortlessly from who you are, just as you need to see it, based on who you believe yourself to be, based on the choices you make on a second-by-second basis. As I stated earlier, this world is built on the idea of lack. Everything in this three-dimensional world of ours supports lack. Our thinking promotes it, and our beliefs propagate it. As a matter of fact, this world is the embodiment of lack. It is our master creation. We created this world to become separate, incomplete beings who must therefore sustain ourselves. We have never-ending needs, and because we are responsible for ourselves, we must get what is needed. Every single thing you do is based on the idea of lack. And because of lack, there is desire. Everything you lack creates desire. You cannot shift your position while sitting in a chair without it being a desire to find a better position because something is slightly wrong with where you are now. **Every single action you take is an attempt to fulfill a desire for a better situation**, and all of those desires support the body and ego. It is subtle and all-pervasive in this life. We spend most of our mental energy trying to compensate for our lack. Lack does not exist in God. If the Son of God had been perfectly content with his situation as the Son, this universe would never have appeared.

The law of creation that God laid over our dream can only reflect the truth of God and, therefore, cannot support lack. It can *manifest* lack, but not support it. Any thinking that believes in lack cannot create anything in this world except more lack to demonstrate to us that belief in lack is self-destructive, and conflicts with the will of God. That lack is a reflection of our deep, human beliefs, and so we receive the lack that we believe in. You must see what you believe.

Your conscious desires can be generally fleeting, so the law of creation does not manifest them if they are subject to change. What manifests are the beliefs that are strong enough to become ingrained. Their power has built up slowly over time, based on the small, regular, subconscious choices you make. If you want something, that simply means you don't have it now. That belief that you lack it is the deeply held belief that is reflected back to you. So, you receive the lack that you believe in, and the absence of the "thing" you want. "Wanting" is the thought that created this world.

Chapter 7 – *Symbols and a Bigger Picture*

It is the lack of something and the hope for it in some uncertain future that defines and creates humans and denies God.

If you want *anything*, then you are supporting the idea that you are not God, because God has denied you nothing, and never could. Your prosperity doesn't come from your thinking; your poverty does, so the most efficient thing you can do is to let go of your thinking. Let go of making your own decisions. We only know the world of form, so when we think we want something, we usually think in terms of this world we occupy as humans. We want "stuff," whether that means money or health or a house or a new TV, human love, peace on earth, or a burrito; things that support our body and ego needs. The things that God has, and has given us, are not part of this world, just as our thoughts of lack are not part of this world.

This was a difficult concept for me for quite a while because I could only think in terms of what I wanted and what I thought I needed in terms of this world. Quite frankly, I didn't really care about those ephemeral things that God supposedly gave me in abundance that I couldn't use in a practical way in my life. Love? Sure, that's great stuff, but my phone needs an upgrade. An important shift in thinking is required to let go of worldly concerns, and to understand the real *connection* between the things God gives you and a happy life here on earth. They don't seem to be related to each other, but they are exactly the same.

The *only* practical use for the law of creation is total, peaceful acceptance of what comes into your life. Do not fight what *is*. Never regret what you don't have or where in life you are. Everything has been set up perfectly by you and the Holy Spirit at every moment. Knowing without doubt that this is all of your own making, and that everything is always presented to you exactly as you need it, the law of creation is always working for you and always offering you something better than what you think you are now. The only "thing" we are all trying to create is the remembrance of the truth and who we really are.

The law of creation is certainly designed to give you the "things" of this world: people, events, situations, challenges, toys, etc., exactly when you need them, just not in a way you can control consciously. The instant you consciously want something, you immediately begin limiting the possibility of creating it because that desire is based on the lack of it. That doesn't mean you won't get it; it means that your conscious desire for it is not what creates it, just as your conscious hate of something will not push it away. You will get what you *need*—always—and if what you subconsciously need matches your *conscious* desire, congratulations! Just remember that everything that appears in your life represents a thought that you have made a part of yourself. It may be a thought that you have held onto for lifetimes without even knowing it because it is so deeply buried, or it may be a thought you are now still consciously aware of.

> *T-12.III.9. The world you perceive is a world of separation. ²Perhaps you are willing to accept even death to deny your Father. ³Yet He would not have it so, and so it is not so. ⁴You still cannot will against Him, and that is why you have no control over the world you made. ⁵It is not a world of will because it is governed by the desire to be unlike God, and this desire is not will. ⁶The world you made is therefore totally chaotic, governed by arbitrary and senseless "laws," and without meaning of any kind. ⁷For it is made out of what you do not want, projected from your mind because you are afraid of it.*

Attempting to create your life consciously means that you are attempting to create a future for yourself that is as desirable or more desirable than your present circumstances. It also means that you are trying to have specific illusory symbols appear in front of you that are more pleasing to your ego than the symbols that the Holy Spirit is currently presenting to you for your liberation from those very symbols. This sounds fairly silly when you understand what really makes up the substance of your life. Your ego wants desperately to see symbolic illusions that please it, even though they would not have any purpose other than the temporary pleasure of one disconnected ego. Accept that everything is perfect at every

Chapter 7 – *Symbols and a Bigger Picture*

moment, and that having illusory, symbolic "things" of your choosing appear in your life is meaningless to life's purpose. You will always have exactly what you need, presented by Someone Who knows precisely what that is. It cannot be any other way. Merely accept life as it is at every moment.

The future doesn't exist, so God cannot support thinking that looks to the future. God exists only in one moment, right now, so the only way to think like God is to accept the present moment exactly as it is, and know always that you are precisely where you are meant to be. It's all being taken care of, if you would only let it be. Let go of all future dreams and worries, and forgive and love everyone right now. There is nothing else to do or strive for. Let go of all of your planning. All of our plans are defenses against our fears of what would happen without our planning. Can the world even think in those terms? Ego control. Instead, trust in the Holy Spirit to plan your life, and it could not turn out better.

There will always be plenty of people who can say that using the law of attraction in the currently accepted way has worked for them, because there are always people who seem to manifest what they want. That's simply because there are many things we want consciously that are in accord with our subconscious minds, and their appearance is in accord with the Holy Spirit's timing. Many times, the lessons we are here to learn can be augmented by the things we consciously want. We can say that those things have come into our lives because we started applying the law of attraction, but those things we believe we created were already in our lives behind the scenes, and on their way to us as potential, and their manifestation was planned long before you even thought of them consciously. The only reason we even wanted them at all might be because they were brought into our conscious awareness from a deep urging for them from our subconscious minds to prepare us for their arrival. The ego mind will easily believe only the obvious, superficial and positive things, and never the subtle, complex or negative things; whatever seems to serve it.

Take a look at life from the bigger picture. Everything that comes from the Holy Spirit is perfect for the entire world. Everything fits together with everything else. The Holy Spirit is creating a vast all-encompassing scenario that includes all of us. The Holy Spirit is creating an unfathomable flow of life just beyond our sight, if we could only wake up to see it. God's law of creation does not function to allow things to manifest randomly in one person's life for the sole purpose of his or her temporary gratification. And once again, things can certainly pop into your life for your temporary ego gratification. But only because the Holy Spirit has decided you need it and, it fits into the entire picture; not because you have decided.

Don't ask yourself what you want to get; ask yourself who you want to be. All of the striving, all of the focus on our personal achievements, all of our quests for status or notoriety, mean nothing, unless they help us gain more understanding of ourselves and the bigger picture.

> T-12.VIII.5. *You have but to ask for this memory, and you will remember.* ²*Yet the memory of God cannot shine in a mind that has obliterated it and wants to keep it so.* ³**For the memory of God can dawn only in a mind that chooses to remember, and that has relinquished the insane desire to control reality.** ⁴**You who cannot even control yourself should hardly aspire to control the universe.** ⁵*But look upon what you have made of it, and rejoice that it is not so.*

The choices we make write the script of our dream. The Holy Spirit helps us to see which choices are correct. The script of life is written, meaning that this will all end and the dream will be over. How we each choose to end it is the script of your personal life, and it is very changeable, but it cannot and will not change if your thoughts don't. The script is written for you personally. If you change your thoughts, you have become someone new and, therefore, require a new script. The *entire* purpose of this dream life from the perspective of the Holy Spirit, and therefore yours, is for us to wake up to the truth. The Holy Spirit's purpose is for this dream to end, and for everything in it to disappear. His job is to become unemployed. Then again, I'm sure God will find something else for Him.

If there really is a reasonable, loving God who is eminently interested in your well-being, who created you but not this world, would you expect Him to do anything less than whatever is necessary to retrieve us from this illusory mess without interfering with our free will to choose what we want? He would take over the fake world as much as possible to change the way it works, not in a way that would coerce us, but in a loving way that would give us opportunities at every turn to give up this life, and remind us of our true nature and origin. He would try to show us over and over again that nothing here matters, not by telling us directly, but by letting us find out for ourselves so we would really understand it and accept it as our own decision, so we would never feel disempowered or condescended to. He would let us find and accept our own power. He would constantly show us our incorrect thinking and if we showed any effort to correct it, He would immediately and gladly accept our attempts. He would offer a perfect assistant to help all of us, if we choose to listen to Him, even those who of us are so oblivious to His plan that we silently curse Him and reject the possibility that He even exists.

As we stumble through a painful life, we are also living a life of pure freedom that we can't even see, just because we still choose to make the false life real and freedom inaccessible. Freedom is right here! Let this go! Let go of the pain you get by letting go of the pain you give. There is another way to see this life and it is wonderful and complete and perfect and right in front of you, if you would only choose it.

The Big Start

Even though the following information is not in the Course, another idea that may help you understand how you create your life is understanding how it starts. Creating our lives starts before birth. Before you are born, between lives on earth, you create a contract with yourself to face and challenge many of the incorrect beliefs you hold onto. This is an incredibly powerful aspect of each individual life. We set up everything to put ourselves in very specific venues that will require us to face deeply held beliefs, and each soul's life map will be unique to its own makeup. These are hugely complex scenarios that include other souls with whom you enter into a lifetime, including many who interchangeably play your family, friends and others.

All circumstances that occur during the course of your life were planned by you with the Holy Spirit for your upcoming life and they remain in place unless you are compelled to change your thinking before they occur. They only change when your needs change, because your thinking has fundamentally changed. We usually don't change before these events occur, and the entire reason we have set up these experiences is to get us to change our thinking. They are powerful influences. Many of these large events may not succeed in changing our thinking significantly because we are so set in our rigid ideas of randomness and external causes, but they will all make a dent in their own way. The timing of these larger experiences is also up to the Holy Spirit. The intensity of your challenges will vary from lifetime to lifetime, depending on your own unique needs.

Everything we have the opportunity to "create" in life stems from our preliminary circumstances here. The freedom, or bondage, we have set up for ourselves in each life is determined by unique circumstances that we are born into right at the start of life at birth. Think about all the things you start with, or without, right at the starting gun; financial status, point in time, gender, location, social status, family, race, cultural background, physical limitations and assets, etc. You are born into a time, body, city, family; a very complex combination of unique conditions that is best for you to get as much out of each particular life as possible, whether it seems that way to you consciously or not. That birth situation, and any subsequent larger situation that flows out of it, determines your life experience. For most people, there will come times when you move into one or more different situations as you go through life, like a promotion or new job, a new city, a new financial situation, health challenges, marriage, etc. Some seem like simple changes of choice; some seem like pure serendipity. Some people never change those original circumstances. Some change them often. Either way, it is all created by you and it is all timed and guided by the Holy Spirit. It is all set up to bring people and circumstances into your life so you can, slowly but surely, understand yourself a little more clearly.

These are the parameters of your life. They are the larger circumstances in which you live. Each one of us lives within our own parameters, and each one of them binds us or frees us in different ways that are unique to each of us. We are limited by what we can *do* based on the circumstances we need to encounter, determined by our earthly parameters and the Holy Spirit's gentle and constant guidance, but we are never limited by what we can think. These larger circumstances cannot be changed by you at all, unless you change who you are. It sometimes seems as if we are in conscious control of them, but we are not. Once again, we are always very anxious to believe that our situation has changed because of what we have done in our lives, but this is simply not true.

We can think that we have pulled ourselves up from our bootstraps and made a success of our lives because of the simple conscious decisions we have made, or that we are victims of circumstance, but that's just what you designed for yourself before you were born, based on the personality traits that you also chose. Yes, you got where you are because of what you did! But you did what you did because of who you believe you are and the thoughts you hold that define you. Even your thoughts were predictable because they were based on choices you were compelled to make based on the deep patterns of your soul that you may not even know you hold. The actions you take exist in the dream, and they are all illusion and cause nothing by themselves. Your subconscious thoughts will persist until you choose to change them, and *the most effective way to get you to change your deepest thinking is to have those thoughts challenged by circumstances that don't support them.*

Opposites

The life you now live flowed out from a place and point in time that was set behind the scenes, when the Holy Spirit arranged for you and your friends and family, antagonists and angels, challenges and opportunities, to come together in a way that He could best use to present many different scenarios to you that would be most effective in facilitating changes in your thinking. As I mentioned before, He emphasizes our conflict with God's will and shows it to us in our circumstances and other people. These people and circumstances were arranged for you personally. Others will be involved in your life but their actions and reactions are their concern.

> T-5.3.11 ²*The Holy Spirit must perceive time, and reinterpret it into the timeless. ³He must work through opposites, because He must work with and for a mind that is in opposition. ⁴Correct and learn, and be open to learning. ⁵You have not made truth, but truth can still set you free. ⁶Look as the Holy Spirit looks, and understand as He understands.*

Again, it doesn't matter what you do. Your actions have no power to change your dream; just to confirm what you already believe. We may think that where we are in life is based on our actions and conscious desires but if you honestly look at where you are in life, you will notice that, for almost all of us, you are not where you set out to be. But, and this is true for everyone at every moment, you are exactly where you need to be.

If you take any action that would lead you somewhere that is not perfect for you, then that action will always come to nothing. All of the actions you have taken that have led you to this precise moment are actions that are supported, and those actions have always been based on the thoughts that came first, by what you believe yourself to be, and on what the Holy Spirit knows you need to move forward. Those actions were supported by the universe to lead you to today, exactly where you need to be.

The contract you have made with yourself before you were born is no small thing. If everyone could be allowed to override their birth contract and, through sheer force of will and desire, become a healthy, attractive billionaire by using some simple visualization methods to control some law of attraction, that would throw off all of what we came here to learn. We *need* to experience certain things, and those things are not our conscious choice to experience. Psychics may be able to tell you about certain things that are coming into your life, but the best psychic in the world will not be able to tell you what you are not supposed to know in advance, because the sudden appearance of certain experiences is the best tool we have been given to learn certain things. If we could consciously choose our lives, would we choose any difficulties? Of course not! That's why we hide those thoughts in our subconscious minds. We don't want them in our lives! But the Holy Spirit knows they need to go away, and the only way for that to happen is for us to consciously face them, sometimes dramatically, and eliminate them consciously.

Chapter 8 – Relationships and Chaos

Special Function

Another part of the bigger picture in the formation of our lives is that Holy Spirit has also given us each a special gift or gifts, as much as He is trying to help us get over specialness. This is an excellent example of how He has taken over the ego's misguided ideas and turns them around to use for our healing. It is what you feel a positive passion for; what the Course calls your "special function." We have *all* been given a talent or two for something by the Holy Spirit, whether it's astrophysics or motherhood or the gift of gab or stacking beer cups. It is that unique talent inside each of us that resonates with our soul. The special function is a gift we can all use to help us find ourselves more effectively.

What you feel intensely can manifest more quickly because you are so invested in it that you have temporarily put your ego aside. Intense focus can sublimate your ego if it is used positively. It can also support the ego if used fearfully. If you have a passion to play music, that doesn't necessarily mean you will be a successful musician, but it might. You may have issues around other aspects of your life that are stronger than worldly success in that field. But that should be unimportant.

We all gain and lose interests as we journey through lifetime after lifetime, so we need to find our current talents. They are there. And we all know that for some people, some talents are obvious and easy to feel at an early age, while some people may go through their entire lives never finding any, usually because their fears make them believe that they need to focus on money or survival first rather than to find any passion for what they do. Those who have no goals or deny their passions are apt to relapse into their fears, and make choices from that dark place.

This place in our minds where we feel intense passion seems to be the point where the conscious and subconscious minds meet. It is a doorway into the depths of our soul, and it is where we are able to glimpse something about ourselves that is beyond this world.

> T-25.VII.7. *Your special function is the special form in which the fact that God is not insane appears most sensible and meaningful to you.*

The many twisted versions of God that we have created make us think God is insane or absent. Your special function can immerse you in a different world, where you may be able to catch a glimpse of a God who is not insane. Your special function is part of your soul, for now, as a resident of earth. Our talents can save us, for that is their purpose. We can and should use them to move ahead in our lives.

When we are immersed in our passions, the Holy Spirit is more able to get through to us, to whisper in our ear that there is a God, and that we are part of Him. For many of us, we may find our talent but seem to achieve nothing material in life. But achieving something material in this life, however you may define that term, is not always their purpose, although it could be.

The real purpose for finding your talent is to grow in awareness, and you will always grow naturally if you have the simple desire to grow. You will also grow eventually because of the Holy Spirit's efforts, whether you are aware of it or not. The Holy Spirit is trying to get your attention by helping engage you in your passion, so you can see the connection. That's just a complicated way of saying that you will always be able to see yourself and the world more honestly when you are living from a place of passion. Find your passion. Live your life passionately. Your passion will help you discover more quickly whether you are on the right or wrong track. Living your passion may speed up your personal growth process, but it's also a very good way to live your life, whether you believe all of this or not.

Relationships

If you are one with everything, that means that there are really no such things as relationships. What do you relate to if everything is you? The love relationship, as well as all other relationships, for that matter, are what the Course refers to as "special relationships." As I said, this means that we believe some people are more special than others. We treat everyone and everything on the planet differently, depending on our perception of them. Some people we treat better, some worse, and we have very different expectations of everyone based on our history with them. You already know that there's no past, so why do we do that?

You pick up a china teacup more delicately than you do a heavy coffee mug, because you remember something from the past about their weight and strength. You treat them differently. It's the same with people we know. That's how the world of form works; everything is different, based on our past experience with it, so everything must be treated differently. To go beyond *this* world, you must *think* beyond it. The ego's use of relationships is one the most powerful methods for keeping us firmly locked into the dream, but the Holy Spirit's use of relationships is one of the best ways to wake up from the dream. The ego has twisted our most treasured relationships into making us think that they are good for us, and that they are helping us grow.

We call these relationships our love relationships, but they are really some of the scariest and most misguided relationships we enter into, and they have precious little to do with love. We all have them, or if we currently don't, we desperately want to get into one, with a few exceptions. They are compelling and overpowering for us. We spend a tremendous amount of time and effort looking for them, nurturing them, and fighting them, but no matter what our current relationship status is, society tells us that they are the correct thing to pursue, and we mostly believe that. That's because society is a giant ego. Love is badly misinterpreted and regularly excoriated in songs from every genre because any romantic relationship of any sort, with any result, is lumped into one strange category called "love." That's not really love; it is ego disguised as love. Maybe we need more song writers who are Course students.

All of our relationships are symbols of who we believe ourselves to be. The other egos that come into our lives are introduced to us by the Holy Spirit, Who sets up our meeting in whatever venue is appropriate, no differently than He sets up all of our experiences. There are no mistakes. The people we meet are reflections of our strengths and weaknesses, supporting and challenging our beliefs.

We believe that we can "find" ourselves in love relationships. But the real purpose of love relationships, as far as the ego is concerned, is to keep the truth, and ourselves, hidden. As with most ideas in the Course, these are difficult ideas to accept and understand, and once again, this is going to challenge what you believe about yourself and the world.

Love is not special, because that's impossible, so let's go back to our definition of God. If you were a perfect God of unconditional love, what would be the best way to treat your children whom you love without reservation? Would it be to treat some better if they pray more passionately? Would it be to give only to those who ask? Would you love some more than others? Would you punish your children for what they do in their imaginary dream while they are asleep, even though they're perfect beings, lying on a cosmic bed, doing nothing but snoring adorably? If God were to grant requests to some and not to others, He would be making those souls special. So, His solution is elegantly simple: He withholds absolutely nothing from any of His kids; you just have to stop blocking His generosity from coming to you with your intense focus on the dream. It's your choice, and He would never interfere with the choices you make because non-interference with your free choice is another aspect of unconditional love.

Chapter 8 – *Relationships and Chaos*

When we are born into this dream world, we see all around us nothing but examples of special love, so as we grow up, we attempt to emulate those behaviors. As far as our non-romantic relationships go—family, friends, coworkers, etc.—we consider those something quite different from our romances, and so we treat them very differently as well. Some are loving, some are mechanical, most are polite but distant. What we are learning, slowly but surely through all of these diverse relationships, is that everyone is your brother and is as deserving of your equal, unconditional love as everyone else.

When you treat someone in your life as special, you are doing a disservice to them and yourself, and keeping yourself locked into fear. By treating someone special you are declaring that all of your other relationships are inferior, condemning all of them, even if it's a subtle, subconscious condemnation, and therefore, imposing your guilt on them by making them less. This is simply judgment. You are saying "this person is better than this one." You are effectively shutting yourself off from the rest of humanity in a subtle but effective way and adding guilt to your soul.

The special relationship is based on sacrifice and compromise. We look to all of our relationships, romantic or otherwise, to give us something. We only need something if something is missing, so a special relationship is based on lack. It is an attempt to fulfill a desire or need in ourselves. It is an attempt at Renée Zellweger/Dorothy Boyd-type completion. Unfortunately, the only way to create a special relationship is to compromise yourself, because your partner wants something from you as well. You both must sacrifice something to get something else. We have outwardly convinced ourselves that this sacrifice is a good thing. We tell ourselves that we should become what our partner expects of us, so he or she will stay in the relationship, because we need to learn about ourselves and grow, and the best way to do that is to see how someone as clueless as we are allows us to feel and behave. But when we sacrifice ourselves, we quietly hate the fact that we are being asked to become someone we don't want to be, whether we were directly asked to or not, and then we project that anger onto our partner, who we feel has no right to expect us to change.

Subconsciously, we are screaming for freedom. So, we want our "space," and this is the humorous belief that more separation can bring us closer together. So, in our effort to find ourselves in the relationship, we are really giving ourselves up, justifying sacrifice and separation, and fostering resentment towards our partners. Ego love. The perfect distraction from the truth.

God's love requires no sacrifice. Unlike God's changeless love, the love we feel in special relationships is constantly changing. Because of the guilt that's a part of special relationships, fear exists within them, just as in everything else in this world. We are afraid of saying or doing the wrong thing for fear of jeopardizing the relationship. If we feel jealousy or anger or manipulation or disinterest from our partner, our feelings of love also seem to wax and wane. There is a constant up and down shifting of feelings within the special relationship. Stock exchange love.

As soon as you agree that you are in a relationship, your entire attitude shifts, doesn't it? You are now attached to that person, and your world is suddenly a different place. You are now beholding to your partner, and you have certain obligations that you did not have the day before. It's all fluffy bunnies and puppies at the beginning. The honeymoon period can last years. Eventually, however, reality sets in and the real relationship appears. The Course makes a very powerful statement when it says that egos always enter relationships with anger, because that's all the ego really knows, so it believes anger is a necessary component of any relationship. That anger is used to make the other person feel guilty, and that becomes the glue that holds the relationship together. More importantly, the job of the ego is to make sure this anger and guilt are not seen clearly. The ego needs to perform its magic and twist what's really happening, so we think we are moving in the right direction, while we tread tepid, ego water.

A romantic relationship, in human terms, means that two people are together. In other words, it has a lot to do with the proximity of bodies. You live together, or spend most of your time together, etc. But minds can go anywhere they want. We judge the success or failure of relationships, not by how we join our minds, but how well we maintain our physical proximity to each other. After all, we need the other person close to us to receive the guilt we want to mete out. We go to tremendous lengths to justify the pain and suffering we feel to remain in our relationships.

The Holy Relationship

I know that many people have maintained long relationships, many of them good, and many tolerable, and many not so good. Whatever the dynamics of your relationship, your partner in a special relationship is a perfect representation of your subconscious mind. We love them. We hate them. They push all of our buttons, and elegantly twist the knife into our psyches. But there is good news in all of this. There is a way to change your special relationship into what the Course calls a Holy Relationship. It's quite simple. It just requires giving the relationship away—to the Holy Spirit. This sounds like some sort of a religious statement, but the reality of it is that once you make the decision to hand over your relationship, it will now, quite literally, be directed by the Holy Spirit. This giving requires that you have accepted the idea that you are here to change your thinking and that everything you see in this relationship is just your personal video of your subconscious mind.

As I said, the ego's purpose in a love relationship is to find happiness within the illusion, while pretending it is finding some sort of completion. The Holy Spirit sets up this relationship for another purpose, which we squander most of the time. It is only when you give the relationship to the Holy Spirit's higher purpose can the relationship fulfill its true function.

As long as you believe that this special relationship is outside of you, just like all of your other encounters with people, and that it is happening *to* you, you will see yourself as a victim of your partner and the relationship. You will continue to suffer and struggle, while attempting to suppress all of your anger for a few moments of peace. When you give your relationship to the Holy Spirit, it will change. Your role is now unconditional forgiveness. You will see your relationship as coming from inside you. Whether or not he or she knows that you are now in a Holy Relationship, your partner's reactions to you will change. And your reactions to your partner will now be based on your personal responsibility for all of the events that you go through together.

The purpose of a Holy Relationship is to see God in your partner. The way to do that is to forgive them. And then forgive them again. All personal relationships are reflections of how you see everything in this world, so use them to practice healing your thinking by forgiving all intrusions into your life, all demanded sacrifices, all burdens and all anger. When you give your relationship to the Holy Spirit, the relationship may not last, because this new relationship paradigm may not be pleasing to one or both of you, but that's OK. Take what you have learned and move forward. The Course spends a lot of time discussing the Holy Relationship because it is so vital to our learning, and because the special relationship is so destructive to it.

Laws of Chaos

Just as the world of separation has a set of physical laws by which matter is governed, the separated egos also have a set of rules which run quietly underneath our awareness and influence us greatly, often without our conscious understanding that they even exist. These unstated rules are part of the bigger picture of the world of separation and hold it in place. They describe our behavior and our reactions in ways that seem frightening but that they exist is beyond question. They are an incredible set of laws that are based on the structure of the ego and what it needs to survive, and have become quietly dominant in all of our lives. The Course calls them the laws of chaos and they are the misguided laws we have subconsciously created and hold onto to keep ourselves from finding the truth.

These so-called laws have caused us to turn our thinking upside down, and keep us from striving to discover more than what we have been brought up to believe. They convince us of our guilt and complicity and limit our growth and behavior by limiting what we believe about ourselves. I am not going to go into too much detail about them because they are clearly described in the Course, but I feel I should touch on them so you know the deep, insane psychological beliefs you and I are up against without even knowing it. They make a lot of crazy sense and explain the behaviors and attitudes we carry that keep us apart, angry and judgmental.

The *first* law of chaos is that we believe that the truth is different for everyone. This is a denial of oneness and the fact that we *are* each other and share the mind of God. It gives us permission to express our ego-selves and justify anything we want to do, no matter how destructive it may be. It confirms our specialness. The **second** law is that we all sin and we ultimately deserve to die because of it. Isn't this the way we all live? Don't we forever attach all people to their past transgressions, including our own? Isn't all sin permanent and deserving of our anger and judgment? This is the permanent wedge between us and God, for if we are sinners, then we not only deserve punishment, but we also can never be free from the sins we have committed because they are part of us.

The **third** law may be the most insidious. It states that if God created us, and God cannot make errors, then God must accept us as we are, including what we think about ourselves and each other. Therefore, what we think about ourselves can only deserve God's hatred of us. How can God be loving or helpful to beings who justifiably hate themselves and were created by Him? We hate Him for creating us this way, and He must hate us because we have gone wrong and turned into jerks. We deserve God's wrath, and the wedge between us is irreparable. How can we go to God for help with our suffering in this scenario and truly expect anything from Him when He hates us so much? And since we can't count on Him, that's a perfect excuse for us to solve our own problems because we are so embarrassed and apologetic and undeserving for what we have become.

The *fourth* law states that the only things you can possibly have had to be taken from someone else. Of course you had to take it from someone, so now they don't have it. This belief leads to us valuing *things*, and securing them from harm and from others, hiding them, fighting for them, fighting against loss, lusting after another's secure treasures, killing to get them. It puts the longing in belongings.

The ***fifth*** and final law of chaos is the icing on the cake and puts everything together. It follows from the other laws that vengeance is justified by us toward everyone and everyone toward us and God toward all of us. Attack by everyone will never end, so death is the final answer because we all deserve to die. God must accept us as we believe ourselves to be: flawed and evil, and that we can only possess what we take from others. This final law states that the only real answer to all of these laws is our death at the hands of God or our brother. This is the law of fear. It is the substitute for love, and we believe it is our salvation. Fear makes death looks beautiful because it is the end of suffering. Someone else's death is the end of our problems with that person, so in their death lies our salvation. Our death is someone else's salvation. Death is now salvation. The existence of death denies the existence of a loving God. We are all treacherous and the only way all of us can atone for what we have done is to perish for it. In our deaths is also God's salvation, for He created us this way, so our death is His only real solution to our evil, just as the death of Jesus was somehow the payment for the sins of all mankind. Sin must be compensated with death.

We are all filled with guilt for the real sins we have committed and we all know that the only way to atone for those sins is our death, because sins are real and permanent, and so they are beyond the reach of God. We are justified in taking from others because we are only trying to protect what is ours, and what they have taken from us, and so the only solution to this is their death. These laws of chaos are the theme of every billion-dollar action and superhero and western movie ever made, not to mention most others.

If we examine these "laws" from the perspective of the truth of who we really are, they are pure madness. Yet we all swear by them subconsciously, live by them, behave according to them, and justify them. They make us all unknowable to each other, angry at each other, and angry at God for creating us this way. They are the fundamental belief structure behind the tiny, mad idea, and they are why we so strongly believe we will die, and *must* die. They seem to solve all of our philosophical problems. But they are not true. They are ingrained in us and need to be acknowledged so we can let them go. The truth is the same for us all, because we are, in truth, one with each other. Sin does not exist: only errors in thinking, which can be easily corrected and, therefore, eliminated. God created us but not our egos, which are our incorrect thoughts about who we really are. We are, and always have been, part of Him, and He has never stopped loving us unconditionally. The things we hold onto in the world of form do not exist and have no meaning. The *only* things we keep are the things we give away. And above all, there is no death.

Your Power

No one else on the planet has any power to create anything inside of your life, your dream, unless of course, you give them permission, which we all do on a regular basis. We allow others to influence us or control us in very meaningful ways. It is another part of our master plan to be small and helpless victims. Letting others be in charge can be a good thing when it's done for the right reasons, but for the most part, it's just egos trying to control other egos. This world has become a game of control and manipulation. We feel the need to control others either physically or mentally in an effort to demonstrate our power to overcome our own fears of weakness and inadequacy. This is the way everything works in the world of the ego, from governments and corporations to individuals. We want to tell others, or force others, to do what we want them to. This is a world of rules and laws and restrictions and papers to sign and requirements to fulfill and behaviors to behave and where not to walk and walls and barbed wire and borders and locked doors. But it is impossible to exert any control over another unless the recipient decides that he or she is a victim. Unfortunately, that's the way most of us think right now, so it's not too hard to find a chain of victims and tyrants, spiraling up without end.

But giving away your power to others is not just making yourself a victim—it is the entire problem we are facing here in these small bodies! We are all-powerful beings, and we have made this tiny body and claimed for ourselves only a miniscule portion of the power that we truly are. In every transaction we have on earth, we are bartering with our limited power, mostly giving it away in an attempt to trade it for something else we don't really want. Reclaiming your power is not something you have to fight for: you already have it. If you feel any negative emotions, you are leaking power. You don't need to be angry with yourself about it. That just proves that your weakness is real to you. The way to stop the leak is to change your thoughts about yourself right now. Forgive yourself and the person or thing you are giving your power to. Remind yourself that your power is unlimited and loving. You must trust that every decision you make to reclaim your power in a loving way will be supported by the Holy Spirit. You must also accept that other people can control your actions all they want, but they can never control your reaction or your perception.

The only purpose of the conscious mind is to decide, and the only thing that matters to you in this dream is how you react to life. The present moment is the only thing you have. In all the spiritual teaching, in all the billions of words written on the subject, if you want any change in your life to occur on any level, there is only one thing you can do about it—change the way you react—right now—to what is happening in front of you. Do *not* react as you used to. Make a better choice in every moment. The moment of *now* is the only moment, and in each moment, you have the choice to be the person you have always been, or someone different. Nothing else has the power to change the course of your life.

Changing the way you react can be very difficult, because it means that you must first pay honest attention to the way you are reacting now, understanding your motivations. Then, you must also have a desire to change it. If that weren't enough, you must then have the self-discipline and courage to change your reaction, because our reactions are like deep grooves in our psyches that are difficult to climb out of. When someone makes you angry, you react angrily. That's it, right? You still see it as an event that is occurring outside of you, in front of you. So, instead of listening to the message of the lesson, we immediately go into denial, and turn it right back on the other person. We ignore the emotional response that the Holy Spirit has presented to us to get our attention. It doesn't matter what they said or did. It only matters that we have to make *them* the problem, so we don't have to look at ourselves. We shift the focus to save ourselves from facing our shortcomings. And in that moment, the last thing you want to do is show weakness by being forgiving and not showing anger. The ego's power manifests in its demonstrations of individual power.

This is how anger works. As I said before, anger *always* means you have decided you are a victim but, because it's impossible for you to be a victim, anger is really your denial that you could ever be responsible for bringing or inviting that event into your life from the deep recesses of your mind. It is also the denial of who you really are. If you are angry, you are angry at something or someone, including yourself. But anger means that blame must be assigned somewhere. And it means that someone really did something, so you think they should feel guilty about it. Anger is the idea that blame must be passed, punishment is warranted, the guilty must suffer. In other words, anger creates guilt, the very thing that keeps us locked into this illusion.

We don't want to admit our own responsibility for our lives or look at ourselves honestly because we are afraid of what we will see. Anger means you want to be powerless over outside events and other people, and when you feel anger, you are always telling yourself that you are small, weak and human. Because you don't want the responsibility for these bad events, you have to blame someone else for them. In other words. you feel guilty about what's inside of your mind but if you can pass that guilt on to someone else, you can pretend the guilt and blame are gone from you and then you can temporarily feel OK about yourself again. Too bad that feeling is only temporary. Changing your reaction means you choose to take responsibility and to no longer be that victim. Your ego will disagree. Your soul will be relieved.

Your thoughts invite your circumstances, so if you see something that doesn't please you, you can either blame someone for it (make *them* the victim in payment for making you the victim, and perpetuate the cycle of suffering on earth), or you can correct the source. You make conscious choices every second of your life, and those choices matter very much, but each tiny choice is a decision you make about what you believe about yourself.

More Magic

Two things occur in present moment. They are the events that occur in your life, and your reactions to those events. Stuff happens, and you react. Something occurs and you make a choice. Because these two ideas are connected, we believe that the choice we make, followed by the action we take, directly effects the outcome of whatever happened. But the connection between these two things usually occurs only on the level of form. The event and the action you take are both worldly events and so, they are both occurring only at the symbolic level, in the world of form.

What is actually happening is that you are being presented with a symbolic representation of a thought or belief you have, and you are reacting to it with a mental choice. If your reaction to any event is an attempt to fix it on the level of form, it will not succeed. It may work temporarily as you see it, but the fix is only superficial and the problem still exists in your mind. You will see it again and again, until you make the correction in your thinking.

This is the essence of what the Course calls "magic" which I mentioned earlier. It bears repeating. Magic is the idea that the physical world has power, so repairing its form or using its form seems to be the way to solve a problem. Working only in the world of form does nothing lasting or real. This is what the ego does with virtually everything. This is why we go to doctors or lawyers or the workplace. We believe our company is responsible for our paycheck, or that a pill or surgery will fix the body, or that a lawyer will settle a dispute with a piece of paper.

When something occurs, and our reaction is to take an action, based on the event's form, our life will always feel like a crap shoot, unless the decision we make and the action we take is based on a consultation with the Holy Spirit. All occurrences are trying to teach us something, so we must always bear that in mind. Nothing is happening. Symbols are just being presented. Nothing more.

Chapter 8 – *Relationships and Chaos*

Two Ways

Having said that, you can only react in one of two ways; with God or with the ego. And I am referring only to your mind. Each event occurs only for you to react to it. Regardless of what action you may take, each decision will always be based on God or the ego. You either believe this is a dream or you don't. It's real or it isn't. If you are living your life from the perspective of your ego, believing that you are really here on earth, and that body you see in the bathroom mirror is the real you, then most of your decisions will be ego-based. All ego-based decisions serve to perpetuate this world and its accompanying suffering. If you see yourself as a perfect soul, having a dream, you are probably working to end the dream and wake up. All God-based decisions are made with the Holy Spirit and are the beginning of the end of this world.

There is also some amount of difficulty knowing the difference between an ego decision and a God decision. The reason is that we have expended a lot of effort identifying strongly with our egos, convincing ourselves how wonderful we are, not to mention how rotten we are at the same time, fueled by our passive-aggressive characteristics and desires to wallow in self-sacrifice, not to mention a host of other self-manipulating mind games we play. We take "nice" actions to hide our anger. We believe it's good to be a martyr, or to mete out justice to people we see as evil, all for the purpose of pretending how God-fearing and loving we are. Each of us thinks that the way *we* think and behave is the best way to be, no matter how painful it may be. In one of the oddest contradictions imaginable, we love fear, and we fear love.

Your purpose is to make choices in response to events in the present moment. You have created those events with your thinking and they are presented to you by the Holy Spirit so you get another chance to look at what you have made of yourself, and decide whether or not to change. Each choice you make further configures your subconscious mind and decides your future projections. What you see can only come from what you truly believe, which is your subconscious mind. That mind does not change easily. It has been conditioned and reinforced over many years and lifetimes. This dream is *your* dream. Edgar Cayce said that the subconscious mind is like an elephant; it's very hard to get it to change direction, but once you do, with extreme persistence, you will find it firmly on a new path. Before you choose, ask for guidance and follow what you feel. But never follow guidance that causes anyone pain or increases fear. Choose God over ego.

See it Differently

We are generally afraid to take the time to actually think about ourselves with any degree of real honesty and so, as I said, we are a collection of absurd, conflicting ideas. These conflicts are the ego's crowning achievement. To honestly examine the motives for our thoughts and actions takes a degree of honest introspection that everyone is capable of, but few ever do. We *say* we really want love but real closeness terrifies us. We love action movies and superheroes because they represent our feelings of powerlessness and our deepest desires to kill what threatens us, yet we still tell ourselves how caring we are. We have accepted violent actions of self-defense as solutions in a hostile world. Our minds are spider webs of intense contradictions that we never choose to look at honestly. But, in the end, there is only God or the ego. Which do you choose?

See everything negative that happens in your life as a choice; you can see it as an opportunity, or you can see yourself as a victim. God or ego. Anger or forgiveness. Love or a call for love. If you react with anger, you are choosing to see yourself as a victim, you have not seen correctly, and the incorrect thought will return at another time, whenever you are ready to see it again, perhaps in a different symbolic form.

Your conscious mind is your connection to either God or your ego. You decide which it is. Every effort you make to forgive, and live in joy, and extend your peace into the dream world will make your life, and everyone else's, that much better—just not necessarily in the way you planned. Each present moment you decide to connect with God rather than the ego brings you closer to the truth of yourself, and begins to undo the subconscious. Don't choose to be a good person because you expect something in return. Do it because you are starting to accept who you really are.

> *T-9.I.4. You have imprisoned your will beyond your own awareness, where it remains, but cannot help you. ²When I said that the Holy Spirit's function is to sort out the true from the false in your mind, I meant that He has the power to look into what you have hidden and recognize the Will of God there. ³His recognition of this Will can make it real to you because He is in your mind, and therefore He is your reality. ⁴If, then, His perception of your mind brings its reality to you, He is helping you to remember what you are. ⁵**The only source of fear in this process is what you think you will lose. ⁶Yet it is only what the Holy Spirit sees that you can possibly have.***

The Holy Spirit brings mistakes to the truth. He is only working to allow us to see our errors, and provide the solution.

> *T-26.II.4. The miracle of justice can correct all errors. ²Every problem is an error. ³It does injustice to the Son of God, and therefore is not true. ⁴The Holy Spirit does not evaluate injustices as great or small, or more or less. ⁵They have no properties to Him. ⁶They are mistakes from which the Son of God is suffering, but needlessly. ⁷And so He takes the thorns and nails away. ⁸He does not pause to judge whether the hurt be large or little. ⁹He makes but one judgment; that to hurt God's Son must be unfair and therefore is not so.*

The Guy

As the Holy Spirit allows your thoughts to manifest at the perfect time with the solution built in, you must also know that He is standing right there at the moment of every presentation in your life, holding your hand and telling you that you now have a choice to make. "You can make the same choice you have always made in the past, or you could see it differently this time. If you choose to see it differently, I will present the solution to you and you can move past this forever."

The Holy Spirit is the Guy. He is in charge of this illusion. If you want help, ask Him. If you need guidance, ask Him. As a matter of fact, you do need help and guidance all the time because you are not in a position to make any good decisions without Him. Our ultimate aim is to hear the Voice for God, the Holy Spirit, all the time, in every decision we make.

When you are listening to the Holy Spirit, you are listening to God and to your Self. When you are not listening to the Holy Spirit, you are listening to your ego. Just as the Holy Spirit does, your ego makes decisions based on judgment. The Course describes judgment very well:

> M-10. 3. *The aim of our curriculum, unlike the goal of the world's learning, is the recognition that judgment in the usual sense is impossible.* ²*This is not an opinion but a fact.* ³***In order to judge anything rightly, one would have to be fully aware of an inconceivably wide range of things; past, present and to come.*** ⁴***One would have to recognize in advance all the effects of his judgments on everyone and everything involved in them in any way.*** ⁵***And one would have to be certain there is no distortion in his perception, so that his judgment would be wholly fair to everyone on whom it rests now and in the future.*** ⁶*Who is in a position to do this?* ⁷*Who except in grandiose fantasies would claim this for himself?*

It goes on to say the Holy Spirit does know the full ramifications of His judgment, so the only decisions that will succeed on every level are His, and not those of the ego. We are here to give up our control to God, represented by the Holy Spirit. We are here to hear

His voice to guide us. We must learn to never let our attention stray from our purpose.

Chapter 9 – Letting Go of Control

The Universal Curriculum

It has been widely reported that many religions are steadily losing their flocks because their messages are out of date, lack substance, or seem discriminatory and so, they aren't attracting younger people. As I learned to understand *A Course in Miracles*, it became apparent that it makes all previous books ever written on philosophy, religion and psychotherapy obsolete, not to mention many other categories. That is no small statement, considering the vast number of books and authors that have tackled these subjects over millennia. The Course is a remarkable book. The Course answers all of the questions that every religion and philosophy ask, and even those questions they avoid asking. It answers all of our questions about morality, purpose of life, personal behavior and responsibility. It tells us that all questions are spiritual questions and can be clearly understood when the context of life is understood.

What is this life and world? The simple answer to everything is that this is all made up. Let go of your control, your planning, and everything about life on earth that you now feel is important, except the love you give. Make all your decisions with the Holy Spirit, and fear absolutely nothing; neither disease nor death nor suffering of any kind. No problem is unsolvable. Everything that happens to you is a gift given to you without any mistake, ever, so that you can make a choice to let go of errors in your thinking and acknowledge who you really are instead of holding on to who you thought you were. It is so powerful a message that it dwarfs everything that has come before, and it is certain that we will all get it someday. I am grateful I found it, and grateful to everyone with whom I have come into contact in this lifetime.

We Like It

If you really understand the Course, especially if you have made that huge intellectual leap and you really accept this is a dream or illusion, it has to be rocking your ego boat in a big way. The Course's description about how our lives manifest cannot help but change what most people believe about their role in creating their lives, and our old ideas will certainly not die without uproar. As humans, we cannot imagine *not* being in control of everything, even though we certainly know that we can't control *everything*. Our egos really want us to be in control of as much of our lives as possible, because not being in control makes our egos feel weak. But remember, we designed this entire universe just to take control away from God.

Therefore, the fundamental problem we have as humans on earth, is that we think that we are directly in charge of the direction our lives take on a daily basis. We put tremendous effort into our striving for small and large outcomes, when we are not at all responsible for them in the way we think. We believe that if something did not go our way, it was because we did not try hard enough, or that luck was against us. If we could understand that the world we see is a massive directorial dream event orchestrated by the Holy Spirit to help us awaken, we could easily stop our stressful lives and live in harmony with each other and ourselves. Our thousands of attempts every day to direct our lives are folly. They drain us and frustrate us needlessly. This world is an exploration in separation, taken over by the Holy Spirit to bring us back to Oneness.

Our belief in our personal control is essential to us because it represents our break from God. Our egos will not let go of our belief in our control because our egos *are* that very control. Our minds split from God's mind so we could take away His control and have control over ourselves. Now, we can't even conceive of a shared mind with anyone, or shared control, or that we are somehow part of something larger that wants to give us a better life than we could ever create individually, if only we were able to get rid of the lies we are telling about ourselves. Our decision for individual control is merely a choice we make, even though we may think personal control our only option here on earth.

The reason we don't want to let go of our control, and we don't want to give up on our current ideas is because **we like it here!** At least for the time being. Most importantly, we don't know any other way to be. We love the drama and the seeming control. We want to see what we can do here, and it has to play itself out until it stops working for us. There is absolutely nothing you can do or any method or doctrine or book or teacher you can follow that will advance you on your spiritual path, unless you have decided that this world doesn't work for you anymore.

There are countless people on a sincere spiritual path, but precious few have really understood what they were truly facing. The goal is to let go of who you think you are. Very few people knew they were signing up for that. I believe most people thought the spiritual path was some sort of an extension of religion. They come once a week to hear a speaker inspire them, or they go further in and begin to meditate or do yoga. They seek a better human life that their former religions could not deliver. Then, suddenly, they come across the real goal, and slam on the brakes because they never realized it was going to be this massive a change. Letting go of your personality, name, body, life on earth, is quite a leap and it may take lifetimes of being aware of the goal before one can truly pursue it. The Holy Spirit's first step in all of our lives is to help us see just that; this world doesn't work.

> *T-4.VI.5. How can you teach someone the value of something he has deliberately thrown away?* ²*He must have thrown it away because he did not value it.* ³*You can only show him how miserable he is without it, and*

> slowly bring it nearer so he can learn how his misery lessens as he approaches it. ⁴This teaches him to associate his misery with its absence, and the opposite of misery with its presence. ⁵It gradually becomes desirable as he changes his mind about its worth. ⁶I am teaching you to associate misery with the ego and joy with the spirit. ⁷You have taught yourself the opposite. ⁸You are still free to choose, but can you really want the rewards of the ego in the presence of the rewards of God?

Control represents our fears. When we feel any fear at all, it's because we feel we are not in control of some thing or some outcome, and we are calling on ourselves to figure out what to do. Lack of control makes us feel fear. Our solution almost always automatically involves taking an action. When the ego lacks control, it feels powerless. Therefore, control is power. It knows that when it loses its power, it will die. This is the ego's greatest fear. Giving your control to the Holy Spirit is your recognition that your ego is unable to guide you in any real sense. In fact, your fear that something bad may happen is the cause of bad things happening.

> M-29.3 ³To follow the Holy Spirit's guidance is to let yourself be absolved of guilt. ⁴It is the essence of the Atonement. ⁵It is the core of the curriculum. **⁶The imagined usurping of functions not your own is the basis of fear. ⁷The whole world you see reflects the illusion that you have done so, making fear inevitable. ⁸To return the function to the One to Whom it belongs is thus the escape from fear.** ⁹And it is this that lets the memory of love return to you. ¹⁰Do not, then, think that following the Holy Spirit's guidance is necessary merely because of your own inadequacies. ¹¹It is the way out of hell for you.

There is no greater theme in the Course. It's hard to believe that there are no accidents, or that things just "happen." If you believe that, then you believe that there is a cause apart from God. There is "something else" making or allowing events to occur. The universe is random, or chaotic with chemical elements bumping into each other without intelligence or reason.

When the Holy Spirit took over this world, He took back control. We are in the confusing space right now of still believing we have the control that we never really had. Being in the midst of confusion, we currently believe that we have direct control over *some* things that come into our lives, but not others, and therefore, we have to engage our focus to maintain control of those things we do. We don't think much about who or what decides which things we have control over. Who says, you have control over this and this, but not that and that? Where is the line? Is it a solid line or a dotted line; sometimes you have control over this but not today? None of this makes any sense at all, yet most of us believe something very vague to this effect because we have a hard time believing in a God Who could actually be so powerful and involved in our lives, and yet so seemingly invisible at the same time.

Our egos will decide what they think we have control over, and then change their minds tomorrow when circumstances change. All of the drama you put into controlling your life, or desire for this or that, or anger or disappointment, is all a distraction by your ego to keep you hooked on the video you are projecting. Your ego wants you to vainly manipulate your life through actions and desire to fill a lack, while supporting your worries and desperation by focusing on the shiny objects outside of yourself. It is frantic to keep you from looking inside at the real source of your life. The ego wants this external life to be important and wants to keep you from letting it go. God just wants you to wake up from it.

Can forgiving everyone and everything really be worse than the life you live now, even if the Course is wrong? The fear of giving up control is the ego's fear of its own death, and it has convinced you that this means you. But you will not die. You will finally come back to life.

Stop thinking of yourself as alone and in charge of your life, lacking connection with anything in a real way. There are no spiritual fixes or shortcuts in this life until you see that it is meaningless. As I said, as long as you still want to experience it, it will remain. On the other hand, there are many of us who believe that this tiny, mad idea really is mad. It didn't turn out as well as we had hoped it would, and now it has run its course, and we are ready to return to something much better.

The idea that you are seeing your own thoughts at a perfect time for you to undo the crazy ones might not sound like the life you are living right now, but it is the most wonderful and clever thing that could happen in this world of seeming chaos, and it requires you to understand what the Holy Spirit is doing and why. God's plan for our escape from ourselves is far beyond a simple plan. It is more incredible than the compelling world that we have made for ourselves, because God is doing all he can to help us, and that is no small thing. There are no exceptions to the ideas that all negative events are gifts, and all people are your saviors. This life is nothing else. If you are willing to dive into the implications of this, you can transform yourself and save yourself lots of time and heartache.

Once the Holy Spirit sees that you are beginning to get it, the events of your life can now become powerfully meaningful. You will probably be faced with some deeply hidden and potent fears and desires, but now you know that these events are coming into your life from deep within your own mind so that you can choose to stop being afraid of them and denying they exist. Many call this the dark night of the soul, and there can be many of them in your life. They can occur before you make any conscious changes to accept your responsibility for life, but the Holy Spirit is using these events to help you along because He sees where you are headed long before you do.

There is nothing to be afraid of, *ever*. When many of your fears begin to go, the larger, underlying fears will come, challenging you to your limits. The depth of your fears must be plumbed, but now you know that the universe in on your side. God is with you at every step, and those large fears that once seemed so vast and all-encompassing will disappear into nothingness because, just as you once gave those fears incredible power, you now give them nothing. Your desires will show themselves to be the hollow idols they are and you will be able to more easily let them go, not because you are sacrificing them, but because you are allowing them to be replaced by something better.

Each incorrect thought you have ever had over many lifetimes has added to a deeply buried reservoir of subconscious beliefs. Every single one of them was created by you and every single one of them must be corrected by you. Even though all incorrect thinking is only one incorrect idea, we have decided that they are separate ideas, so we will correct them one-at-a-time, or as connected bundles, as the Holy Spirit decides. All of those thoughts *must* manifest in some form at some point in our human existence until we understand that they are all the same problem, because every one of your thoughts will exist until you undo it! You have chosen these ideas in your life, because you are their creator and have made them your dear, sweet children. Thousands of tiny psychotic urchins, destroying your happiness.

You will most likely not even know beforehand that these negative thoughts existed within you until they manifest in your life as some sort of strange or unpleasant emotional events. Recognize your role in the appearance of *everything* in your life, and consciously choose to see these negative things as nothing and **let them go**. This is helping us realize that there truly are no bad events. Shakespeare said (through Hamlet), "...*for there is nothing either good or bad, but thinking makes it so.*"

No, Not Frozen

Giving up your control, or rather, giving up your belief that you *can* control, is a major step to finding out who you are; a step we must all take. Discovering that you do not control the timing of events that come into your life is the entire gist of the Course. Yet, giving up our desire for control is an almost ridiculous concept to imagine for us egos down here on planet earth. It is a simple matter of trust. It is required. Do you *really* believe in God? Do you really believe that the small, frustrated person you are with extremely limited knowledge and resources could make better decisions for you than God, who knows everything and who knows where this is all leading? To the ego, letting go means fear and uncertainty. But certainty is of God. Keeping our belief in control is the source of all guilt, and guilt is what keeps us in the illusion.

Can you see where life is leading us? This is an entirely different way of looking at this life on earth. This is not what any religion tells you, or what any other teacher on earth will tell you. *A Course in Miracles* wants you to see your life in an entirely different context. This life is not what we think it is! This life doesn't mean anything and it doesn't even exist. I imagine at any given time on the planet, there are very few people who even consider this idea, yet it is the most important concept you will ever embrace. Absolutely nothing you do matters at all, unless it helps you get closer to the exit. Spend some time with it. Don't consider it only for the amount of time it takes to read this paragraph. If it's true, it's the only thing you have ever thought that will make any difference in your life.

The Course is not another book; it is a description of the truth that is all around you, invisible, yet more real than the life you are now living. This three-dimensional life has an incredibly powerful grip on us all and defies questioning. Please, start questioning. What the Course describes is radical, profound and very, very different from anything you have previously understood. How do you undo all those years of believing in something and exchange it for something else that seems so weird and hard to understand? But your beliefs in humanity eventually will and must reveal themselves as nonsensical.

If you have been able to grasp the idea that your life as an ego means absolutely nothing, then you may begin to realize what a dramatic and all-encompassing task lies ahead for you. Is there any sense to what the Course describes? It's pretty far out there. Can you see or admit that you have created everything in your life, that you are not in charge of the short-term results or the direction your life takes? If there is a God and He gave you one function—to wake up through forgiveness—then why would you spend one minute of this phony existence focusing on anything else? You are only seeing what you have made projected in front of you so you can forgive what doesn't work. That's it. The whole enchilada. These are our lives.

Over millennia, we have imagined every possible scenario in our desire to explain this life, including where it came from, what it's for and how it works. We fill in all of our denial with the games of the ego. We have given importance to it all; the eating, drinking, sex, the money, playing, as well as the manipulation and judgment and pain and suffering. We truly want life to be this way in every aspect, or it wouldn't be. We love the chaos and the confusion. We want to see people punished for what they do. We want ourselves to suffer for the deep guilt we feel. We want to see injustice all around us to justify our unending anger. Every story on the news must include someone to blame. We are invested in this game very powerfully. We really, deeply want to believe that we are consciously in charge of what happens to us in our own lives. Being in command of creating our lives is so important that we have created elaborate rules for how that happens, and repeated them over and over to each other to get support for that false scenario. The Course has made a case for a very different scenario. Everything we now live and believe is merely life on the surface and, according to the Course, it is not life at all.

What does this amazingly different context of life mean to you personally? This is all leading to one very obvious conclusion about how this world is structured and what we all need to do about it.

Let go.

Let go of everything. Let go of your control over your life, other people and all situations. Let go of your stress and pain. Let go of the drama. Let go of results. Let go of all of your hopes for what you want in this life, not in a depressing, suicidal way, because if you do, you will shut yourself off from the incredible possibilities of what God is trying to give you, more real and powerful than you can imagine.

Letting go is no small thing. It is a profound change of life, and it is the result of your new belief in who you are and why you are here.

Letting go isn't something you just decide to do; it's something you must single-mindedly grow into as you understand the real nature of your human existence. Letting go of your control is learning to turn over your control and trust to God's control—without any external proof that it exists. We have all heard it said over and over again that we need to "let go," whatever that is supposed to mean, but if you believe that you are in charge of your life and that you are creating your life from your conscious mind, and you enjoy living that false premise, then that phrase will have little meaning beyond just another spiritual slogan. Letting go is not a catch phrase; it is a conscious, ongoing decision to let go of your humanity, your identity and your life as you know it. It is the scariest idea a human being can face.

    Letting go is giving up the ego. It is the result of forgiveness but the magnitude of its power only makes sense when you have begun to see that it's working. Letting go is the unbelievably profound discovery, deep inside you, that you are the Son of God. This is not an intellectual discovery. It is the certainty that all the power of God is within you because you have let go of the small, insignificant power that your ego wants you to cling to. You can give all your illnesses, problems, shortcomings, fears to the Holy Spirit effortlessly and completely, without hesitation or a second thought, because you are falling into complete acceptance of Who you are, and your True power.

    Why would you not want to let your true mind, the mind of God, be in control? If the decisions you now make are intended to move your life forward with an expectation of results, then you have misunderstood. Your purpose is to choose in each moment for God, without any other agenda, without any hope of any particular results. A desire for results is just another type of control. If you *have* to stay in control, and letting go is impossible, your life will be limited to the wants of an ego, separate from the will of God. The most vital idea to let go of is the complete context of how you think this world works because it does not work the way we think it does (if you haven't picked up on that by now). You must shift away from the idea that the choices you make in every second are for some result in this world. Use your choices simply to reclaim your soul, peacefully. It doesn't matter what's out there ahead of you in time.

Letting go means giving up the fear of not having control. What happens if you get a serious illness? Or you have a financial setback, or you lose your home? Can you trust God to fix it? How can you not be afraid of serious setbacks and want to do something about them? There will come a time, and perhaps it is still a long way off, where you will see that giving these important issues to God or the Holy Spirit is exactly what you should do. There will be no fear involved, and no doubt. This is not an experiment or game, and it requires complete faith. God will handle every situation, and tell you what to do, if anything, and you will understand completely, without a moment of hesitation, that He is taking care of it.

At some point in your understanding of yourself, you must come to accept the incredible underlying power that drives this life. Everything that happens in this life comes from your deep desire for it to happen, no matter how disconnected from those real, hidden desires you may be. God would never impose anything on you that you did not create, nor would He deny you anything you did create. There is no randomness at all! The more screwed up you feel your life is, the more out of touch you are with your own power, creativity and subconscious wishes. Accepting the way the world works means letting go of the control you want to have, **which you do not possess anyway**. Truly understanding how your life is created is vital to your happiness.

> *T-14.III.9. Whenever you choose to make decisions for yourself you are thinking destructively, and the decision will be wrong. ²It will hurt you because of the concept of decision that led to it. ³It is not true that you can make decisions by yourself or for yourself alone. ⁴No thought of God's Son can be separate or isolated in its effects. ⁵Every decision is made for the whole Sonship, directed in and out, and influencing a constellation larger than anything you ever dreamed of.*

The Holy Spirit is running a vast organization. Everything that happens here is perfectly coordinated with everything else. You can make any decision you want and do anything you want but not one action you decide to take can manifest without the Holy Spirit allowing it because its effects will touch many other people. No events can be avoided if the Holy Spirit deems them necessary at any given moment.

You are God. How could you not be extraordinarily happy every moment? If you need to be somewhere or do something, you will be there and you will do it. If you are not meant to, you won't. And no matter where you are, it is perfect, and you should recognize that in a powerful way. When this idea really sinks in, you will understand that there is nothing for you to concern yourself with—ever! You are not a human. If you give your absolute trust to Who you really are and let go of your limited, stressed-out, not very bright ego, you will never worry about anything for the rest of your human life! Why do most of us ignore a promise as wonderful as that?

Because the ego won't let us. But you can override your ego at any time. Look back at your entire life. Do you see that everything that needed to happen to you actually did happen? And all of the things that didn't happen, even though you may have wanted them to happen, were the things that just didn't fit you?

Any inability you have to let go of your own desires and control is only a reflection of your ego's unwillingness to go away. You will always be led to where you need to go, so why work so hard, stress so much, and fight so hard for control that you don't even have? Get out of your own way. Thinking with your ego mind and human brain will not make things work better. This world will always coalesce in front of you around your personal, subconscious attractions and put you exactly where you need to be. Whether you are evil-minded or spiritual, loving, full of fear, wizard or muggle, you will always find yourself right where you need to be and experiencing exactly what you need to experience. Your job, your friends, your health, your financial standing are all exactly what you need right now. Nothing is happening *to* you and nothing happens from the outside. It *all* happens from the inside out. Stop trying so hard! It's all going to happen easily, effortlessly, with or without your conscious consent. And it's always going to be perfect for you. The more you accept that your will and God's will are the same, the easier your life will become.

I understand that this control issue will be a hard concept to implement. It seems inconceivable that our hard work and actions and stress didn't get us where we are today. How do you let go of an ego, so obviously in control, when the human race mind of seven billion other people also believes in that conscious control? This Course is asking you to give up what everyone else believes, and to start believing in something that very few believe and even fewer are able to live. If we didn't want this familiar ego life so much, we never would have tried for it so hard, right?

We want to see justice and punishment and poverty and hunger and struggle because it is all deserved by those miserable sinners. If you believe in hard work and walking over others to get what you need, then that's the world you will see and live within. If you believe that getting money is a competition, it will be. If you believe in stress and failure, in spite of your hard work, then your life will reflect that. What you think you believe is most often not what you carry subconsciously. Life will always give you what you need, based on your deepest beliefs, no matter what you do on the surface of your life.

You will always take actions exactly when you need to take them. If you take actions that don't lead you in the direction you need to go, they will come to nothing. You *will* feel compelled to take actions that lead you where you need to go, and I must stress here that you *should* take action in this life. If you don't take an action you should, you will get another opportunity because the results may be important for you. Either way, your actions will always be based on your subconscious beliefs and desires with the help of the Holy Spirit. Right now, our actions are always leading us to the things we need to forgive. And please understand once again, letting go does not mean not taking action! Letting go means trusting the Holy Spirit to direct you to the best actions, without any stress on your part. As you let go more and more, your actions will lead you to better and better outcomes, and those outcomes will be based less on the ego happiness you used to desire, and based more on a much more satisfying happiness that is the desire to connect with your fellow non-humans.

Defense

There is an extraordinary piece of writing in the Course, nestled within many other extraordinary pieces of writing. It is the workbook lesson 135. In just a few short pages, it presents an important summary of how dramatically different your thinking must become. It is about the defenses we have built up against everything. This is a world of attack. We are afraid of people we don't know and people we do know. We are afraid anyone might find out what we're thinking. We are afraid of what's going to happen in the future.

It then takes the idea of attack to the next logical step. Since this world is one of attack, we have made it one of defense. The only way to defend yourself from all the attacks of this world is to think about all of the possible things you are afraid will happen, and then plan and take action to make sure they don't. We must come up with ways to defend absolutely everything we can think of. We have to think about what we or others have done to defend in the past in this situation. We have to think about what we want to happen and then organize ourselves right now to fortify our lives against every possible scenario that's important to us. We plan against every possible contingency we can think of.

Is our door strong enough? Is our insurance up to date? Are we taking enough of the right pills? Is our computer protected from hacking? Will our lifestyle cause us to get some terrible illness some day? Have we covered our butts at work? Will we be able to survive financially? Is another country going to start a war with us? Will our own inevitable death be long, horrible and painful? What happens when I get old? Will I have to go into a home where I'm mistreated? Is my job really stable?

Whatever we can worry about, which is everything, we also try to plan against. But it doesn't matter what the subject of fear or attack is. It's all the same; it's always a fear of not being in control. Ultimately, we always plan out of fear. We have to try to stay one step ahead of life. We have to decide what happens to us before it happens on its own, without our input. We took control away from God so we could experience life without Him. So now, the only solution is to exercise as much individual control as possible, and do as much as we humanly can to prevent everything unwanted that could possibly occur.

Lesson 135 states that making plans is an error. That's quite a powerful statement. Planning is done out of fear, fear of attack, to gain an edge somehow, to protect what needs no defense, because the ego is obsessed with control. The ego makes decisions to allay fears and to propose a future that we think we want. But the fears don't go away because what we think we're afraid of is not what's causing the fear. The source of all fears is not outside of us. There is only one fear, and that is the fear of being separate, alone and vulnerable. There is only one way to live and that is in and with God. It is the opposite of the ego's way that we currently pursue. The Holy Spirit is already planning your life, and if you replace His plan with your own, you will only cause yourself all of the suffering and stress and pain you are planning to stop. Don't worry about the small plans you make on a daily basis to run your life in the short-term, although it would still be a good idea to ask for help with those as well. But the Course is not trying to get you to avoid living your life, and that includes making those short-term plans to help it run efficiently.

The word "defenselessness" is not only a good summation of the Course but also a very accurate description of the historical Jesus as well, and one of the most difficult concepts for the ego mind to understand, let alone accept. It is also another way to describe letting go. Defenselessness means, quite simply, that each time you defend yourself from anything, you are stepping into the role of being your own god, maintaining the illusion of this life, along with the struggle and pain of attack and suffering. You are giving reality to illusions. There is simply nothing to defend because everything is God, so there is also nothing that is not you. If you believe in protecting yourself, that means that you believe you are subject to attack from something outside of yourself, and that you are actually trying to control your life by planning it. It also means you believe you are weak and must strengthen yourself, and it means that you live in fear. None of these things is true but believing they are is the very cause of all attacks.

> *W 135 L 2. You operate from the belief you must protect yourself from what is happening because it must contain what threatens you. ²A sense of threat is an acknowledgment of an inherent weakness; a belief that there is danger which has power to call on you to make appropriate defense. ³The world is based on this insane belief. ⁴And all its structures, all its thoughts and doubts, its penalties and heavy armaments, its legal definitions and its codes, its ethics and its leaders and its gods, all serve but to preserve its sense of threat. ⁵For no one walks the world in armature but must have terror striking at his heart.*
>
> *3. Defense is frightening. ²It stems from fear, increasing fear as each defense is made. ³You think it offers safety. ⁴Yet it speaks of fear made real and terror justified. ⁵Is it not strange you do not pause to ask, as you elaborate your plans and make your armor thicker and your locks more tight, what you defend, and how, and against what?*

Who are we defending ourselves against? Well, what we're really afraid of is our brother, who is just us. We defend ourselves from ourselves because we have created a hideous monster of our brother, based on how we need to see him to justify and match the fear we have nurtured in our own hearts, and to mask our guilt so we can blame him for our suffering.

Planning our lives is folly because the only way to truly live is to act on the guidance you are given from God at the moment you need it. That is why defenselessness is very closely tied to how we create our lives. Defending yourself by building ups arms and heavy doors is simply planning for and choosing to experience a very negative event in the future and therefore, making those attacks real. The desire for money is the desire to protect yourself against a future of lack.

As I said, defenselessness contains the entire idea of the Course in one word. Everything you need to know about yourself can be summed up in this concept. Because you are God (and there is only God) then what could you ever need or want or defend against? Who can hurt you? What has power over you? What do you lack? Where does anything from your current life fit into the real idea of a God of unconditional love? God will never protect you or forgive you, because there is nothing that threatens you, and there is nothing you can ever do that needs to be forgiven. Can you bring that feeling from deep inside your heart into this world? Can you understand that all of those people you see on the news every night, doing all of those awful things, are actually your brothers, who are merely another aspect of your own mind? There is nothing to fear from them if only you could understand that your fear of them is what will draw those threats to you in this dream life. Your absolute faith in God, and your willingness to give up your control and give it back to God is the only safety. By truly giving up the need for defense, you will never be drawn into situations that require it.

The idea of defenselessness represents the hurdle we must all jump to let go of this world. This is why the Course, which is simply the truth of this universe, is so daunting. It represents giving up all your control or the belief that planning your life will make it better or safer. Control defines this world and the ego. Giving up control requires that you give up all of your fears because your faith in God and the truth of who you really are so powerful that you know without doubt that you are invulnerable because you are safe in the arms of an unconditionally loving God. It requires forgiveness of everyone and everything you come into contact with because it takes away the idea that you can be a victim of anyone or anything. Defenselessness is knowing that there are no enemies, so you cannot see this world full of brutality the same way. When God denied our request for specialness, He knew it would have these devastating consequences.

Holy Spirit

This life is simple, easy and carefree because God will take all of our problems, all of our concerns, all of our difficulties and give us unlimited unicorns and candy canes. Of course, that's the big problem, isn't it, trusting God to take over? That means we have to stop letting our egos solve our life problems, and have absolute faith that every problem is presented to us with the solution and the potential for our healing. This is enormously important to do, enormously difficult to do for egos, and as simple and easy as your faith that there really is a loving God out there somewhere who really cares about you, and is really invested in your happiness. Get out of your own way.

> *T-17.VIII.2. This simple courtesy is all the Holy Spirit asks of you. ^{2}Let truth be what it is. ^{3}Do not intrude upon it, do not attack it, do not interrupt its coming. ^{4}Let it encompass every situation and bring you peace. ^{5}Not even faith is asked of you, for truth asks nothing. ^{6}Let it enter, and it will call forth and secure for you the faith you need for peace. ^{7}But rise you not against it, for against your opposition it cannot come.*
>
> *T-17.VIII.3. Would you not want to make a holy instant of every situation? ^{2}For such is the gift of faith, freely given wherever faithlessness is laid aside, unused. ^{3}And then the power of the Holy Spirit's purpose is free to use instead. ^{4}This power instantly transforms all situations into one sure and continuous means for establishing His purpose, and demonstrating its reality. ^{5}What has been demonstrated has called for faith, and has been given it. ^{6}Now it becomes a fact, from which faith can no longer be withheld. ^{7}The strain of refusing faith to truth is enormous, and far greater than you realize. ^{8}But to answer truth with faith entails no strain at all.*

Living in truth is waking up. When you live in truth, you are no longer living within illusion. That is when everything in this world falls into place, and when we are promised that life called the happy dream, which is a temporary arrangement on earth. It is the time when everything makes perfect sense, and all of your actions are guided clearly and easily by the Holy Spirit. It is the end of stumbling in the dark, fighting, worrying, hoping and stressing. It is also the subject of the last chapter.

We are trying to reconnect with the mind of God. The dream is powerful. It is as strong as your mind makes it, which is the most powerful thing in the universe. We have to erode the dream through constant attention; what the Course calls vigilance for God and His kingdom. This cannot be stressed enough; the amount of time and effort that we currently put into this world must be countered with equal, and eventually greater, attention away from this world. It is very difficult to engage in a normal life with all of its demands for your mind's attention, and still be vigilant for God. Being vigilant for God simply means to *always* keep the idea at the forefront of your mind that this isn't real, and to forgive everything that comes into your life, most notably, the constant evaluative choices you are making of everything you see; the insidious judgments that never seem to end, and then to forgive yourself.

The Holy Spirit is our behind-the-scenes assistant/teacher in everything we do in every moment of the day. He is the solution to everything. We do not have to play the game; indeed, we are not even part of the game, because it doesn't exist.

I know how hard it is to read a book like the Course, and change it from reading material into an actual concept and a lifestyle that you understand and live.

- *This world is not at all what we think it is*
- *In our effort to feel special we, the Son of God, have made a fake world of definition, opposites, perception, opinion and judgment*
- *We have replaced God's oneness with a dream of duality.*
- *This experience is just like your nighttime dreams. You are not here*

- *This dream is consistent to convince us it is real*
- *The Holy Spirit is God's complete stand-in in this world of three dimensions*
- *Your mind is the cause of everything in your life*
- *Cause and effect work exactly the opposite as we understand them on earth*
- *What happens to you in life is exactly what you believe about yourself*
- *You cannot change your life by manipulating the world of form*
- *This world and everyone in it are perfect. The only problem is your perception of it*
- *All anger means you are a victim and demonstrates your desire to make others guilty*
- *There is nothing to fear, and nothing to attack. You are perfectly safe*
- *The bliss of living in God cannot be put into words*

Lucid Dream

Many of you who are reading this have had lucid dreams. For those of you who have not, a lucid dream is simply a nighttime dream in which you wake up inside the dream and realize that you are you, the same waking person that you are during the day, with a name and address on planet earth, but your body is still asleep and you are still inside of your own dream. Your waking, conscious mind is engaged. Once you wake up within a dream, you realize that you can now do anything you want, like fly, go anywhere in the world or beyond, etc., as long as you can maintain the lucid state. Here's an example of a lucid dream I once had.

I was in a restricted, cement, underground parking garage of some sort that led to a secret office. To get through a certain door to that office, you needed a magnetic striped card, which I didn't have. There were some men standing and talking who were about to go into the secure office. I wanted to follow them through the door without them knowing it, so I had to act nonchalant. As they stood and talked, I walked past them towards the door and then pretended to have dropped all of the cards and everything else out of my wallet so they would pass me by as I picked everything up. My plan was that they would get to the door first and as they went in, I would quickly reach over and stick a card in the door to keep it open.

As I was looking at all of these cards I had strewn about on the garage floor, I realized that there were more and more of them, and the more I tried to pick them up, more and more appeared. I realized the humor of it, and said to myself, "This is like what happens in a dream." As soon as I said that, I realized that I *was* dreaming. I got excited and realized that I was having a lucid dream. I immediately stopped caring about the wallet and the garage and the men. I knew that this was all a dream and I was now in total control of it, so I wanted to explore. The first thing I wanted to do was fly, so I merely willed myself to fly, lifted my arms up and I rose up. It was the most wonderful feeling. I had a big dream smile on my face. I flew out onto a lawn and up to a house. I stopped to tie my gym shoes and noticed that the colors were extremely intense. I made a mental note of it. The grass was *very* green and the shoes were *very* white and the colors were stunningly beautiful.

There is quite a bit more, but that's all that matters. The point of telling this story is to illustrate that forgiveness is not a dramatic, serious attempt to focus on something terrible and then try with all of your might to forgive it. It is a simple letting go as I did in my dream. It is turning your head away from what happened, not in denial, but because it isn't true or real. It is meaningless. It is neutral. Move on from all negativity you see or feel because it comes from yourself, and you just have to let it go.

This waking dream we are living is no different than our nighttime dreams. The moment I realized I was dreaming was the moment I realized who I really was, at least from my nighttime dream perspective. It was the moment when everything in the dream became unimportant, and I forgave it. As I saw those cards on the floor multiply, I woke up, and immediately forgave everything I saw in front of me. Nothing mattered. The men weren't really there; they were only shadows. The frustration with the wallet was nothing. The desire to get through the door was gone. Being trapped in a concrete parking garage wasn't real. The forgiveness I felt inside of that dream wasn't a dramatic forgiveness of assessing what happened or analyzing anything, or reluctantly letting go of a negative or dramatic event; it was a simple letting go of its importance. It wasn't a deep engagement or struggle or finding some deep feeling for the event in my heart, and then releasing it. I simply made the past disappear by giving it no importance or meaning. My entire past inside of that dream consisted of being in a parking garage with two men and having a desire to get through a door. I let all of that go because I realized that I had made it all up and it didn't exist. It was easy to do, because it was a very small dream with a very small past, dreamt by one person. This is what forgiveness truly is; the acknowledgement that this life isn't real and therefore, unimportant. Forgiveness is merely turning your head away from an illusion and toward the Truth.

By contrast, this dream here on earth is a vast, complex dream shared by all of the souls that make up the Son of God. The past is huge. Our lives are complex. Our ties to our past are dramatic and shared. The dream is consistently solid and seems intensely real. It was easy for me to give up a simple past, consisting of about one minute of history, not shared with anyone, containing very little to hold onto, and obviously spawned by my own thoughts. Yet now, we are asked to give up a much more compelling dream, consistent, huge and dramatic, going back millions—even billions—of years, shared by billions of brothers and sisters who are all telling us how important it is. And now there is one quiet voice telling us, with all the love of God, that there is a better way: maybe we are all incorrect about this world.

> *T-22.V.1. How does one overcome illusions? ²Surely not by force or anger, nor by opposing them in any way. ³Merely by letting reason tell you that they contradict reality. ⁴They go against what must be true. ⁵The opposition comes from them, and not reality. ⁶Reality*

opposes nothing. ⁷What merely is needs no defense, and offers none. ⁸Only illusions need defense because of weakness. ⁹And how can it be difficult to walk the way of truth when only weakness interferes? ¹⁰You are the strong one in this seeming conflict. ¹¹And you need no defense. ¹²Everything that needs defense you do not want, for anything that needs defense will weaken you.

Acceptance

Letting go is really acceptance of the truth. The truth is that whatever is happening in your life is not under your conscious control, so you must merely accept that—know that—without question. Your life is made by your choices, and the only choice you need make is to accept that you are the Son of God. You have to truly accept that you are God's Son and incorporate it into your life in a real, substantial way. It has to bleed into your illusory life until it takes over.

You work and sweat and play the game we all play because you are afraid. You are afraid that if you didn't, you would probably get kicked out of your home or lose your car or not be able to buy nice clothes, or you would get sick, or just be generally broke or helpless or alone.

So, as a personal experiment, try to project yourself into the future, and imagine the worst thing that could happen if you gave up trying so hard. Find your fears and go into them. What's the worst that could happen? Lose your home and your car and your health and life. Let go of your body and your earthly existence. How do you feel when you're in that position? Admit that you are striving desperately so that you can control the future of your body. Even though you know that death is inevitable, give in to it and all of the other terrible things that might happen if you didn't retain your desperate control.

See those results, and then accept them, and then, and then. . . give them all to the Holy Spirit. Once you have admitted what's really going on in your subconscious and you have seen the things you fear that make you strive and seek and desire and sweat, only then can you let them go.

The Holy Spirit cannot take away the things you fear until you acknowledge them. But once he takes them, you no longer need be concerned with them. This might sound easier than it really is, but that's simply up to you. It's a matter of desire and choice.

Chapter 10 – Guidance

God's Mind

The ego's reasoning will always be able to point to many, many situations where it seems obvious that we took conscious control and made things happen in our lives, but that is simply the ego's choice, because that's what the ego wants to believe and see. Because this is a dream, your actions are part of the dream and do not exist. Actions do not cause anything because they are themselves, effects. Only mind exists. Your world will always verify your beliefs, just as it does for everyone else, even though others don't believe the same things you do. Your beliefs about controlling your life are reflections of your subconscious mind, and they are reflected in what appears in front of you. You can easily interpret this as your ability to consciously control your life. But nothing can happen unless you need it. Nothing can be avoided if it's needed.

Your mind and God's mind are the same. Your will and God's will are the same. Whenever you choose to think apart from God, or choose differently from God, you are creating conflict by believing something that isn't true. The thoughts you and I think are universally insane. We stress out, we worry, we make uncertain decisions, we take control, we get angry, we judge, etc. We are disconnected from real knowledge or sane understanding, separate and wandering aimlessly. The ego is a thought that you are having that describes a fake being. The thoughts you think that are from your ego do not exist!

Part of letting go of this world also means letting go of results. There is a powerful need in all of us that believes in the future. We want to know the future and we want to make the future, and we want to extend our hope into it. It doesn't exist. Can you let go of your hopes? Can you let go of all your plans? Can you accept the idea that you are not in charge, so none of your ideas about the future matter? Anticipation is a powerful driver. I suspect that the reason for those who find themselves in the throes of depression is that, in essence, they have lost all hope for the future. It is tied directly to the loss of control by the ego. But there is another way to look at it. If you understand that letting go of the future is simply giving it to a better decision maker, the Holy Spirit, and letting go of your investment into creating your life and desires for certain outcomes, then you will truly begin to experience freedom and joy. Trust in a future that will come to you without your intervention. Accept the present as it is.

> T-15.IV.2. *⁶Give over every plan you have made for your salvation in exchange for God's. ⁷His will content you, and nothing else can bring you peace. ⁸For peace is of God, and no one beside Him.*
> *T-15.IV.3. Be humble before Him, and yet great in Him. ²And value no plan of the ego before the plan of God. ³For you leave empty your place in His plan, which you must fill if you would join with me, by your decision to join in any plan but His. ⁴I call you to fulfill your holy part in the plan that He has given to the world for its release from littleness. ⁵God would have His host abide in perfect freedom.*

Our *only* purpose on earth is to correct the mistake we have made, and the only way to correct it is to make different choices in the present moment; choices that support a much different picture of life. You are consciously in charge of the choices you make but not consciously in charge of what happens in your life. By that I mean, of course, that you are not consciously in charge of which symbolic representations of your choices will appear at any given time. Choices that are in conflict with God's will don't exist because they support an existence that isn't true. Nothing in God is untrue, so untrue thoughts cannot fit into the body of God, which is the only thing that is real. So, where is the *you* in this scenario? What is real? What's left? Who *are* you?

We have taken our true Self, the part of us that is in turn, part of God, and buried it so deeply that it is suffocating under layers of ego. We have created a massively fake self and fake world to live in, to cover up who and what we really are. We need to dig ourselves out with a heavy-duty shovel. The devastating idea of the Course is that we have to give up everything we think we are; that is, individuals with separate thoughts, apart and alone, special and disconnected. It doesn't mean physical death but it will certainly be our demise as humans. As long as we focus on what we will be losing, we will not be able to see that we are gaining a most incredible, powerful, satisfying and perfect existence.

The only thing about you and me that is real is the mind that we use that is still part of God. That's it. But we access it all the time in a half-hearted sort of way. It is our essence. You know it's in there. What we need to do is bring it out into the open by letting go of the ego part that seems to dominate us right now. As we grow more and more into the Truth, we will naturally let go of our bodily desires, which covers just about everything we do all day, every day. We will let go of all of our fears and denials and anger and judgment and guilt.

Does it make you feel disempowered to think that your mind and will are God's mind and will? Does it make you feel small and unimportant, considering that there are billions and billions of your brothers who also share the same mind? Are you aware that the uncomfortable feeling you have when you think about letting go is the original tiny, mad idea perpetuating the universe?

We must each choose on our own to give up our egos but we will only give them up when we see that they don't work. God isn't demanding that you rejoin the Borg because resistance is futile. He is asking you to come home to a place better than you could ever imagine. He is merely asking you to let go of the dream of pain. This universe was a short experiment by the Son of God to experience specialness and life without God, a life separate and alone, without connection or love.

One of the phases we will all go through in our journey back to God is realizing the futility of life on earth while suffering a great degree of deep personal hopelessness and loss, until we realize that there is something else beyond this. What's left after you take away all of the illusions of a fake life and fake thoughts, is an unbelievably powerful, happy, permanent, real piece of God, made of love. Do you feel close to that part of yourself, or far away from it? You can also understand that in giving up this world and this life, you are giving up nothing.

Guidance

If you can see that your ego thoughts don't exist, then you can see the importance of cultivating the thoughts that you think with the God part of your mind. That part of your mind is the part you share with the Holy Spirit and with God and with all of your brothers. The moment of Now, when you make all of your choices is where everything happens, and every choice that presents itself to you lets you decide from this moment on who you want to be. When that guy in front of you drives 20mph in a 40, or when your significant other pushes your buttons, or when your boss yells at you for something you didn't do, will you react in anger with the ego mind or with the mind of God? When you want guidance or help of any kind with the choices you make, make them with the God part of your mind. Let the Holy Spirit make those choices for you/with you.

In the Course, the Holy Spirit is referred to as the Voice for God. But there is a problem: how do you know when you are hearing that voice and getting real guidance? How can you tell you are connecting with something really wonderful and truly helpful? This is probably the most often asked question by all people who are trying to get in touch with their "higher selves." If you look at the

Chapter 10 – *Guidance*

context of your life from the point of view of *A Course in Miracles*, then you have to know that you are getting exactly the guidance you need at every moment. You are getting as much conscious input as you can handle, and from behind the scenes, you are being led precisely to the correct actions, all of the time. There is nothing to fear and nothing to plan or control. This is true for every person on the planet at every moment. So, the real question becomes: How do I become more consciously aware of the guidance?

The real answer is: it doesn't matter. It doesn't matter in the least because the plan for your life will always work for your benefit in returning to God. If you truly wanted to do exactly as the Holy Spirit suggests and have every one of your thoughts agree with God's will, you would hear Him effortlessly. The truth is, we don't want to hear Him that badly, because our egos have their own message.

If you make a decision that is out of alignment with the Holy Spirit's guidance, then the Holy Spirit will recalibrate His work in your life. He will present different choices with the same loving guidance. You will choose again, and yet again. You can never make a mistake because He anticipates your mistakes and compensates for them. You will never end up where you are not meant to be.

Now, having said that it doesn't matter if you become more aware of the Holy Spirit's guidance, it is also extremely important for you to ask for it. The answer that you *want* to hear (and have already heard countless times) about that quiet guidance is that it takes practice to hear it. The practice it requires is changing your thoughts, changing your mind, becoming someone different, someone who is closer to God; not using a "technique." If you want to hear God, move closer to Him by becoming more like Him. The problem, as with everything else, is the willingness to set aside your ego, which has a much louder presence, and which really wants to inform you and keep you locked into its reality. Hearing the Holy Spirit doesn't involve trying; it involves letting go.

The desperation we feel to get an answer is the biggest block to hearing that answer, because that desperation is based on the desire for a better situation, which is the tiny, mad idea and the voice of the ego. As long as it is engaged, it will drown out the quiet Voice for

God. The first step in hearing that quiet voice is accepting that you aren't in charge anyway. We think we want to hear the Voice because we want advice on the correct actions to take to lead us to something better; something that we want in this world, hopefully in the near future. What we really want is control. We *want* to know what to do, so our actions can lead to a happier dream. We want to be in charge! But the correct and best things will *always* happen in your life. Let go of your desire to know about them in advance. It doesn't matter! The desire to become psychic or hear the voices of your guides is just an extension of the desire of your ego to control what you can't control. You want to know the future? There is no future. You want to know what to do now? You will always do what leads you where your soul has already decided you want to go. Always. Do you want to be prepared for what may happen? Why? What could happen to you that could harm you or lead you to where you were not meant to be? What could the Holy Spirit present to you that He feels you are not prepared for? What would God allow you to face accept those things you need to face? No matter how psychic you are or not, you will always have exactly what you need for the journey you are on. Let go of the desire to control it or know it in advance. If you need advance knowledge, you will get it in spite of yourself. All the help you will ever need will always be available to you.

You can certainly practice listening for the Holy Spirit, and that's a good thing to do because it means you are becoming more aware of your true nature. You practice by slowing down and calming down. Your mind needs to be quiet and as blank as possible, which is another way of saying that you need to keep your ego thoughts quiet. You have to let go of your desired outcome. You have to put your mind in a place that accepts a direction that is best for everyone involved. It must be based on love. When you don't listen to the Holy Spirit and you make decisions that lead you in the ego's direction, that choice still teaches you what you need to know by teaching you what not to do.

There is one more absolutely vital piece of information about accessing the Holy Spirit's guidance; when you are asking for His

Chapter 10 – *Guidance*

guidance and doing your best to consistently ask for and follow that guidance, you are no longer responsible for your decisions. That means that you will have nothing to feel guilty about! Please read this excerpt carefully.

> M26. 2. ⁶*The curriculum is highly individualized, and all aspects are under the Holy Spirit's particular care and guidance. ⁷Ask and He will answer. ⁸The responsibility is His, and He alone is fit to assume it. ⁹To do so is His function. ¹⁰To refer the questions to Him is yours. ¹¹Would you want to be responsible for decisions about which you understand so little? ¹²Be glad you have a Teacher Who cannot make a mistake. ¹³His answers are always right. ¹⁴Would you say that of yours?*
> *3. There is another advantage, -- and a very important one, -- in referring decisions to the Holy Spirit with increasing frequency. ²Perhaps you have not thought of this aspect, but its centrality is obvious. ³To follow the Holy Spirit's guidance is to let yourself be absolved of guilt. ⁴***It is the essence of the Atonement.*** ⁵**It is the core of the curriculum.*** ⁶The imagined usurping of functions not your own is the basis of fear. ⁷The whole world you see reflects the illusion that you have done so, making fear inevitable. ⁸To return the function to the One to Whom it belongs is thus the escape from fear. ⁹And it is this that lets the memory of love return to you. ¹⁰Do not, then, think that following the Holy Spirit's guidance is necessary merely because of your own inadequacies. ¹¹***It is the way out of hell for you.***

If you are on a spiritual path, you may think that you need to continue searching for the next method, the next healthy food, the newest teacher; that salvation or enlightenment or release from this world requires our striving for better methods and circumstances. But the truth is that we are being given everything we need to release ourselves from this world. Instead of wanting to know the future, use your energy to let go of the future and to accept the true purpose of this life, which is to give it all to God and to stop wanting to be in charge or to want anything else. Our only task is to forgive what comes into our lives, and our continuous searching for that next craze is actually hindering our progress.

The real progress comes when you let go of the striving, accept your life where you are right Now, and focus on changing your thinking. Allow yourself to be exactly where you are right Now. Be willing to accept life as it is Now! Focus on the task at hand, forgiving what's in front of you. Focus on the peace of God. You will always be shown the path you need to follow, and if you calmly expect to be shown, with perfect faith in the process, it will happen that much more easily.

If you are always being led to the perfect place, why should you work so hard to figure things out? If the place you are being led to doesn't seem perfect for you, that's because you are being led to a place you need to forgive. The next step is to trust that God is really there beside you. That is also known as faith, but faith is not a simple word; it is fundamental change in your attitude about life; a knowing in your heart that there is something real behind this life that you cannot currently see or hear. This is about firmly accepting the idea that God is always with you, and no matter what happens to you, you will always be in the perfect place. So, you must powerfully believe in God in a way that you haven't before.

Faith is not a casual ego word that means that you "hope" there is a God, or that you believe in God but you don't deserve His help, or any number of other watered-down versions of your commitment to another, better idea of life. Faith is all-in. No doubts. No fears. No backtracking. No mind games. You are now willing to take the leap of faith that says God will always take care of you if you let go of trying to take care of yourself. That is not an easy thing to do. It starts as an intellectual decision but it must be solidified in your thinking by application. Our faith has to become more valuable to us than the fears and doubts we so love.

If and when you do start getting those advance answers about your life, the first responder will probably be your ego. The ego's voice is the loudest, and it needs to stand up for itself first. Let that first answer go and wait for another, quieter answer. If you get a second answer, then feel it for kindness, love and peace. If the second answer calls for anger, violence or pain for anyone, then it cannot come from God. If you get an answer you just aren't sure about, but seems positive and does not harm anyone, follow it.

The emotions you feel are also very important when receiving guidance. They are your inner wisdom when you learn to trust them. The Holy Spirit uses your emotional response to show you that forgiveness is called for. He does not use it when He gives you intuitive guidance. The Holy Spirit is always serenely peaceful. If you feel you are receiving inner guidance but it is accompanied by fear or any feeling that's not just a pure "knowing," then it is likely an ego response. The guidance of your ego is usually very emotional. The Holy Spirit may not give you obvious answers, but you will always be led to the correct and best answer, as long as you believe you will. Even if you don't believe it, you are always being directed. It's up to you to follow that direction or not. Becoming more intuitive should not be thought of as a goal; it is a side effect of becoming closer to God and your real self. The solution to using your intuition, and to all other problems, lies in your acceptance of God's presence.

No Decisions

Everything you need will come to you, so stop *needing* poverty and anger and sickness and control. The only decision is right Now; God or the ego. When you start forgiving everyone and everything in a real way, you will also start to see how trifling all of your desires have been. Your desire for answers from the Holy Spirit will become much less important as you realize that you are already being safely guided. Your desire for the things you thought you wanted won't seem nearly as important, and your ability to choose will become much easier. If you already know that you are being given what you need at every moment, and you are being shown what you need to forgive, why do you need to know anything ahead of time? Your only real job is to stop mis-creating, mis-choosing, so you don't see more negative things in your life. It's simply about changing your mind.

This entire process is all a matter of how much importance you put on this life, versus how much you want to give it up. It is as easy or as difficult as you choose it to be.

You will also slowly begin to see the decision-making process from another angle, when you can wrap your head around the idea that as long as you are choosing, you don't know who you are. Making a choice means you are engaging your ego mind and you don't know what to do. Choice is uncertainty. When you become Who you really are, there will be no choices to make because knowledge will replace all uncertainty and you will simply know, without choice being involved. If you keep seeking better and better ways to get answers, you are missing the point. You have the answers. You are God. You just need to let go of the ego's version of decision-making, which is what most of us use most the time.

Dropping Away

So, if you're on that spiritual path and trying to see within yourself who you are and what you should do, is it OK to swear? What about drinking or smoking or eating fast food or hunting or taking sticky notes from work or telling off-color jokes? Are these minor infractions OK? Are they even infractions? At what point have we crossed the line? If we are aware that this is a dream, does any of this really matter, since it's nothing? The short answer is, stop worrying about it. As we evolve, our behavior changes naturally. Certain things drop away from us because they no longer serve us. Most of us don't murder other people anymore. I suppose some of us may have stopped killing because it's just so hard to get away with it, and then there's all that blood and stuff. But other people have stopped killing because they realize it no longer serves them.

When you come to a point in your personal evolution where you understand that killing someone doesn't make the problem go away, you will simply not do it. You will understand not that killing is an error, but that killing another person would only be a reinforcement of your belief in the importance of this world and its drama, and that person's death would only be your own false validation that ending a physical life solves a problem that you have

Chapter 10 – *Guidance*

made up in your mind and also, that one day, you will have to experience that same attitude from another person, directed towards you, for the purpose of helping you see the error in your thinking.

In other words, as we evolve, we learn. We don't "choose" not to kill, so much as the idea of killing just falls away from our thinking as we learn to take full responsibility for Who we are and to recognize our True selves. This is the same for every act we engage in, including all of the behaviors I mentioned at the beginning. You will stop telling off-color jokes when you naturally begin imagining yourself as the person in the joke. You will stop swearing when you can feel the energy those words carry that all of society has imposed on them, in spite of your own previous belief that *you* may have overcome that energy, and also how ineffective those words are at providing quality communication. Other words simply work better, and you will stop swearing naturally when you feel the desire for a higher quality communication.

If you give up something you like because you feel it is hindering your spiritual progress, you are essentially sacrificing it. You will know in your heart that you still want to hang onto it, and you will subtly resent God and yourself for making you give it up. God never demands sacrifice and your gesture will probably not work. A better way might be to first examine your behavior and ask yourself if this is really something that is serving you and if it is something you would like to keep. If not, let yourself give it up because you really want to and let it fall away naturally and easily.

All of the sacrifices demanded by all the religions of the world and all of the dictates by religious leaders to give up certain behaviors will ultimately come to nothing, simply because a sacrifice is the giving up of something you want. No guns or edicts or any control by parents or dictators can change your desires, and God's law of creation guarantees that your deeply held desires always be given you, even if it is to experience them so you can see that they do not serve you. After all, that is precisely why we're here.

Another behavior I have seen demonstrated among seekers; I have come across some Course students who believe that because they understand that this life is a dream, that they can do anything they want, as long as they keep in mind that it's just a dream. They feel they can eat decadent, non-nutritious food, or judge others, as long as they remember they're only eating dream food and judging someone's ego and not their true spirit. They can swear or commit what they used to consider to be minor sins but because they are now aware of their context, and they now know that these actions and thoughts aren't important or real, they also aren't worth worrying about or correcting.

Unfortunately, this misses the whole point of the Course. The Course maintains that the solution to escaping the illusion is an all or nothing affair. Believing that you can eat anything you want implies that your eating habits are based on your desires, and those desires are caused by ego thoughts. That's perfectly OK to do, but what they neglect to understand is that these behaviors are still based on those ego desires, hiding behind self-righteousness. The point isn't simply to *know* that life isn't important; it's to *experience* life as unimportant. The Course is not a lesson of intellectual knowledge; it is a lesson in experiential knowledge.

Desires change as we evolve. As you evolve, you will find it more difficult to eat red meat, and sugar and pasta and other heavy foods, simply because your body will be vibrating at a different rate and you will not crave those things anymore. All conflict in all areas of your life will fall away as you become nearer to God and who you really are.

What do you want?

The real surprise in the search for God and the spiritual path many are following is that we don't really want to wake up, as I mentioned before. This is something we all need to examine honestly. Do you really want to let go of your humanity? Many of us are so lost in the game that we don't even know that the game has a goal. We want to find our purpose in this world by becoming more loving or compassionate or present or kind or some other characteristic. And that's not a bad thing, but it is only the beginning. Many of us pretend we are trying to wake up but don't really want to because that would mean we would actually have to face our ultimate fear, which is not being a special individual who drinks Chardonnay and wallows in self-pity and joins book clubs and buys and sells stock. We would have to give up this life that contains everything we cherish. We would have to look at ourselves honestly.

We say we want to be closer to God, but we really want the best of both worlds; the Chardonnay part and the God part. Except we aren't so sure about the God part because we don't really understand what that part is, and the wine part is ever so tasty. We know the God part is supposed to be good but it also seems very different from this mess of a life we have grown accustomed to. We all know we're going to get sick and die, and go through lots of crap while here on this globe, but we have accepted that. It's *our* crap. We hope our sicknesses and our deaths aren't too lingering or horrible but we like what we're familiar with and our egos don't know God and so we fear God and the process of awakening, whatever that is. We have even changed what the word "awakening" means because we want awakening to still include a "me" in some way, with all of our dreams and possessions.

So, we keep reading books and going to retreats and listening to other spiritual people talk about their spiritual experiences and garden pixies and astrological influences and Kombucha mushrooms and power vortices, and we settle back into a self-satisfied reverie, knowing that we have done all we can for today and so there is nothing more required until the next book or lecture. We never quite come to the realization that the only way we are ever going to actually wake up is when we stop looking outside of ourselves and actually change who we are. The Course tells us to do that by changing what we believe about ourselves and the world.

The problem with all of this is the very powerful force at work in our lives called the ego, which has decided the path we should take, and that path certainly doesn't include waking up. It includes the illusion of waking up, by playing a spiritual game of hide and seek. The ego, which is you for now, knows without doubt that waking up means your death. This is not something that is spoken out loud or acknowledged by many spiritual teachers or aspirants. But it is the reason most people never quite make it out of their earthly slumber. We don't want to wake up! We don't always like *this*—whatever it is— but we certainly want to maintain it. Waking up is a catchphrase, as foreign to humans as astrophysics or cellular biology. It is so far beyond our understanding or reach that it's not even on the radar for most of humanity. We are locked into the human being, and all of our efforts to awaken must include remaining much like we are now, only with special powers somehow, like superheroes in action movies.

The Path

We have a path that we have to follow, and it is a prolonged path designed by the ego to stretch out as long as possible, forever really, if the ego had its way. We began by simply falling asleep and finding ourselves within this remarkable dream with high fructose corn syrup and cool breezes and snowboarding. We are initially innocent and get caught up in it easily because it satisfies that tiny, mad idea of specialness and separation from God. We are bodies, and we love it! Then we begin to go through the various phases of awareness as humans. We start out slowly as we learn about this life, afraid to do too much except observe. We usually start out our journey with lifetimes as soft-spoken, don't-rock-the-boat people, many who live in small towns and villages, or working menial jobs, and we may spend lifetimes getting up the courage to stand up for ourselves against the smarter, older egos who are taking advantage of us.

As we go through this phase, we examine ourselves within the dream and come to realize we can have more than our small lives have gathered so far. We slowly build up courage as we get angrier and angrier at the way we are treated, as well as tempted by the wealth we see all around us. We work our way up through the ranks, lifetime after lifetime, learning the games, preparing to make our move. We can have the money, and we can have that power over others. With control over others, we can make them do our bidding with our power and also make ourselves lots of money which, for a time, seems to make many of our fears go away. We don't have to grovel anymore; we can push and force our way to happiness. The

Chapter 10 – *Guidance*

more we can control this dream, the less we fear. Our fears of being so alone and small are so great that we will do whatever is necessary to keep ourselves safe from all the threats out there, including our own thoughts.

Of course, we don't realize that what we are doing is just suppressing the fears, but that doesn't matter at all. We kill others and steal because the more stuff we can get, the happier we will be. We build walls and moats to keep our stuff safe and make weapons that are always a little bigger than the last weapons we made because they keep making better weapons and better armor. They want our stuff as badly as we want theirs. Over many lifetimes, we aggressively assert ourselves, push others farther away, and try harder and harder to control all the things that are important to us; all the things that seem to allay our fears.

Eventually, that fighting and anger wears us down so much that we feel compelled to move beyond that desperation, and we enter another phase of trying to see the dream a bit more kindly. We still want all of the money and we really like all of the stuff we can buy with it, and we are still afraid, but now we address our fears a little differently. We begin to see the beauty of this world, and so we turn our fears toward more positive pursuits. We start to use the world in a slightly better way, in spite of the fact that we are still terrified and lost in our own desires. So, after the long trip through the ranks of power, we loosen our grip, and we become a little more creative in some way.

We have exhausted our desire for overt killing and stealing for protection, so we simply continue killing and stealing a little more creatively. We may involve ourselves in a more shared lifestyle that includes other people but a huge undercurrent of very sick beliefs still drives us, but now, we acquire money and power more cleverly because we are still afraid of everything out there. We still equate stuff with happiness because stuff is all we know. We may become store owners or artisans or lawyers or one of many other professions. Our interests shift over lifetimes from one thing to another because our egos keep finding the next thing for us and hope that we latch onto something that holds our interest for as long possible as we lose interest in the previous thing. We become foodies, and pill popping health fanatics, experts in a certain field, accomplished scientists or musicians or athletes or speakers. We collect things; Cabbage Patch dolls, Beanie Babies, Pez dispensers, Tibetan tapestries, crystal vases or silver tea sets or fine art. We try our hand at any number of fun and compelling trades, all the while stuffing down into our subconscious minds the guilt and fears and evil we know ourselves to be.

Throughout all of these phases, the idea of a god pops up now and then. We examine it and join religions and other groups to see how the idea fits. Most of the time, a god concept is just another ego distraction to immerse ourselves into, instead of an actual endgame. We pretend it works, and we may even participate in these groups more formally. But our ideas of a god are still just like our collection of antique snuff boxes; it's fun until it stops working because ultimately, it makes no sense.

Nothing on this earth works, and ultimately, everything makes no sense. When it stops making sense, it is then the ego's job to find the next thing for you to focus on, to keep you as distracted as possible from ever finding anything real or true.

There will finally come a time when you get to a point where nothing is working for you anymore, and the ego is starting to get frustrated and scared. It is a point we must all come to in our vast series of lives. It is the point where you actually slow down and start asking yourself some real questions. You become a seeker. The problem with this phase of your life is that none of the answers are going to make any sense. It's going to get more frustrating and painful. You have always tried various types of mind-altering substances throughout your journey of lifetimes, but now, you may turn to them in earnest. Suicide is also still a distinct possibility, as it has been in most of the previous phases.

This phase will lead to a deep questioning of everything that you cherished. There will be no other way to see it except as meaningless, and that will most likely rankle you mightily. God or Neil deGrasse Tyson may be blamed. All manner of philosophy must come into question. All things will be examined and reexamined until you stumble upon something that works. Then surprisingly, that and the next thing will also cease to work and you will continue to stumble in the dark until you realize there is something beyond this external life. There is something much more.

Near the end, after all of the degradation, power, fun, frustration, searching and striving, you must eventually come to the realization there is nothing left but for the ego to die, because as everything on earth has proved itself to be meaningless, at last, so has the ego. The problem is, it seems that the ego is the one who must make this decision. So, the ego must be its own executioner, because it seems that we, who believe ourselves to be ego, must now decide to kill ourselves. We have already gone through that suicidal phase and realize killing the body doesn't work, and we really don't like the idea of dying on any level, and so the ego smiles a deep-down secret smile, knowing that it is simply not capable of declaring its own end.

This begins another new phase of finding the "real" answers, which aren't real at all, but they are still necessary to pursue, so you will eventually see them for what they aren't. Now, you become an earnest seeker. You find a guru or a book or a movement or a group and you get together and sing and share, but eventually your guru turns out to be an axe murdering heroin addict, and so then you move on to another, better guru, better book, better group, better movement and sing in a different key and share some more. This phase can last a long time. The ego loves it because this is the time when you think you are finally moving ahead. You have found the answers to life after all of that trial and error, and all those wasted lives of standing on 5th Avenue with a megaphone exhorting people to accept Jesus into their hearts, or handing out pamphlets denying God and promoting your new, cool cult of the Golden-Beaked Raven or the Grand Exalted Crystal-Dwelling Sun Bear. All that time, you now realize, you may have just been treading spiritual water, even though you were also learning what didn't work in spite of yourself, and you were avoiding the final decision you must make; you must let the ego die.

This is the point where all of the gurus, and teachers and books and retreats must face their truth. This is the point where something higher than the ego must step in, something higher than what you think you are must come in and make the final call. All of that teaching and reading and striving and coal-walking and nasal cleansing was all just more crap devised by the ego to stay alive for another lifetime or five. It's time to let it all go. It's time to let go of the external teachers and finally trust something deep inside you that doesn't answer to your name and social security number. It's the final release of all of the things you have spent thousands of years releasing, and it is the most difficult release of all, because you still hold onto the idea that this thing you are letting go might be you, and that scares the daylights out of you. But it's not you, even though it seems to look and smell like you. It is the final and true leap of faith, out of darkness into light, from illusion to truth. You will be gone, but it will be just fine. You hope.

You can take *A Course in Miracles* in one of two ways. You can see it as the next spiritual book, and read it and go to group meetings and study it and share your feelings about it on social media, or you can use it to shut off your ego. You probably won't be able to do both, because these paths seem to be mutually exclusive for the most part, not because you can't do both but because they come from different places inside you. If you need external support for your journey, you will always get it, but it's rare to find that support from people who have already made the trip and awakened, so you have to settle for those who are still lost and walking in circles just like you, and want you to stick around because they don't know any better. Your ego will certainly do everything it can to convince you that you can participate in a group setting and still be independent enough not be influenced by those around you who are merely the water-treaders, doing whatever they can do to stay stuck in their tepid, changeless lagoons.

A Course in Miracles is a self-study course. It states in the preface that, "It emphasizes application rather than theory, and experience rather than theology." And also, "Without the practical application the Workbook provides, the Text would remain largely a series of abstractions which would hardly suffice to bring about the thought reversal at which the Course aims." The Course stresses doing something, and the cessation of jabbering about it, as I'm doing here. It is time now to admit your complete responsibility for your life, and to wake up from a self-imposed dream of specialness and separation.

Hear This!

We will all see synergies and coincidences, good and bad luck, inconsistencies, surprises and the mundane. This is just life going by in the usual way, but we will usually ignore the beautiful purpose of everything or, for a few seconds, we may see the miraculous in the interesting ways everything seems to unfold. The entire time, throughout your life, without forcing you to learn, the Holy Spirit is whispering in your ear to let go of the negative things you see by forgiving them, and whispering to you that you are God. One day, you will hear that voice, by your own choice, and you will remember that day as the day a miracle happened in your life. The healing has begun.

We are reminded that we are God by seeing the things that do not work in our dream. We will see them over and over again, relentlessly, until we finally start to see the futility of fighting life, until the day we understand the miracle of letting go. Only then will we begin to know who we really are. There is no reason for life on earth other than God's intention to help us discover what we already know. We have to peel away the layers of black tape that have obscured our knowledge of who we are. You are God. You are not human. You are not male/female, white/black, rich/poor, healthy/sick, or any other description that you think may apply to you. You are a pure and perfect thought in the mind of God. You *are* God!

As long you see this world as real, it will be impossible to let it go, because you will resist having to mourn your loss of it. Every moment you let go of this life, even for a second, you are allowing a miracle to enter into your life. Miracles are able to collapse time, to make the past disappear, and to heal. If you let go of the past, the dream falls apart. The Course states that miracles are habits and should be involuntary. In other words, when you start changing your mind about who you are through forgiveness, and letting go of your control, life can flow through you, not blocked by the black tape of your misguided ego thoughts. Miracles are the moments when you allow yourself to see through the veil. Real life is a miracle and miracles are not subject to the laws of physics or this world.

Dying

Before you can have a different life, you must die to this one, figuratively, of course. All change requires letting go of what you used to have and be. It will likely be a tremendous loss, depending on your love for who you are and what you have. But God doesn't ask for sacrifice, so you cannot truly let go until you are ready to let it fall away of its own accord. That's why people usually don't look for God until everything they used to love has stopped working for them. The spiritual journey is not simply dying to your self and discovering God; it is dying over and over again to the beliefs you once held. Each belief you have that conflicts with God's will must be relinquished. Each belief you release is another small death. Each small death is a step of discovery along the way to your true nature. Seeing this life as a dream is dying to the old self you used to know. Letting go of all you have worked so hard can be a painful death. This is where you can re-interpret that idea of what it means to be born again, as some Christians believe. Being born again might mean that in every moment you are alive, you are choosing to die to what you were before, and becoming something new. Every lapse you have back into this world will require yet another death, and another rebirth. Letting go of your control over your earthly life is a painful death. Letting go of judgment and anger is another. But they are also powerful rebirths.

Waking up to the Truth can only mean letting go of the lies. But the lies are who we thought we were for so very long. Letting go of them is a mourning process, and you will feel it when you embrace the ideas of the Course. There will be a lot of resistance from your ego, as I said, because your ego does not want to die, but that is exactly what is happening. When you finish digesting the ideas in the Course, it will be time for a huge decision in your life. You will sit and stare out from those eyes and wonder what your next move will be. You might feel that it doesn't matter if you stay in your job or not. It doesn't matter whether you water the plants, or eat healthy food, or see a doctor, because your life has become meaningless. You will accept that you are dreaming, and life has lost its meaning. This is the moment to tell yourself that what you can do *now* is the most important thing you have ever done. Stay in your job, water the plants, eat a healthy snack, visit the doc, and then start to change your thinking one day at a time, one second at a time. Start listening for guidance. Start forgiving. Start to wake up.

> *Lesson 243: I will judge nothing that occurs.*
> *"Father, today I leave creation free to be itself."*

God offers us peace but this peace is not the peace you may currently be aware of. You cannot tell the ego about peace or letting go because the ego has already decided what those words mean. True peace of God is a peace beyond human understanding. It is the absence of any fear or stress. There is no running background monologue about your credit card bills or your work or your children. Like every human, I thought I had an idea of what the word "peace" meant for over 40 years. When I began to experience it in my meditations, I realized that I didn't at all. And I still realize that I haven't truly experienced it yet; just a taste of what it must truly be, and it is remarkable and words cannot describe it. The ego cannot learn what it thinks it already knows. Peace is not something you practice; it's something you experience when you give your life back to God. It is the same with gratitude. You can practice gratitude, but even though we all have a sense of what it is, you will truly only feel real gratitude when you begin to see the results of your seeking, and it will be so powerful, it will bring you humbly and gratefully to your knees.

There is much more to the Course, as there is to life. It is a rich book, filled with the scary ways we manipulate ourselves into believing in this life and all of the rotten things we do to each other, and then justify in the name of the ego. It is beautiful poetry and profound psychology. It is full of hidden treasures and complex ideas. It is insightful and kind, and it never waivers from its pure message of love. It describes the God that, deep in our hearts, we have all hoped would be there for us, but we were never able to find in any book or religion or teacher before. The true characteristics of God are lightyears beyond human characteristics and understanding, and the Truth scares us with its immensity.

We are afraid of everything and so, we feel we must defend ourselves against it all. Does that represent a god you want to spend eternity with? You are loved, and you are love. There is something infinitely better than this life, waiting for us to decide to live it. It must be our choice, for it can never be forced on us. It can only be offered. Let's all choose something better than hurting each other, living in fear and lack and struggle and pain, ending in death. Let us all choose life and never-ending love.

Chapter 11 – The Two Worlds

W-249.1. Forgiveness paints a picture of a world where suffering is over, loss becomes impossible and anger makes no sense. ²Attack is gone, and madness has an end. ³What suffering is now conceivable? ⁴What loss can be sustained? ⁵The world becomes a place of joy, abundance, charity and endless giving. ⁶It is now so like to Heaven that it quickly is transformed into the light that it reflects. ⁷And so the journey which the Son of God began has ended in the light from which he came.

"I am incredulous that people would spend real time—valuable time—doing much of anything but seeking this thing that somehow fell into my lap. It's that amazingly wonderful. Oh, all these stupid words: *wonderful, amazingly, valuable, incredulous*. It's all I can do to keep myself from running up and down all the streets and shrieking, at nobody in particular, *Your life is not at all what you imagine. You think you have good times? You think you have love? You ain't seen nothing yet.*

I want to tell people—to take them by the arms and plead with them, *Drop everything. Take all the effort you've been putting into the stuff of regular life and put it into this.*

And they would do that, every single person would do that, if they knew what *this* was like—if they knew what they were missing. The

trouble is, they are unable to imagine it. Which is why I ache to share the reality of it. However impossible a task that may be."
–Jan Frazier, When Fear Falls Away

There is something incredible going on here. Even if you are a student of *A Course in Miracles*, I believe most of you do not realize the immensity of this incredible plan. There is something going on here behind the scenes that makes this world the polar opposite of what virtually everyone on earth is doing here. We are living small lives of tedium and insignificance, no matter what our status here may be, instead of being aware of this remarkable Atonement plan that is mentioned countless times in the Course.

You are here for a totally different reason than you think, and this world does not function the way we have all convinced ourselves it does. But because most people are not aware this, the Holy Spirit is quietly waiting for you to get it. In the meantime, your life will go on as you choose, full of chaos, uncertainty, stress, fear and missteps and pain, as you continue living the life of a human being, making more mistakes that need to be corrected, in a seemingly endless cycle of suffering and disappointment. There will come a point when you will take a breath, step back from this life, and weep with happiness when you realize that this process is the most amazing thing that you could ever imagine, and you have been totally missing it for lifetime after lifetime in your vain pursuit of happiness on an earthly level.

> T-15.I.1. Can you imagine what it means to have no cares, no worries, no anxieties, but merely to be perfectly calm and quiet all the time? ²Yet that is what time is for; to learn just that and nothing more.

In the excerpt at the beginning of this chapter, Jan Frazier is describing the incredible feeling of being awake. She is not a student of *A Course in Miracles*, but what she describes is beautifully illustrated in the Course as the Real World. This real world has been described by many people over the centuries, including some people currently alive in physical bodies like Ms. Frazier, who are able to give a tremendously clear idea of what this world is like. When you awaken from this dream, you will still see what appears to be the same world pass before your eyes, but your perception will change from night to day. It is a world where judgment is not possible. It is a world without drama or stress or anger or striving or desire or urgency of any kind. It is a world where you will naturally *know* what to do without question in every circumstance, because you will not be making your own decisions; you will be making them with the incredible flow of knowledge that washes over and includes everything, called the Holy Spirit.

There is no sickness or separation, and only loving thoughts are thought. There is no death, not because the body doesn't die, but because it is seen for what it truly is; a temporary, unimportant container that, without pain, is simply laid aside at some point. It is the earth as we know it now, but without the guilt, fear or suffering. There is no suffering, not because others don't suffer; but because suffering is seen for what it truly is: a call for help. God created the real world in response to this false world we made. God's version of our world is a perfect version of earth, and it is where we will stay for a short time before we move on. It is our gentle transition to the majesty of heaven. It is the world where we are awake from the illusion we are currently living. We will see nothing false anymore because we are living within the Truth.

This chapter is about the two worlds. The one in which most of us now live is an illusion based on a tiny, mad idea dreamed by the Son of God. To replace it, and help us in our transition from this phony place, God has created another version of our world, where we can live for a short time after we awaken, while still within a separate body. While awake in the body, we do not perceive our separateness. We do not feel fear or stress of any kind. Our perception is healed, so we see the Truth and nothing else.

> *W-pII.8.1. The real world is a symbol, like the rest of what perception offers. ²Yet it stands for what is opposite to what you made. ³Your world is seen through*

eyes of fear, and brings the witnesses of terror to your mind. ⁴The real world cannot be perceived except through eyes forgiveness blesses, so they see a world where terror is impossible, and witnesses to fear can not be found.

W-pII.8.2. The real world holds a counterpart for each unhappy thought reflected in your world; a sure correction for the sights of fear and sounds of battle which your world contains. ²The real world shows a world seen differently, through quiet eyes and with a mind at peace. ³Nothing but rest is there. ⁴There are no cries of pain and sorrow heard, for nothing there remains outside forgiveness. ⁵And the sights are gentle. ⁶Only happy sights and sounds can reach the mind that has forgiven itself.

W-pII.8.3. What need has such a mind for thoughts of death, attack and murder? ²What can it perceive surrounding it but safety, love and joy? ³What is there it would choose to be condemned, and what is there that it would judge against? ⁴The world it sees arises from a mind at peace within itself. ⁵No danger lurks in anything it sees, for it is kind, and only kindness does it look upon.

W-pII.8.4. The real world is the symbol that the dream of sin and guilt is over, and God's Son no longer sleeps. ²His waking eyes perceive the sure reflection of his Father's Love; the certain promise that he is redeemed. ³The real world signifies the end of time, for its perception makes time purposeless.

W-pII.8.5. The Holy Spirit has no need of time when it has served His purpose. ²Now He waits but that one instant more for God to take His final step, and time has disappeared, taking perception with it as it goes, and leaving but the truth to be itself. ³That instant is our goal, for it contains the memory of God. ⁴And as we look upon a world forgiven, it is He Who calls to us and

Chapter 11 – The Two Worlds

comes to take us home, reminding us of our Identity which our forgiveness has restored to us.

My Fake World

I'm writing this from my fake world. I made it all up. And it is designed by me but managed by the Holy Spirit so you can't get in unless we have something to learn from each other, whether you're my significant other or the guy in front of me who is driving way too slowly. In my world, which I alone can see, the Holy Spirit is trying to show me some things that I believe but that I may not admit to, or be aware of, on a very deep level. Virtually all of it just isn't true, and because my beliefs make my world, I am living in a world that isn't true. I can choose to ignore Him if I wish and continue to live in my strange, badly designed, poorly functioning world. There are over 7 billion worlds here on earth. My world is exactly as it should be. If I see anything in my world that causes me any stress or conflict, I have just forgotten that I invited it in, and everyone and everything is merely doing exactly what I asked them to do. They are all my guests and my saviors, even though it may be difficult for me to see them that way. They are my saviors because they are giving me the opportunity to see myself in them, forgive us both, and erase the incorrect thinking. When I finally see my world as perfect, then it will no longer be a dream of suffering, and I will be seeing correctly. At that point, my will is the same as God's and my world will then match the Real World He created and laid gently over this one, unknown and unseen until now, but always there. Thank you to all of you who have entered my world and helped me see more clearly Who I really am. All I can say for certain is that the fellow who drives too slowly in front of me is extremely wealthy, because each day he is driving a different car.

Which world do you live in now? Which world do you want to live in? For you have chosen many worlds at once. Do you choose to live in a world where war can be justified? Is corruption acceptable if it serves a higher purpose? Do you believe it's OK for individuals or governments or institutions to torture or control others with their will? Do you believe that if someone does something evil, they should be punished? Is pain or jail or hardship justified if it comes to those who deserve it? Do you believe in justifiable anger, or accidents, or luck? Maybe you choose a world where murder is justified in certain circumstances? Do you believe that innocent, well-intentioned judgments of others are a part of the world? Do you believe the body is important? Do you value what society values? Is it OK if someone steals something, especially if they are deserving of it, or are in hardship, or if the item won't be missed? Do you believe that your actions make your life? Do you believe God is absent or flawed or vengeful?

Virtually anything that you believe in your heart is the world you have made. If you believe in a world where these things, and any other things—good or bad, are acceptable on any level, then this is the world you inhabit, and these are the gifts your world will offer you and all those who share your beliefs. It matters not whether you are the giver of your world's gifts today, for tomorrow, you will be the receiver of the same gifts. It is the world that surrounds you and holds you in its embrace, because it is the world that you have made with your beliefs. It is your world, your choice. It is a world you made from many hidden beliefs, tacitly approving of pain, suffering, anger and sadness. If you believe those things are OK for others to receive, then you believe in those things for yourself as well.

When the Holy Spirit took over this world, He gave *no one* the power to hurt you or have any control over you at all. You are not subject to illness of any kind, nor can you be a victim of deceit or any injury. No one can betray you or steal from you. No one has that ability. If any of these things happen to you, it is because you have chosen to experience them. You have not just allowed them, but chosen them, and now you have the single purpose of learning that they are not true. You made them up and you brought them into your world, your experience, and you can get rid of them by changing what you believe about yourself, by forgiving yourself for believing in a world that simply isn't true.

There is another world. It is that one God created, and it sits quietly above the rest of the worlds that we have each made. It is the earth from the perspective of an awakened state. It is waiting for us to believe in it, so that it can become our temporary home by fully accepting it as true. I spoke previously of the blanket that God placed over the world when He created the Atonement, led by the Holy Spirit to help us through this mess that we made. As part of the Atonement plan, He included the Real World as part of that blanket that covers the entire illusion. It is right here, right in front of you, more real than the world you are living in now, and absolutely invisible to the ego. There are some people living in that Real World right now, and you may pass them on the street every day without knowing it. This world is not metaphorical, or merely a slight change in perspective; it is a radical, completely altered reality that is exactly as we now might imagine a perfect world created by God. The ego's world of illusion does not appear to change as far as the body's eyes and ears see and hear it. But in this real world, the body's senses are not the method of seeing and hearing any longer. The ego is all but gone. Only a tiny sliver of it remains; just enough to allow the body to function. All conflicts, pain and anger are perceived perfectly as calls for help and not of judgment. Sickness is not perceived, because only the perfection of Christ is seen in everyone.

The people who inhabit this real world live in a place that is not in conflict with God's will because they are living *in* God's will. They have let go of the ego and they exist with no conflict, in pure love. These people walk through life able to help the rest of us because they have direct access to the Voice for God, Who is the Holy Spirit. They have no need of a will of their own, because they have let it go and live the will of God. They are the Saints of God. They are the healed healers.

The path to this world has many names. In the Course, it is referred to as waking up, the Christ vision, healed perception, the birth of freedom, the forgiven world, the real world, knowledge, and the happy dream. In other belief systems, it has many other names. It is called enlightenment, the release of kundalini, samadhi, satori, moksha, nirvana, self-realization, jnana, and many others. The Course also refers to it as the Atonement, but the Atonement is also the process and principles used along the way to accomplish the end of the dream. It is a bridge that we all must, and will, cross.

Waking up from this dream is not an intellectual change in thinking or a better attitude, or an "Ah ha" moment, or comparable to an altered state of consciousness brought about by drugs or alcohol. It is not an intellectual awareness. It is an unbelievable, ineffable, permanent and massive transformation that is inconceivable to the ego, and unknown by anyone who is not enlightened. It is radically transformative and powerful and unworldly. It is the death of yourself as you now know yourself to be in all respects, and the birth of a new you in God. To attain it, you must want it. To want it, you have to stop wanting this life and this world. It is not a part-time hobby. It is not something that happens to you or something that you strive for; it is Who you already are. Once you awaken, it doesn't go away. Becoming enlightened is a natural unfoldment into the future you that is inevitable for each of us. It has already happened. To find it, you must merely change your mind about the Truth of it.

> *T-16.6.[6]Across the bridge it is so different! [2]For a time the body is still seen, but not exclusively, as it is seen here. [3]The little spark that holds the Great Rays within it is also visible, and this spark cannot be limited long to littleness. [4]Once you have crossed the bridge, the value of the body is so diminished in your sight that you will see no need at all to magnify it. [5]For you will realize that the only value the body has is to enable you to bring your brothers to the bridge with you, and to be released together there.*

I believe there are still many spiritual seekers and students of the Course who believe that their seeking will not result in anything tangible in this world. They are convinced that they will live one lifetime and get their reward in heaven when the body dies. This is a holdover from the indoctrination of religious thinking that has become part of who we believe ourselves to be. This is not what the Course says. This is not what people who are currently awake and alive on the planet say. This is not what enlightened masters have written for thousands of years. A profound change occurs in your life. It is what Jesus and Buddha and Krishna have all experienced and it is real, and most importantly, it is available to everyone. It is your transformation from a small, limited individual into the Son of God.

Those who have written of their waking experiences, no matter what their background, have all described a world that is impossible to imagine by anyone who still sleeps. It is a world where there is no "I" and everything can be perceived as part of One Thing, where nothing exists separate from anything else. Each human experiences enlightenment slightly differently simply because they are still human in some respect, and each carry with them the insignificant remnants of an ego, along with its nominal baggage to varying degrees, in order to continue functioning in a body. But once enlightenment has occurred, the learning is over and all further progression comes from God. It is the point when the body begins to heal naturally because all personal incorrect thinking has gone.

The Holy Spirit has no more negative symbols to present in the world of form, because all incorrect thinking is gone. It doesn't mean illness or injury is impossible; just much less likely, and it will not have any important affect. To use an old term, your karma has all been burned away. There is no more striving or stress or worry. There are only varying degrees of joy and contentment, and a sense that there is nothing left that needs to be done. What remains of each individual is directed by the Holy Spirit, even though many enlightened individuals do not use that name. The say "the flow" or "the presence" or "the current" or ideas to that effect. Many are compelled to teach while they remain for a short time on earth. Others will come back for another lifetime for various reasons; either to complete the waking process or to continue to help humankind evolve. Most will simply leave this dream forever, content to move forward into the bliss of God.

This is why we are here. There is no other reason. It is our only function. There is no striving for money or fame or attention or any other worldly goal. Those are the ego's functions, and you must give them up before they can be replaced by your true goals. Giving up the ego's goals is not sacrifice. As long as it feels that you are sacrificing something you want, you are not ready yet to wake up. The things you think you want will fall away from you naturally when it is their time to go, and you will let them go gladly as you see their unimportance. The end of this world of suffering is the end of your belief in it.

Three Levels

There are three very general levels of understanding that each of us must experience. The first is where the vast majority of people are; it is living in a fear-based world in which the belief that actions cause results is the persistent paradigm, that the problems of the world are addressed through taking actions to solve what appears to be in front of you. This is the level of ultimate frustration, where randomness, chance and luck seem to reign. Stumbling through life without certainty or context or understanding.

The second level is when you understand that there is something much more profound going on here, which is the Atonement plan that God has laid over the earth and given to the Holy Spirit. It doesn't matter how you discovered it or what name you call it. This is a rare level experienced by a very small percentage of people, and a revelation in personal thinking. This level will bring a new understanding in which you now see that you alone are responsible for everything that happens in your life, and that you can change the world only by changing your thinking about the world. This second level is the intellectual understanding of what is true.

The third level is the Happy Dream. It is also called enlightenment, the borderland, Christ's vision, the journey's end. It is the manifestation of the second level; the actual experience of a life lived in Truth. This is when you are still in your body, but you encounter this earth, this life, this universe, in a totally transformed way as the real world. It is you without your ego. It is you with healed perception. It is you without being you.

> *T-17.II.4. ⁴The perception of the real world will be so short that you will barely have time to thank God for it. ⁵For God will take the last step swiftly, when you have reached the real world and have been made ready for Him.*

After a time living in the real world, God then comes and picks you up by the scruff of your neck and lifts you into heaven, there to stay forever.

There are many people alive on earth today who are living this Happy Dream. Many of them don't even know what it is, or why it happened to them, or what it means or what comes next, because enlightenment is different for everyone at this point. There are still remnants of the ego, but, at this point according to the Course, your work is done and the rest of the work is not done by you but by the Holy Spirit. And when we have all come to see Who we really are, when the dream is over, the real world will disappear back into God.

Here are some examples of descriptions of being or becoming awake:

"One morning during the Christmas of 1937 I sat cross-legged in a small room in a little house on the outskirts of the town of Jammu, the winter capital of the Jammu and Kashmir State in northern India. I was meditating with my face towards the window on the east through which the first gray streaks of the slowly brightening dawn fell into the room. Long practice had accustomed me to sit in the same posture for hours at a time without the least discomfort, and I sat breathing slowly and rhythmically, my attention drawn towards the crown of my head, contemplating an imaginary lotus in full bloom, radiating light.

I sat steadily, unmoving and erect, my thoughts uninterruptedly centered on the shining lotus, intent on keeping my attention from wandering and bringing it back again and again whenever it moved in any other direction. The intensity of concentration interrupted my breathing; gradually it slowed down to such an extent that at times it was barely perceptible. My whole being was so engrossed in the contemplation of the lotus that for several minutes at a time I lost touch with my body and surroundings. During such intervals I used to feel as if I were poised in midair, without any feeling of a body around me. The only object of which I was aware was a lotus of brilliant color, emitting rays of light. The experience has happened to many people who practice meditation in any form regularly for a sufficient length of time, but what followed on that fateful morning in my case, changing the whole course of my life and outlook, has happened to few.

During one such spell of intense concentration, I suddenly felt a strange sensation below the base of my spine, at the place touching the seat, while I sat cross-legged on a folded blanket spread on the floor. The sensation was so extraordinary and so pleasing that my attention was forcibly drawn towards it. The moment my attention was thus unexpectedly withdrawn from the point on which it was focused, the sensation ceased.

Thinking it to be a trick played by my imagination to relax the tension, I dismissed the matter from my mind and brough my attention back to the point from which it wandered. Again I fixed it on the lotus, and as the image grew clear and distinct at the top of my head, again the sensation occurred. This time I tried to maintain the fixity of my attention and succeeded for a few seconds. But the sensation extending upwards grew so intense and was so extraordinary, as compared to anything I had experienced before, that in spite of myself my mind went towards it, and at that very moment it again disappeared. I was now convinced that something unusual had happened for which my daily practice of concentration was probably responsible.

I read glowing accounts, written by learned men, of great benefits resulting from concentration, and of the miraculous powers acquired by yogis through such exercises. My heart began to beat wildly, and I found it difficult to bring my attention to the required degree of fixity. After a while I grew composed and was soon as deep in meditation as before. When completely immersed I again experienced the sensation, but this time, instead of allowing my mind to leave the point where I had fixed it, I maintained a rigidity of attention throughout. The sensation again extended upwards, growing in intensity, and I felt myself wavering; but with a great effort I kept my attention centered round the lotus.

Suddenly, with a roar like that of a waterfall, I felt a stream of liquid light entering my brain through the spinal cord.

Entirely unprepared for such a development, I was completely taken by surprise, but regaining self-control instantaneously, I remained in the same posture, keeping my mind on the point of concentration. The illumination grew brighter and brighter, the roaring louder. I experienced a rocking sensation and then felt myself slipping out of my body, entirely enveloped in a halo of light.

It is impossible to describe the experience accurately. I felt the point of consciousness that was myself growing wider, surrounded by waves of light. It grew wider and wider, spreading outward while the body, normally the immediate object of its perception, appeared to have receded into the distance until I became entirely unconscious of it. I was now all consciousness, without any outline, without any idea of a corporeal appendage, without any feeling or sensation coming from the senses, immersed in a sea of light simultaneously conscious and aware of every point, spread out, as it were, in all directions without any barrier or material obstruction.

I was no longer myself, or to be more accurate, no longer as I knew myself to be, a small point of awareness confined in a body, but instead was a vast circle of consciousness in which the body was but a point, bathed in light and in a state of exaltation and happiness impossible to describe.

After some time, the duration of which I could not judge, the circle began to narrow down; I felt myself contracting, becoming smaller and smaller, until I again became dimly conscious of the outline of my body, then more clearly; and as I slipped back to my normal condition, I became suddenly aware of the noises in the street, felt again my arms and legs and head, and once more became my narrow self in touch with body and surroundings."

–Gopi Krishna, *Living with Kundalini, The Autobiography of Gopi Krishna*

"Imagine this: Whatever has weighed on you suddenly no longer weighs. It may still be there, a fact in your life, but it has no mass, no gravity. All that has ever troubled you is now just a feature of the landscape, like a tree, a passing cloud. Every bit of emotional and mental turmoil has ceased: the entire burden, some form of which has been with you as long as you can remember. A thing familiar as your closest friend—as much a part of you as the language you speak, the color of your skin—is utterly, inexplicably *gone*.

Into the startling emptiness flows a quiet joy that buoys you morning, noon and night, that goes everywhere you go, into any kind of circumstance, even into sleep. Everything you undertake happens effortlessly. You are happy, but for no reason. Nothing bothers you. You feel no stress. When a problem arises, you know what to do, you do it, and then you let it go. People who used to drive you crazy no longer do. While you feel compassion for others' suffering, you don't suffer yourself. Activities that used to be tedious are fun. You don't need therapy; you don't get bored, anxious, or moody. Except when needed for a task, your mind is at rest. Your life is entirely fulfilled—without your having to do anything to fulfill it. Because your equanimity is disconnected from anything in your outer life, you know that no matter what challenge you are handed—*for the rest of your life*—the peace will sustain. Never again will you be afraid, desperate, lonely. Whatever comes your way, this causeless joy will hold. Imagine it."

–Jan Frazier, *When Fear Falls Away*

"Ego-death as a means to no-self—abiding non-dual awareness—is what this journey is all about. That's the reason behind the devotion, the prayer, the meditation, the teachings, the renunciation. Anyone headed for truth is going to get there over the ego's dead body or not at all. There's no shortcut or easy way, no going under or around. The only way past the ego is through it, and the only way through it is with laser-like intent and a heart of stone. The caterpillar doesn't *become* a butterfly, it enters a death process that becomes the birth process of the butterfly. One thing doesn't become another thing. One thing ends and another begins."

Chapter 11 – *The Two Worlds*

–Jed McKenna, *Spiritual Enlightenment, The Damnedest Thing*

"The Presence is silent and conveys a state of peace that is the space in which and by which all is and has its existence and experience. It is infinitely gentle and yet like a rock. With it, all fear disappears. Spiritual joy occurs on a quiet level of inexplicable ecstasy. Because the experience of time stops, there is no apprehension or regret, no pain or anticipation; the source of joy is unending and ever-present. With no beginning or ending, there is no loss or grief or desire. Nothing needs to be done; everything is already perfect and complete. When time stops, all problems disappear; they are merely artifacts of a point of perception. As the Presence prevails, there is no further identification with the body or the mind. When the mind grows silent, the thought "I Am" also disappears, and Pure Awareness shines forth to illuminate what one is, was, and always will be, beyond all worlds and all universes, beyond time, and therefore without beginning or end."
–David R. Hawkins, *The Map of Consciousness Explained*

From *A Course in Miracles*...

> *T-17.II.1. Can you imagine how beautiful those you forgive will look to you? ²In no fantasy have you ever seen anything so lovely. ³Nothing you see here, sleeping or waking, comes near to such loveliness. ⁴And nothing will you value like unto this, nor hold so dear. ⁵Nothing that you remember that made your heart sing with joy has ever brought you even a little part of the happiness this sight will bring you. ⁶For you will see the Son of God. ⁷You will behold the beauty the Holy Spirit loves to look upon, and which He thanks the Father for. ⁸He was created to see this for you, until you learned to see it for yourself. ⁹And all His teaching leads to seeing it and giving thanks with Him.*

T-17.II.2. This loveliness is not a fantasy. ²It is the real world, bright and clean and new, with everything sparkling under the open sun. ³Nothing is hidden here, for everything has been forgiven and there are no fantasies to hide the truth. ⁴The bridge between that world and this is so little and so easy to cross, that you could not believe it is the meeting place of worlds so different. ⁵Yet this little bridge is the strongest thing that touches on this world at all. ⁶This little step, so small it has escaped your notice, is a stride through time into eternity, beyond all ugliness into beauty that will enchant you, and will never cease to cause you wonderment at its perfection.

T-17.II.4. The stars will disappear in light, and the sun that opened up the world to beauty will vanish. ²Perception will be meaningless when it has been perfected, for everything that has been used for learning will have no function. ³Nothing will ever change; no shifts nor shadings, no differences, no variations that made perception possible will still occur. ⁴The perception of the real world will be so short that you will barely have time to thank God for it. ⁵For God will take the last step swiftly, when you have reached the real world and have been made ready for Him.

T-17.II.6. All this beauty will rise to bless your sight as you look upon the world with forgiving eyes. ²For forgiveness literally transforms vision, and lets you see the real world reaching quietly and gently across chaos, removing all illusions that had twisted your perception and fixed it on the past. ³The smallest leaf becomes a thing of wonder, and a blade of grass a sign of God's perfection.

W-159.3. Christ's vision is a miracle. ²It comes from far beyond itself, for it reflects eternal love and the rebirth of love which never dies, but has been kept obscure.

³Christ's vision pictures Heaven, for it sees a world so like to Heaven that what God created perfect can be mirrored there. ⁴The darkened glass the world presents can show but twisted images in broken parts. ⁵The real world pictures Heaven's innocence.

W-pII.10.1. Christ's Second Coming gives the Son of God this gift: to hear the Voice for God proclaim that what is false is false, and what is true has never changed. ²And this the judgment is in which perception ends. ³At first you see a world that has accepted this as true, projected from a now corrected mind. ⁴And with this holy sight, perception gives a silent blessing and then disappears, its goal accomplished and its mission done.

Vigilance

If you're going to let go of this world and your vice-grip control over everything, it seems likely that you've got to find something else to latch onto to replace it. I hope this convinces you to some small degree that waking up to the real world is something worth striving for. The corollary to the idea of letting go is vigilance for God and His kingdom. This means regularly, continually, putting your trust in God rather than yourself, asking for guidance from the Holy Spirit, trusting something much bigger and more powerful than you are. Vigilance for God and His kingdom simply means that you focus on something beyond this life and this world, knowing it is there without having anything solid, at least for a while, to base that on.

The Holy Spirit has taken over control of this world and your life and made waking up to the real world our single purpose. *That's all we're here to do.* He has done it in a way that is so unobtrusive that the vast majority of humans have absolutely no idea about it. As the Son of God, we have the absolute right to believe this plan doesn't exist. But it is also available for us to tap into instantly and totally, if we are willing. There is, right now, beyond our comprehension, a massive support system that has been put in place for us, that functions quietly and all-powerfully, discreetly, and perfectly. It is a vast engine of assistance that is trying to get our attention, and it will never stop until it succeeds, and even then, it will continue to steer us, offer us all the guidance we need, until every single one of us awakens to the Truth of Who we really are.

Nothing your ego does makes any difference in your life. All it does is hinder your progress. Do you realize that nothing happens here on earth! *Nothing!* This isn't a real thing. The real Self of yours and mine is sitting serenely and permanently in God. How much effort do you want to continue putting into nothing at all? Every decision you make without the Holy Spirit means nothing. It will come to nothing. The only thing that happens here is a fake dream character flailing around for a while and then disappearing back into God when he finally gets it.

> *T14.IV.5. [2]Your function here is only to decide against deciding what you want, in recognition that you do not know. [3]How, then, can you decide what you should do? [4]Leave all decisions to the One Who speaks for God, and for your function as He knows it.*

Most of the people on the planet do not have any inkling that there might be something else going on here, or even consider that it's possible. I also know that just typing it into a book will not get you to change your mind about this world. But now that I've said it, maybe you will at least think about it. Vigilance for God is a concept in the Course that can't be emphasized enough. Yet, it's very clear that this is an important task. We have to change our habitual thinking to change our lives, but until we shift our focus to something real, we will keep re-making illusions. We must remember to forgive. Without the purpose that we thought it had, this world leaves us with very little to look forward to from a human point of view. I have written quite a bit about the dream and spent a lot of effort trying to help you understand more clearly why this life might be an illusion, but until you can accept that idea and put your entire focus, day in and day out, on the real goal, which is waking up to the kingdom of God, your progress will be slow or non-existent. The Course has us follow a set of lessons that turns these ideas into a practical, usable framework. I urge you to do them.

Change what you think about this life. Think of it as nothing more than a training video. It is called *Enlightenment Training*, brought to you by the School of Advanced Dream Relinquishment. In every moment, everything that you see in front of you on the screen of life is trying to show you what works and what doesn't. Everything happens for you to learn from it. It's up to you to hear the narrator suggesting better choices than your ego's. You won't know what works until you try a forgiving approach to your life. When you can see your life that way, you will finally learn what it means to choose God. Creation will light up and tasteful cosmic horns will sound and biodegradable confetti will fill the air because the Holy Spirit has finally been able to remind you that you are God, and your life will change.

Going to Heaven is not a change of venue. "You" don't go "there." You are already there. The part of you that freshly experiences heaven is the part of you that drops the baggage that you have been carrying. That baggage is your personality, your character traits, your likes and dislikes, your judgments and fears, your possessions. It is your ego. The you that is left after the ego goes away is not a being separate from other beings. Heaven isn't a place where your earthly desires are all manifested. You have left those desires behind. There are no mansions with doors that close off others and leave you to yourself. Heaven is merely the oneness of God, where you are a part of everyone.

> *W-189.3. This is the world the Love of God reveals. ²It is so different from the world you see through darkened eyes of malice and of fear, that one belies the other. ³Only one can be perceived at all. ⁴The other one is wholly meaningless. ⁵A world in which forgiveness shines on everything, and peace offers its gentle light to everyone, is inconceivable to those who see a world*

> *of hatred rising from attack, poised to avenge, to murder and destroy.*
> *W-189.4. Yet is the world of hatred equally unseen and inconceivable to those who feel God's Love in them. ²Their world reflects the quietness and peace that shines in them; the gentleness and innocence they see surrounding them; the joy with which they look out from the endless wells of joy within. ³What they have felt in them they look upon, and see its sure reflection everywhere.*
> *W-189.5. What would you see? ²The choice is given you. ³But learn and do not let your mind forget this law of seeing: You will look upon that which you feel within. ⁴If hatred finds a place within your heart, you will perceive a fearful world, held cruelly in death's sharp-pointed, bony fingers. ⁵If you feel the Love of God within you, you will look out on a world of mercy and of love.*

Truth

When you begin to see beyond the surface of the events of your life, you will hardly believe the immensity of what is now happening. There is a transformation of immeasurable proportions taking place that is opening you up to another world of energy and wonder and love that was right in front of you the entire time, but you never before felt. You are remembering Who you really are. To get rid of the illusions we hold on to, we must see them face-to-face, and tell them to go away through forgiveness. You cannot see the real world if you don't get rid of the illusions. You can't get rid of them until you see them. You can't see them on your own because you deny them and are afraid to look at them, so the Holy Spirit shows them to you symbolically by letting them take form in this world.

> *W-193.⁷Forgive, and you will see this differently.*

We access the real world through forgiveness. For most of us, it happens slowly. As we forgive our brothers by realizing, one episode after another, that none of this is true, we also slowly realize that our brothers are starting to forgive us, even if we have just met. We are letting go of the illusion, so our brothers are beginning to see us as we really are, as we see them as they really are. We are moving out of illusion into truth. We are attracting into our lives more and more events and people who support our efforts and reflect our new thinking. "Sin" and suffering and stress and conflict are slowly melting away as the world begins to transform right in front of our eyes. As you let go of your judgment, it can no longer come back to you as one who is judged by others. It is happening slowly, naturally and beautifully as we begin to wake up.

Again, this world is not at all what we think it is. Billions of people suffering, striving for the meaningless, full of anger, fear and stress, firmly believing in the importance of fleeting illusions, sacrificing, controlling, hurting. It doesn't have to be this way at all, if we could even understand on a superficial level that there is something much different happening here.

It may be hard to accept, as the Course describes, that the Holy Spirit has taken all our thoughts that conflict with God and let us see them in our lives, even if we finally understand their purpose when we look back on them from many years in the future. We are not in this world, yet we make an incredible drama of it. We are not dramatic. God is not dramatic. God is absolute serenity. The gift of peace is who you really are. It is accepting what is true, and none of this life is true. If you believe the truth about yourself, nothing can harm you. If you give up your trust in God and go back to being a human, then you will experience the unnecessary pain of this world in the same way you always have. The Course then goes on to say:

> T-17.VIII.3. [7]*The strain of refusing faith to truth is enormous, and far greater than you realize.* [8]*But to answer truth with faith entails no strain at all.*

What you see in front of you is what you have faith in. Having faith in this fake world causes more strain than we realize and is, in effect, the entire difference between being God and being human. Our lives are stressful because we want to be in control of them, but as egos using our limited perspective, we have no idea what we're doing. Yet our goal is to pretend that we know exactly what we're doing. We are proud and cocky about how smart we are and how we are able to accomplish so many wonderful things. No matter how good certain isolated things may be for you, God wants more good for you than you could possibly imagine, so let Him take over in every detail, in every second. Let go of your life and the drama and the importance, and give all of the events and your reactions to those events to your true Self and God. And be at peace.

This is a much bigger topic than words can describe. On this planet, living in these bodies, we maintain the unspoken idea that what we "believe" can change in a moment, depending on our mood or a number of other factors. "Meaning" has very little meaning. When we say we believe in something, we really mean we hope it might be true, like our "belief" in God, our belief that a stock will go up, or our belief that our team will win the Superbowl/World Series/Stanley Cup, etc. In other words, we always keep open a pathway out of our commitment to an idea, and therefore, we split our loyalties. We believe in something, but we are always ready to change that belief if something a little more "true" comes along to challenge our belief.

Faith is beyond belief. This is the time to commit to an immutable faith in a God who loves you unconditionally, who exists outside of your present perception. It's time to throw away the half-heartedness of this life, represented by the lukewarm ideas and commitments of the ego. Look at this life honestly. Yes, you like parts of it but now it's time to get serious. This life doesn't work. It isn't what God chooses for you because it's not worthy of you. This life isn't good enough for you! Why continue to accept a watered-down version of God and of what life should be? Step up to Who you are. There is nothing to fear. Your desire for control and your fears create the very things you fear. Let go to a trust in God that you have never felt before—for anything. Everything will be taken care for you, if you believe it will.

You are not this small, weak human, dependent on your body and the whims of this earthly life for temporary pleasure in exchange for all the suffering and the certain end of the body in death. There is something real and permanent and incredibly good beyond this wisp of a dream world. Grab it.

Letting go of your control of your life is the ultimate belief. Every fear you feel, you must give away to the Holy Spirit. Every challenge you face, you must give away. You must **know** that everything will be alright by giving absolute control of your life to God in all things. We all have doubts and God understands this. What He asks is willingness. Willingness to change, to see things differently, to accept help for the things you have trouble letting go. Doubt is just mistrust in God's control. Doubts are a natural part of the process, but giving up your doubts is the goal.

Religions are popular because they only require an easy belief in God. It's not too much work or trouble and no changes are really required to demonstrate to the world that you belong in the group. You are rewarded when you die. The Course doesn't ask you to do anything either, but it also warns you of the self-imposed consequences of your inaction, Now. It merely describes a context for life that is remarkable and gives you the choice to act on it or not. But if you decide that this life doesn't work for you anymore, the Course shows you what you **can** do about it, Now. You can choose again.

> *T-26.III.2. There is a borderland of thought that stands between this world and Heaven. ²It is not a place, and when you reach it is apart from time. ³Here is the meeting place where thoughts are brought together; where conflicting values meet and all illusions are laid down beside the truth, where they are judged to be untrue. ⁴This borderland is just beyond the gate of Heaven. ⁵Here is every thought made pure and wholly simple. ⁶Here is sin denied, and everything that is received instead.*

> T-26.III.3. This is the journey's end. ²We have referred to it as the real world. ³And yet there is a contradiction here, in that the words imply a limited reality, a partial truth, a segment of the universe made true. ⁴This is because knowledge makes no attack upon perception. ⁵They are brought together, and only one continues past the gate where oneness is. ⁶Salvation is a borderland where place and time and choice have meaning still, and yet it can be seen that they are temporary, out of place, and every choice has been already made.

Who are you? There is no you. There is no me. There is a Son of God, and a small part of His mind drifted off into a fantasy and fell asleep. This tiny part of His mind decided He would imagine Himself as Bob and Betty and a lion and a mosquito and a mountain and a river and a galaxy; a universe of separate things and autonomous beings who thought for a moment that they were on their own and the center of their own lives. This is just a dream and none of it exists. Nothing is happening here. Nothing is real. Nothing has ever happened here. And when the Son of God wakes up, He will realize that nothing He made up was real at all. All of these pieces and people and separate things were all just a silly fantasy He thought up to imagine for a short moment that He wasn't God.

> T-24.VI.4. Forget not that the healing of God's Son is all the world is for. ²That is the only purpose the Holy Spirit sees in it, and thus the only one it has. ³Until you see the healing of the Son as all you wish to be accomplished by the world, by time and all appearances, you will not know the Father nor yourself. ⁴For you will use the world for what is not its purpose, and will not escape its laws of violence and death.

When we each wake up, we will be waking up a small part of the Son of God from His tiny dream until all of us wake up to complete the task, and then the Son will then rub his cosmic eyes and say to Himself, "Wow, what was I thinking? I'm not doing that again."

When we each wake up, we will experience the real world and become part of the happy dream. We will still see the dream, but it will be from a changed perspective; one that knows the truth and understands what's really going on. Then, after a time, God will come for us and bring us out of the real world and back into His light. And that will be that. . .

Love

I haven't spoken much about love so far, so maybe it's about time I did that. It really defies explanation, but I'll try anyway. It is what you are but in a way you are not aware of at the moment. It is the all-encompassing goop that holds everything together. It is just another name for God, you and me, and life. It sounds like a characteristic or a trait, but think of it more as the substance of everything. It is total connection and completion.

What we as egos have done to love is very sad. Love is very different for the ego. The "love" that we experience as egos here on earth is a small, twisted, sick version of what love really is. Just as we have created a painful, illusory life, based on a mad idea, we have also created a perverted idea of love that fits in perfectly with the discomfort.

Because we *are* love, and we don't know ourselves, it stands to reason that we don't know what love is in our current state. As humans, we have many definitions of love. As I stated in the section on relationships, we believe that love is different for different people and things. Ego love singles out certain individuals, bestows its blessings on them, and discards the rest. Real love doesn't do that. It can't, because real love can't withhold or limit itself. Real love can only see things for what they really are, and that is part of, and one with, everything else.

Love is unconditional. The phrase 'unconditional love' is redundant of course, like free gift, or tuna fish. Love does not have any compromises or conditions or enemies. It is the totality of who we are together as the Son of God. It cannot hurt or take sides or go away or deceive. It is Truth. Every person, thing and event in this universe is on the same side as you are, because there are no sides. There is only a collective us. Until we let go of our egos and this world, we will remain divided, without real love, yet continue to think that we are experiencing real love, because this tiny, angry, jealous, manipulative, ego love is all we know. Because we have defined and used love so poorly, we have come to despise it. That black tape over our light bulb I spoke about earlier is covering the love that we are. No matter how much love you think you have or feel, it's time to throw out that idea because love is way beyond what you and I can feel as human beings.

You don't have to try to love your neighbor or the guy who cuts you off in traffic because the Course tells you to, or because you read it in a book; you should try to love those people because love is what you are, and it is also the only thing that works! It works because, if it is expressed correctly, it is the honest expression of the connection we all have between each other and God. Even though the love we feel here as egos is only a small amount of the real love within us, it is so powerful that if you can kinda sorta put aside your ego and use it, nothing can resist it.

Letting go is not about stopping your life; it's about starting it over from scratch from the only perspective that works. When you relax your hold on all outcomes and stop fighting everyone and everything, especially yourself, and begin to see past the facade of this life, you will feel the only thing that's left to feel, and that is love. This is not a forced love. It is the love of real connection and complete openness with everyone on the planet. The universal love that you are able to muster and feel will heal the people you feel it for, whether either of you are aware of it or not. Love is beyond everything in this world and all of the things the ego thinks are important. Love is the knowledge that you are part of everyone, no matter what you may *think* you think about them.

Think about all of the people you don't like, especially infamous, cruel people on the world stage; dictators, terrorists, corporate heads, etc. We absolutely justify the love of a mother for her child just as we justify our hate of Hitler or bin Laden. But these are the people who need your unconditional love and forgiveness most of all. The hate they felt when they were alive is still there in our collective mind, and we all own it. It can only be healed with love; never with judgment or hate. They need to be forgiven for the things they haven't done, no matter how heinous or disgusting those things may seem on the surface. They need to heal themselves through their own evolution of understanding but it's not up to us to step in as judges, as tempting as that is, and as pervasive as that bad habit is today.

It's your attitude and mine that needs healing. Until we can see every person on this planet with equal love, and every evil action on this planet as a call for love, we will not understand love, and we will not change our dream lives or the planet. There is nothing wrong and no one to fix, because nothing is broken—only our own perception. No matter how much your ego may insist that we are here to fix each other and the known universe, it is not true. We are only here to awaken to ourselves by shifting our focus to one of truth. You can only heal the world by healing your own thoughts because nothing is happening on the outside.

The Course states that are only two emotions; love and fear. It also states that, in truth, they are not really opposites, because fear is an illusion and love is all-encompassing. Fear is something we dreamed up so we could experience the absence of love, and so fear is what we represent while pretending to be egos. But that's impossible, because love is all there is. The power of love is everything, but it's hard to understand that in this world of the ego. So, consider this; every time you face a tough decision, ask yourself what your response to it would be if it were based on love, and by listening to the Holy Spirit. Take a deep breath and let go of all of the things you are making up in your mind about your decision, and ask yourself whether you are acting out of love or fear. Let go of your desire to be right. Let go of your desire to fix things or change others. Any decision you make based on fear will eventually fail, simply because it is not supported by anything real.

Love is all there is, so if you express anything less than perfect, unconditional love to anyone, including yourself, you still have more to learn, because you are just saying something that isn't rue, and so you are not expressing yourself as you were created, and you are not making your decisions with the One Who is love. Every judgment of anyone, no matter how small, is an attack on love and, ultimately, yourself. Anything you see as imperfect is a misperception. This perfection is already ours but it can only be rediscovered through forgiveness. When you forgive someone, don't just convince yourself that they haven't done anything; feel a warmth and connection of love with them to acknowledge that they are your brother and savior.

The Course also states that love is not something to strive for, nor can it be taught. So let that go as well. You will experience love very easily and naturally as you peel away the layers of black tape through forgiveness. You are love, so all you need to do is start seeing yourself for who you are, and stop seeing yourself as your ego does. The love will shine through. It is unstoppable.

Change

If there is anything to take away from this book, it's that you can do whatever you want because you have been created with total freedom. And you are doing exactly what you want to do right now, at this very moment, and you always have. You and I are making this illusory world out of our desire to do just that. The world we each live in is our own, complete with pain and suffering and things going wrong and missed opportunities and snubs and sickness, as well as the positive events. Our world is a perfect reflection of what we each deeply desire.

If what the Course proposes is appealing to you, you can learn it, but you have to *want* to lean it more than you want this world. There is more to life than this small earthly being you think you are, and you can experience it if you choose to. Everything reflects your incredible power of choice. Your mind is the most powerful thing ever created. I can tell you to forgive, or let go, or anything else, but the only way anything will happen in your life is when you make the profound, life-changing decision that you no longer *want* this life, you no longer *want* to be the same person you are, and you are certain that the path you are currently on is not the one you want to follow anymore, and you now want to follow another. Then you must live a life that supports your decision.

Change means that you cannot remain the same person you were yesterday, reacting the same way, saying the same things, thinking the same way. If you make this decision to change, your external life will change, simply because that's what you want. It won't change the way you think it will, but it will change. Your life will always be led in the direction you desire, as long as the desire is real, firm and consistent. If the Course can help you, you will be led to it. If another path is better for you, you will find that also. Helen Schucman, the woman who put the Course on paper, thought the Course was only for very few people because it is so overwhelming. She thought that printing about five copies would be enough. You have to decide if you're one of them.

Until this world stops being practical or appealing to us, we will not seek for something else. For many people here on earth at this moment, we *are* looking for another answer, another way. This world *isn't* working. For many, that means trying to fix the world, while many others have finally realized it cannot be fixed. The ego will always choose separation and pain over unity and love. Desire got us into this mess, and it is now up to us to use that desire to exit. Desire is a choice we made to create the world, and only a desire that is just as strong to choose something better can eliminate it. If you are unsure, or still intrigued by this world, your path will reflect your doubts and desires. You can only see one world. You and I have chosen this one. But, just as understanding love means that we must eliminate the barriers to it, to see a better world, we must withdraw our attention from the world of illusion. We have to make our choice, and when we do, this world of illusion will start to fade from our thoughts.

The Context

A Course in Miracles is not a religion or a philosophy containing any accompanying dogma or incense or rituals or threats. It is a personal, self-study course with an accompanying text to explain the workbook. It is simply a description of this universe and how to make it, and all of the pain in it, go away. *A Course in Miracles* describes a context for life that explains everything, beautifully and simply. I have not read words from any great man or woman that explained life on earth in a way that covered every aspect of behavior and purpose. No philosopher, guru, novelist, theologian, historian, or great thinker of any kind has explained life in a way that satisfied me before the Course, and rendered all previous words written on all these subjects obsolete. Of course, you don't know me and shouldn't take my word for anything, and so you must come to that conclusion, or some other one, on your own, if at all. I hope that for you, as it was for me, that will be the moment you have been waiting for.

There is nothing more important for any of us to understand than that this universe isn't real. You aren't here, and the part of you that believes it is human is a false construct, made to have you experience a false premise; what it is like not to be God, to be special and different and separate.

The real world that we are living in right now without being aware of it, is a world so wonderful that we will never again think of this painful, conflicting chaos of a world. Even though it is a real world, it will also eventually disappear just as your nighttime dreams disappear when you wake up in the morning. But before we wake up to the real world, and leave this world and our bodies behind, there will be a short time when we are still here, awake in the illusion.

A Course in Miracles doesn't ask you to "believe" in something or to repeat words or blindly bow down to an unshaven, mythical being. It asks that you examine life—your life—and consider what is real. Does this really work for you? Could a God of love really be responsible for this world? The Course asks that you examine all of this and change the way you see yourself and what you are and what you're doing here. Can you even understand what it means that you may be unlimited? Can you begin to accept the Course's description of you, and then use that knowledge to undo years of self-deceit? Can you change the way you see life? Can you redefine yourself so significantly, that you wake up from your self-imposed dream?

Chapter 11 – *The Two Worlds*

We wake up one at a time, even though we are all in this together. Waking up is a personal journey that involves all of humankind. You must acknowledge not just a connection between you and everyone else but a merging into a common mind called the Son of God. The real world:

> T-28.II.12. *This world is full of miracles. ²They stand in shining silence next to every dream of pain and suffering, of sin and guilt. ³They are the dream's alternative, the choice to be the dreamer, rather than deny the active role in making up the dream. ⁴They are the glad effects of taking back the consequence of sickness to its cause. ⁵The body is released because the mind acknowledges "this is not done to me, but I am doing this." ⁶And thus the mind is free to make another choice instead. ⁷Beginning here, salvation will proceed to change the course of every step in the descent to separation, until all the steps have been retraced, the ladder gone, and all the dreaming of the world undone.*

I cannot emphasize how ridiculous and nonsensical the Course is. It says you are insane. It says you are not special, and there is no such thing as sin. It says that your eyes can't see. It says time isn't real. It tells us that locks on our doors are worthless, and that the only way to be safe is to know without doubt that you are invulnerable. It goes on to say that there's nothing to defend and no one can attack you. It says that any attack you make at all on anyone, no matter how small, is murder. It says we have love relationships with each other because we are trying to push God away. It says that any time you make any plans, you are just afraid of not being in control. It says that this world doesn't exist. It says that if you see anyone as a body, you are seeing them incorrectly. It says that cause and effect are reversed. Any decisions you make alone are destructive. It asks you to give no thought to yourself but then it says that there is nothing but you. It says we only keep what we give away. It says having and being are the exact same thing, not to mention giving and receiving.

Yet, everything the Course says makes more sense than anything else I have ever come across. The Course is asking you to give up this charade we call human life on earth. This isn't who we are. Letting it all go seems a daunting task, I know. Stop fighting what's happening to you. It's only God trying to get your attention and let you know that there's something better: *you* are something better.

If you use the information in the Course to get started on a new path, that's wonderful. When the message it's trying to pass on really sinks in, your life will change forever. The negativity we hold is frightening. But we have to face it and get rid of it, including our very identity and, in the beginning, you may feel that you have a lot you don't want to let go of. It may seem hard to do, but it is as easy as waking up when you understand that there's nothing really there. You don't have to change your external life much; you just have to change the way you see it and interact with it. You may even appear to be the same person you've always been on the outside, but the radical shift that occurs within will reveal something powerful and immense inside of you that you have always wanted to latch onto. Once you experience it, it is impossible to go back to living the same way in this world again.

Like every book, *A Course in Miracles* contains many words and descriptions and we read it in a linear way, from front to back. But if you read the Course enough times, all of the words begin to fall off the page and the list of things we should and can do give way to a beautiful three-dimensional textile with moving, interwoven meanings; a beautiful tableau in which you can begin to see a simple yet unfathomably complex pattern of love and interconnectedness, where this temporary error drops off of the permanence of love's fabric and fades away into the nothingness it is. It is written for every level of student, so that each time you read it, you gain new meaning from each new level from which you approach it. It repeats ideas over and over, but always from a slightly different point of view, with new twists that add fresh meaning. The majesty of the real life that awaits us is breathtaking and appealing and more exciting than anything we can now imagine, while the facade that is this life slowly loses its luster as we remember again Who we really are.

The time has come in this current version of humankind's history that enough of us have come far enough to hear the truth of this world and this life we are living. Communication through the internet and the evolution of our technological society have made it possible for us to hear this unexpected and incredible message from God. The transmission of the information in the Course is no accident in timing. We are ready for it, as life on earth becomes more threatening. It may not be for everyone, but a vast number of us who would never have advanced in our thinking without its help are now ready to move forward in our personal evolution in astounding ways.

Consider this for a moment. I believe that *A Course in Miracles* is no less than the Second Coming. But only if you can understand your role in healing the Sonship. The Course states, "The Second Coming is merely the return of sense," (T9,IV,9,4) and "The Second Coming is the awareness of reality, not its return." (T9,IV,11,10) It may be saying that the Second Coming applies to our collective healing, or it may just apply to each of us on our individual journey. I believe the Second Coming is merely *represented* by the Course's existence. The Course is nothing, unless it is given reality by those who learn it, like a dormant gene, powerful and silent, waiting to be awakened, triggered by a mind that finally understands the deep and profound purpose we have, different from what we ever imagined. A mind that understands that life for hundreds of thousands of years on earth has been misunderstood and squandered by the ego's lust for specialness. Use this ineffable writing to totally change your mind about yourself. It is now time to become Who you truly are—the Son of God. You are God's perfection.

> *T-27.VII.13. You are the dreamer of the world of dreams. ²No other cause it has, nor ever will. ³Nothing more fearful than an idle dream has terrified God's Son, and made him think that he has lost his innocence, denied his Father, and made war upon himself. ⁴So fearful is the dream, so seeming real, he could not waken to reality without the sweat of terror and a scream of mortal fear, unless a gentler dream preceded*

his awaking, and allowed his calmer mind to welcome, not to fear, the Voice that calls with love to waken him; a gentler dream, in which his suffering was healed and where his brother was his friend. ⁵God willed he waken gently and with joy, and gave him means to waken without fear.

T-27.VII.14. Accept the dream He gave instead of yours. ²It is not difficult to change a dream when once the dreamer has been recognized. ³Rest in the Holy Spirit, and allow His gentle dreams to take the place of those you dreamed in terror and in fear of death. ⁴He brings forgiving dreams, in which the choice is not who is the murderer and who shall be the victim. ⁵In the dreams He brings there is no murder and there is no death. ⁶The dream of guilt is fading from your sight, although your eyes are closed. ⁷A smile has come to lighten up your sleeping face. ⁸The sleep is peaceful now, for these are happy dreams.

About the Author...

James K Anderson is no one in particular. He's just a guy who did a lot of searching on his own while living a relatively normal life, mostly in Chicago. A few remarkable incidents in college compelled him to search for God as soon as he graduated. Because he felt certain that God would not be found in religion, at the age of 22 he began reading books based more on individual accounts. He read Edgar Cayce, Carlos Castaneda, Jane Roberts, Yogananda, and a few hundred others.

He made amazing discovery after discovery on his personal quest. First of all, it turned out he wasn't looking for God as much as he was looking for himself. Next, he came to realize that his search was not an intellectual one, but an experiential one. Nothing demonstrable happened in his life that reflected his unrelenting search until he began to actively change his approach to it, and himself. But he also understood that he had to let go of expectations of any immediate results in his life, because that was not the point, as much as it would be nice.

He realized that, in spite of his affection for people, he really didn't like this world and the direction it always seemed to be headed. Collectively, the human race is like a virus, with each individual connected to the whole as a society but severely disconnected when it comes to making collective, intelligent decisions. It seems that each is out for him or herself and there is no effective way to change society's direction.

When he finally found *A Course in Miracles* at age 59, he was embarrassed that someone like him, who was so avidly searching and who had read so many books, after many attempts, had just not been able to read it for 20 years after he bought it. He just wasn't ready.

After certain events, when he finally was able to read it, it had an immediate and powerful effect. He was able to apply it to everything he had gathered in his head for the last 37 years or so, and yet go far beyond what he now knew was his very limited understanding of God and life. The Course was a vastly different book from anything he had come across before, and it seemed obvious to him that it could not have been written by a human.

It was breathtaking and insightful, beautiful and consistent, clever beyond description, and every time he read it through, he felt as if he were reading it as a different person and learning more that had been previously shielded from him until he was ready to assimilate it.

He has been meditating for over 30 years, reads the Course every day, still lives in Chicago quietly taking up a small amount of space, hoping this book will help at least one other person see life differently than they had before.

Bibliography

A Course in Miracles. Foundation for Inner Peace; 3rd edition (January 1, 1975)

Gary Renard. *The Disappearance of the Universe.* Hay House Inc; Revised edition (November 1, 2004)

Christopher Hitchens. *God is Not Great: How Religion Poisons Everything.* Twelve; 1st edition (May 1, 2007)

Jess Stearn. *The Sleeping Prophet.* Bantam (October 1, 1989)

William Shakespeare. *Hamlet.*

Gopi Krishna. *Living with Kundalini, The Autobiography of Gopi Krishna.* Shambhala; 1st edition (November 9, 1993)

Jan Frazier. *When Fear Falls Away.* Weiser Books (May 1, 2007)

Jed McKenna. *Spiritual Enlightenment, The Damnedest Thing.* Wisefool Press (February 27, 2010)

David R. Hawkins. *The Map of Consciousness Explained.* Hay House Inc. (October 20, 2020)

Made in the USA
Las Vegas, NV
14 August 2023